DATE DUE FOR RETURN

RECLAIMING OUR PASTS

RECLAIMING OUR PASTS
EQUALITY AND DIVERSITY IN THE
PRIMARY HISTORY CURRICULUM

Hilary Claire

tb

Trentham Books

First published in 1996 by Trentham Books Limited

Trentham Books Limited
Westview House
734 London Road
Oakhill
Stoke-on-Trent
Staffordshire
England ST4 5NP

British Cataloguing in Publication Data
A catalogue record for this book is available from the British Library
ISBN: 1 85856 025 X

Designed and typeset by Trentham Print Design Ltd., Chester and printed in
Great Britain by Bemrose Shafron (Printers) Ltd., Chester

Contents

Preamble   1

PART 1 KEY STAGE 1

CHAPTER 1
An Introduction to the Issues   5

CHAPTER 2
Themes and topics in Key Stage 1   21

CHAPTER 3
Using stories to support Key Stage 1 history   39

CHAPTER 4
A place in the hall of fame   63

PART 2 KEY STAGE 2

CHAPTER 5
The Key Stage 2 curriculum   81

CHAPTER 6
Study Unit 1: Romans, Anglo-Saxons and Vikings in Britain   95

CHAPTER 7
Study Unit 2: Life in Tudor Times   103

CHAPTER 8
Study Unit 3a: Victorian Britain   123

CHAPTER 9
Study Unit 3b: Britain since 1930   163

CHAPTER 10
Study Unit 5: Local History   181

CHAPTER 11
Study Unit 6: a past non-European society   203
General issues and an exemplar: Benin

PART 3 RESOURCES

CHAPTER 12
Lives of distinction connected with Britain   223
Resources for KS 1 'Famous People' and KS 2 — Study units 3a and 3b

CHAPTER 13
Annotated Resources   241

CHAPTER 14
Organisations and Bookshops   271

Appendix 1
'Who's afraid of the Big Bad Wolf?'   275

Appendix 2
Immigration and Emigration Patterns in Britain over the past two millennia   279

Index   283

Thank you to

Jack — for helping me in more than a hundred ways,
and keeping me on my intellectual toes

Gillian Klein — for encouragement and enthusiasm and
sensitive editing

Sue Adler — for directing me to some good resources and help
with the index

Clare Midgeley — for material about Sarah Parker Remond

'John Adamson' for responding to my questions about his memories
of fleeing Austria in 1938

numerous students on the BEd and PGCE Primary Courses at South
Bank University for helping me formulate ideas, trying out in
practice and giving me feedback

friends at Letterbox Library for help with books for children

Cu San — for permission to use her pictures and story.

This book is for
the four generations of my immediate family
spanning the century and spread around the world;
my mother Dorothy;
my sister Gabrielle and my brother Jon;
my children, Thembi and Alexei;
and my granddaughter Natasha;
with love

PREAMBLE

An inclusive history curriculum

This book offers some thoughts on how to develop an inclusive curriculum for primary history: inclusive in content and in educational purpose, recognising the value of history as training for the mind, and one of the most fascinating of all the curriculum subjects because — potentially — it takes on all human experience. The book is not and never could be an attempt to put on paper all possible ways of working within the Key Stage 1 and 2 history curriculum.

Honouring the requirements of the National Curriculum Programme of Study, I suggest ways to offer broader perspectives, to avoid exclusively Eurocentric or male-centred approaches and to consider how to include working class history. Bruner's belief that any subject can be taught in an intellectually honest way to anyone inspires and guides me. As a primary teacher who is also an historian, I have combined academic subject knowledge with my commitment to the implementation of equal opportunities principles, to identify ways in which the teaching of history in primary schools can be transformed.

History as a training in rational and analytic thinking

The National Curriculum not only brought primary history formally into the curriculum but focused on the weaknesses in the way it had been taught, if taught at all. Since 1989 there has been an ongoing debate about the nature of school history, broadly summarised as content vs. process. Even when the process aspects are agreed there is often dispute about the content — British history vs. world history.

The processes or concepts of history were encapsulated in the three attainment targets of the 1991 Order and have more or less survived the transmutation into level descriptions for the single attainment target in the 1995 Order. Unfortunately, the new attainment target is less clear about what the historical concepts are, so that teachers who have not themselves been trained in history could be unaware that chronology, change and continuity, cause and consequence, appreciation of bias and perspective, interpretation and evaluation of evidence remain at the heart of school history, just as they do in history practised by historians.

Quite apart from arguments about knowledge of one's roots, and the fascination of history, there is another fundamental argument for doing history: the intellectual rigour and training for the mind which its concepts demand. Surprisingly, this argument is seldom heard in primary schools. History shares with science and mathematics reliance on logical thought, use of evidence and need to marshal information in the service of abstract categories. Unlike science and mathematics, history does not work towards provable certainties and this is perhaps one of its greatest strengths. Though science does concern itself increasingly with values, history works overtly with values in human lives. History tries to make sense of human lives, working with the values and moralities of those who lived them. It also requires interpreting 'what was going on' using hindsight and our own contemporary values and appreciating that this is what we are doing. In this way history is never just about the past, but always involves reflection on the present.

History involves accepting uncertainty and conflicts in interpretations and in values; it means using imagination and creative thinking — but always bounded by the limitations of the evidence. It involves being able to communicate with passion and clarity — and still honour the evidence. History is neither a straight narrative of 'what happened' nor a simple celebration of the past. Theme park versions of the past which ignore the downside and paper over ambiguities do not deserve the name of history. They are merely propaganda. At the same time, the power of narrative in helping us make meanings should not be underestimated. Bruner (1990) reminds us that stories are not just accounts of a sequence of events, but always involve trying to reconstruct, explain and make the world comprehensible.

The practice of history is thus truly educative because it develops human powers, concepts, skills, knowledge and reflexivity. An inclusive history curriculum makes pedagogic sense. Without inclusivity history loses the moral complexity which is at its heart and at the heart of grappling with historical concepts.

One of the striking differences between history and say, language development, mathematics or science in the primary school curriculum, is that they have benefited from the insights and efforts of academics and specialists to keep the school subject in line with the sort of work that goes on by 'real' scientists, mathematicians and linguists. Perhaps because of the lead taken by Piagetian developmental psychologists, there are several well known Maths and Science Education Centres in Britain and both disciplines produce a considerable amount of research about children's development and learning. Language development has benefited from both the needs of a multilingual society and concern about literacy.

In comparison, the research and publications about primary school children's learning in history are paltry. Furthermore, although secondary school history teachers — who typically have a history degree — are usually aware of and involved in the controversies and debates of academic history, there is little evidence that primary teachers even know about such perspectives. Given that few primary teachers have an equivalent academic history training to secondary specialists, or are specialist subject teachers, this is hardly surprising and certainly not their fault. But it does have important outcomes for the ways in which primary teachers approach this curriculum area. Faced with the demands of the history programmes of study, they are neither anxious to critique it nor to look for ways to complicate their already difficult job.

This book is designed to support teachers who would like to extend their sense of what history is about, and use these insights to understand how and why an inclusive history curriculum is not just possible, but academically respectable and viable.

Chapter 1

An Introduction to the Issues

Keeping to task in Key Stage 1

After a long period in which history was hardly touched on in the infant school, some KS 1 teachers did not know what they should now teach. The 1991 Order, the 1993 history Standard Assessment Tasks for 7 year olds and non-statutory guidance encouraged work about e.g. Guy Fawkes or Boudicaa or the Victorians, and some infant teachers got started on some of the compulsory KS 2 curriculum. The Victorians are certainly an enticing prospect, especially as there is so much evidence about children's lives but, sadly, much of what is done with infants is so stereotyped and does so little to develop any historical concepts other than chronology, that it hardly deserves the name history. When it comes to working with even earlier periods, such as Romans, Vikings or Tudors, which are well beyond living memory, for which real people can't be interviewed and for which the artefacts and sources are generally less accessible, there are good reasons to wait till the junior school.

This does not mean that we should fail to respond to and acknowledge children's personal knowledge about, for example the Mary Rose at Portsmouth, or the Jorvik Museum in York (gained perhaps through visits with their parents). One of the best ways to help children contextualise such out-of-school knowledge and experience is to place a postcard or a photo on a time-line, to show how long ago the period was. Educational psychologists like Bruner have convincingly argued that children should be introduced to material in a simple form, laying down a foundation of understanding and familiarity which they can return to later in greater depth. The way to establish this foundation is through learning historical skills and concepts in familiar contexts, rather than working on remote periods.

Some aspects of late Victorian life may well be accessible to infants, although I believe that 'intellectually honest' historical study of earlier periods should be held over. The combination of remote time, more complex concepts, more difficult evidence and the absence of 'real people' often leads to poor historical understanding, oversimplifications, misconceptions and a-historicity, all of which is hard to shift later.

The Key Stage 2 curriculum and overlaps with Key Stage 3

Having used 'child development' arguments for keeping the main focus on the twentieth and possibly the late nineteenth century for Key Stage 1, I would use pedagogic arguments to urge Key Stage 2 teachers not to avoid issues that first occur formally in the Key Stage 3 curriculum. In the interests of historical honesty certain issues cannot be omitted in the primary years and will deepen and enrich pupils' understanding of the Study Units. The possible outcome of a narrower version of history in the primary years could be quite racist, fostering partial understandings and erroneous impressions that non-European people hardly featured in Western history till the twentieth century, and only had a history in very early times (e.g. Assyria, Egypt) and remote places (Mexico, Benin).

Once you concede that the overlap might prove positive rather than something to ignore, Key Stage 3 material offers some useful resources for the primary school. Infant school teachers are well accustomed to adapting material intended for older children, but the physical divisions and the different training for teachers of the primary and secondary years seem to have discouraged collaboration between teachers of juniors and young secondary pupils.

Equality issues in the history curriculum

The 1992 DES discussion paper on curriculum organisation and classroom practice in primary schools, by the so-called 'Three Wise Men' emphasised that concern with equality ought to be translated at the individual and group level into concern with task match. Although they scoffed at the idea that equal opportunities should try to counteract an elitist curriculum, they also suggested that social disadvantage should not be used to explain away educational failure or as a pretext for low expectations. Reading between the lines, one might surmise that many children are capable of taking on more than we credit (see DES, 1992, paras 107 — 110).

Olive Stevens' research in the early 1980s into primary children's knowledge and understanding of contemporary political events revealed the extent to which they obtained information and learned their attitudes about the world through television. More recently, there has been a considerable amount of research corroborating and emphasising the huge influence of the media, particularly television news, on children's interest in and knowledge about national and international issues, particularly about 'race', gender and class.

There are good arguments for a more inclusive history curriculum for the primary school:

☐ children need to contextualise the information they are getting through the media in order to understand it better

☐ they are interested anyway

☐ a eurocentric and male-centred curriculum fails to prepare children adequately for life in the coming century

☐ a eurocentric and male-centred curriculum is basically unjust and biased about the contributions and history of women and non-European people

☐ this limited curriculum continues to support sexism, racism and class misunderstanding by perpetuating out-dated attitudes.

Equality issues: some historiography for non-historians

The ideas which follow are recognised within historiography (the study of how history is written) but may be unfamiliar to non-historians. Arguments for inclusive history do not rest merely on trendy 'political correctness' within the teaching profession, but are central to the kinds of debates that go on among historians who are not particularly concerned with school issues.

a) The relationship of British and world history

Despite being an island, British history has never been divorced from the rest of the world and it is difficult to make sense of most British history without a sense of what was going on elsewhere. History which acknowledges these influences and connections is more complete, less biased and hence 'better history'.

b) Avoiding Whig history

The great nineteenth century English historians (e.g. Macaulay) and some of their twentieth century followers (e.g. Trevelyan) were steeped in the prevalent optimism about British institutions and ways of life. They felt that British political and economic pre-eminence in the world reflected Britain's superior social, technological and political systems. They noted with approval the visible results in the economy at home and in British territories abroad of the industrial revolution, the development of a democratic two-party system, the fact that, unlike most European nations, Britain had avoided revolution and civil war since the seventeenth century. They wrote the history of Britain as a 'march of progress' in political, social and economic terms. They spent little time on the failures, false starts and *culs de sac* and even less on the experience of marginalised or less fortunate groups — such as the colonised, or the poor who were the victims of developing capitalism — since such emphases tend to draw attention away from history perceived as the celebration of Britain's mighty and progressively improving past. This tendency to write history as if it were the story of progress is known as Whig history and discredited in many academic circles now, for its obvious biases and overt political agenda. However, many primary teachers do not realise how far the perspectives of Whig history still permeate textbooks used with pupils. Some teachers perpetuate falsely rosy pictures of a British past (albeit unintentionally), relying on historical understanding dating from their own schooling, which never challenged these views.

c) Imperialism and Eurocentrism

The biases of imperialism and eurocentrism are related to the problems of Whig history. The eurocentric and imperialist perspectives of the late nineteenth and first half of the twentieth century are themselves now the subject of historical study. They were part and parcel of a period when Britain (along with other European nations) was occupying, colonising and consolidating its hegemony in other parts of the world. Imperialism involved economic, political and cultural control, which was justified with arguments about the inferiority of the peoples and countries which were taken over, and the benefits not just to the mother country but to the colonised countries, of British civilisation, commerce and Christianity.

Eurocentrism is the other side of the coin of history thus written. It has been well documented. Briefly, the colonised peoples' experience of imperialism is interpreted in terms of the supposed benefits to them, and their history is included only in so far as it impinges on the European presence. Black people generally become the bit parts (often unheroic or childlike) in a drama about white people's activities. The residue of imperialist and eurocentric biases in British history clings insidiously, in the assumptions, inclusions and exclusions that exist in much primary school history. A similar chauvinism affects the way history is written about foreign nations, including those that are 'white'. Part of the purpose of this book is to help teachers recognise this hidden agenda in the textbooks and activities their children will work with, so that they can consider how to counteract it with alternative resources, or through helping the pupils themselves to critique them.

d) Countering male-centred history

Sheila Rowbotham's book *Hidden from History* (1977) was one of the first to explore in a popular format an issue which was already acknowledged and being addressed by women historians. British women's history has developed with the twentieth century women's movement and is a respectable part of mainstream work on the continent as well as in Australasia and America, with several journals and regular conferences. It tends to have two objectives: firstly to research and make visible the unacknowledged contribution of women in the past, including the histories of ordinary women as well as those who were exceptional; and secondly, to critique history which has been written from a purely male perspective. Much as imperialist and eurocentric history uses a set of assumptions and values which affect both content and judgements, so male-centred history has marginalised or ignored the work and experiences of women and failed to take account of how gender determined life experience in the past, as indeed it does now.

e) History from below

There is a school of modern historiography which challenges the way history was and is written as if only the powerful and privileged were worth research and academic interest. Calling itself 'history from below', it counteracts elitist history and offers 'perspectives from below'. It tries to reach into the lives of those whose evidence is often unofficial, harder to find, and who may have been the losers or unsung heroes. Allied with such history is an interest in customs, attitudes and ordinary practices which brings history closer to anthropology or ethnography than the political history of governments and international manoeuvres.

Primary history, an inclusive curriculum and children as learners

The previous pages in this chapter have concentrated on academic arguments for an inclusive approach to primary history, to bring it into line with contemporary historiography in the wider domain. This next section briefly outlines ideas to do with children as learners, arguing that an inclusive curriculum provides the necessary *psychological* foundations for learning history. This history will interest and engage children, allow them to build towards the unknown from what they know and meet needs related to self-esteem and valuing others. It follows that a *non*-inclusive history curriculum must fail or disadvantage some children, possibly precisely those we are most concerned to encourage.

I will develop two main ideas in the next few pages: they are closely interlinked. The first acknowledges the important differences in children's own characteristics and suggests that, as teachers, we cannot act as if our pupils are homogeneous — whether ethnicity, sex or social class is at issue. The second theme is to do with the content of the curriculum, and how far this maps onto children's personal sense of identity, how they relate to the curriculum and what they learn from it. I am considering the interface between teaching and learning, and how far what we offer in the curriculum develops and supports children's enthusiasm and interest. There is not space in this book to develop the ideas in any depth, only a summary in point form, with brief notes, drawing together ideas which may be reasonably familiar in other curriculum areas but which have not, to my knowledge, been emphasised formally for primary school history.

Primary school history should take account of:

'race' and ethnicity

- ☐ to support the learning, self-esteem and identification with history of black and ethnic minority children

- ☐ to give white children non-Eurocentric approaches which help them understand the modern world and counteract ignorance and prejudice

gender

- ☐ to counter sexism and marginalisation of women's contribution, as part of the education of boys

- ☐ to offer girls positive role models and foci for identification to support their interest and motivation in learning history and a sense of their own potential agency

class

- ☐ to make sure that working class children are able to have some point of entry and identification with the content of history

- ☐ to empower children by challenging the view that change has always been the work of the rulers and the powerful

- ☐ to give children the opportunity to start learning about the difficult and painful paths towards democracy.

In the real world, everyone belongs to all three categories, since each of us is female or male, *and* middle, upper or working class, *and* from an ethnic minority or the dominant 'white' English group in British society. In an inclusive curriculum, there are good reasons for not treating 'race', gender and class separately, not just to match the real world, but also to avoid the dangers of creating hierarchies or forgetting the links. In the past, white historians writing 'history from below' have ignored black people; historians concerned with including black and ethnic minority history have ignored the contribution of women — black or white; white feminist historians stand accused of racism because of marginalising the history of black women or writing as if their experience as whites (often middle class) were synonymous with that of black women (seldom middle class).

However, it becomes very complicated in a book like this to try and include all three issues at every juncture. Because I am anxious to make my arguments clearly and they don't always overlap, each issue is explored separately in this introductory chapter.

AN INTRODUCTION TO THE ISSUES

'Race'/Ethnicity and Eurocentrism

'Race'

'Race' is a problematic word, conventionally put in quotation marks these days to indicate that it is not a real biological entity but a construct with social and political meanings and its own history. Mid-nineteenth century 'scientists' like Francis Galton were responsible for the idea that people from different areas of the world, with some distinctive physical, cultural and linguistic features, could be divided up scientifically into a hierarchy of 'races'. The theory exploited new Darwinian ideas, and positioned white European people — i.e. those who had developed the theory — at the apex of this hierarchy, and black people of African origin at the bottom. This so-called scientific ordering of the peoples of the world came just when Britain was expanding her empire into Africa and consolidating with force her two-century-long presence in India, which would become the 'jewel in Victoria's crown'. The institutionalised power imbalance between black people and whites, which the slave trade had established in the sixteenth century, survived and was extended in the nineteenth century. Despite the formal end of British involvement in the slave trade in 1807 and full emancipation of British-owned slaves in 1838, Britain continued to exercise hegemony over the Caribbean colonies. From the early nineteenth century, Britain extended colonial control over Southern Africa and later, parts of North, West and East Africa. Spain, France and Portugal, who had also been major participants in the earlier European imperial ventures into Africa, America and the East, maintained and extended their control, joined in Africa by Germany and Belgium. Twentieth century racism is rooted in this power relationship, underpinned and justified by an ideology of white superiority.

The ways nineteenth and early twentieth century sources use the word 'race' in connection with British people, and not just 'other races' resonates uncomfortably with later Fascist discourses. The word often carries explicit connotations or strong overtones of white racial superiority, race efficiency and even aspirations to racial purity. In the twentieth century, scientists like Steven Rose (1984) have effectively demolished the idea that the peoples of the world can be divided into races in any meaningful way, and that any biological differences are scientifically significant.

Ethnicity

Ethnicity refers to communities linked by culture, language and religion. Usually, but not always, there is a strong territorial connection as well. Many people feel they have a 'mixed identity' and what they choose to foreground will depend on the context. We all have ethnicity, though the majority group tends not to notice and regards its own group as 'normal', and others as 'different'. Some people only become aware of their own minority and ethnic status in the wider world if they travel abroad. Others live with their minority status all the time. Recent writing has emphasised the political and not just the cultural aspects of ethnicity, pointing out that membership of an ethnic group always has implicit, explicit or potential implications for relative power in a community.

Eurocentrism

One of the important arguments for an inclusive curriculum is that no British child at the end of the twentieth century can count on living in a closed community cut off from a wider world in which the majority is neither white nor English speaking. Many teachers are very anxious to find ways to make sure that the history curriculum is inclusive and does take on the implications of teaching towards 'race' equality. Londoners and residents of the other major British cities with large proportions of ethnic minority residents, are sometimes accused of metrocentrism and of assuming that everyone is, and should be as interested in 'race'/ethnicity as they are. However, a great many teachers in rural or largely white areas are concerned with equality teaching, even if they don't have black or ethnic minority children in their school. This is because they recognise that all children are growing up in a changing world and do not want to perpetuate ignorance, intolerance and injustice by default. Moreover, the presence of black or ethnic minority children in a school community is a necessary but not a sufficient condition for the inclusion of black history. In other words, white schools need to take on the inclusive curriculum as much as schools with black children, although for different reasons.

Some people accept the necessity of including black or ethnic minority history in the curriculum when their pupils come from those groups, but use the same rationale to support a 'white' curriculum for 'white schools'. This idea needs to be firmly challenged. Several researchers have effectively argued that the problems of prejudice and racism are far more likely to develop in areas where children don't have their stereotypes challenged through meeting black or ethnic minority people. Some excellent resources for working on race issues with white school pupils have been produced (e.g. Sealey and Epstein, 1990, Brown et al, 1991). My discussion about the importance of a broadly based historical curriculum builds on their ideas.

The statutory curriculum in the 1995 History Order has possibilities for an inclusive curriculum but also makes it quite easy to avoid teaching anything but white history, or history from a white-only perspective (not quite the same thing). Study Unit 6 is such a small part of the whole, and the treatment can be quite tokenistic. In any event, Ancient Egypt is frequently chosen and taught as if this civilisation were actually white.

Health warning: Racism and the importance of a whole school policy on equality

The Rampton and Swann reports (1981 and 1985) were the first official documents to point to racism in schools as an underlying cause of black children's underachievement (in this case chiefly children of African-Caribbean origin) although writers such as Bernard Coard (1971) from the black community itself, had made this accusation ten years earlier. More recently, research in nursery, infant and junior schools [e.g. Hatcher and Troyna (1992) and Wright (1992)] has provided a scathing indictment of adult and pupil racism, even within schools that profess an equality policy. Troyna and Hatcher's work is relevant because they explain how work done in class, for instance on slavery, obviously intended to give the children some understanding of the historical roots of racism, backfired on black children, who found themselves victimised and teased in the playground for being 'slaves'. In slightly different vein, Wright's work points to how teacher insensitivity and their stereotyping of very young black children soured relationships with parents. Where this was occurring, there would be little point in overt work on black contributions to the community and little chance of successful invitations to parents to become involved with curriculum work. There is an unavoidable lesson here about the necessity of a whole school policy: curriculum issues or multicultural resourcing cannot be separated off from parental involvement, issues of stereotyping and expectation, and of responses to name-calling and bullying in the playground.

The Programme of Study for Key Stage 1 encourages work that is drawn from the children's own family life and community ('changes in their own lives and those of their family or adults around them; adults talking about their own past'). Some teachers find that, despite good intentions, they have considerably less success at involving ethnic minority or non-English speaking parents in the life of the school, and that this has consequences for work in class. There is not space here to go through the variety of reasons why such parents might not feel thoroughly at ease with the teachers and the school and be less forthcoming with artefacts, pictures and stories from home than white indigenous parents. However, a number of studies make it very clear that the fault lies less with the parents' disinterest than with the quite subtle ways in which parents feel disadvantaged, patronised, stereotyped or even pejoratively judged by teachers. In my years in teacher training in the inner city, I have been shocked by the stories that I regularly hear from black and ethnic minority students about not-so-subtle racism they and their parents experienced from some white teachers when they were pupils, and which, sadly, they continue to pick up in the staff room.

It is not possible to initiate an inclusive curriculum with respect to ethnicity and race, while vestigial feelings of superiority, condescension or 'victim blaming' linger on among the staff of a school. Minority-group parents are always sensitive to these attitudes and cannot be expected to respond wholeheartedly to requests for information, resources or help when they sense ambivalence beneath the veneer of interest. And individual teachers who are working with total commitment towards equality, may well find their task made difficult in a school which does not have a general, open and thoroughly worked-through policy about race equality.

In both infant and junior schools, teachers have to be aware of the life that goes on among the children, often out of sight of adults. It is here that bullying and victimisation can occur and, as Troyna and Hatcher point out, such behaviour may actually be *fed* by the way children distort or exploit the information they are learning through the curriculum itself. There is no guarantee that learning about the history of another culture or community will lead to tolerance for different customs, let alone sympathy with an exploited people's plight. Children, just like adults, are perfectly able to use evidence of difference and inequality to reinforce their own prejudices, to blame the victim and justify continued oppression. I would therefore like to make very clear, right at the beginning of this book, my conviction that work on extending the history curriculum must always be part of a broader project which takes on children's and adults' attitudes and respect for each other, and is set within a framework for social justice.

Gender

The Second Wave Women's Movement in Britain dates from the 1960s and generated a wealth of material critiquing virtually every aspect of a world it identified as male-dominated and oppressive. In educational research, the main focus was initially on the poor performance of girls in so-called male areas like maths and science, on the ways in which girls were marginalised and undermined through the hidden curriculum and on the sexist bias in curriculum resources. From the early 80s there was a ground swell of interest in policy, and on the active intervention of feminist teachers in curriculum and practice, from nursery to higher education.

However, the impact of all this concern with gender has been minimal on the history curriculum. Pre-National Curriculum, if history was taught at all in the primary school, teachers concerned about sexism tried hard to find 'famous women' to match 'famous men', and set Boudicaa, Elizabeth 1, Joan of Arc or Florence Nightingale against helmeted Vikings, Henry VIII, Drake or Louis Pasteur. There was little evidence in primary schools, even in the most dilute form, of the thinking that was going on in feminist academic circles. Post-ERA, the Programmes of Study seemed to strait-jacket most teachers' attempts to think creatively about a feminist perspective on statutory history.

Gender and 'race'

Feminism has never offered just one critique, perspective or programme for change. Although the early challenges to history and historiography from academic feminism incorporated neither a 'race' nor class analysis of difference and oppression, in the last decade or so, black women have objected to white feminists' claims to speak on their behalf.

Most of this challenge has come from the disciplines of science, sociology, psychology and literature. What about history? From the 1980s, books started to appear that documented the presence and contribution of black men in British history (e.g. Fryer, 1984, File and Power, 1981). In America there is a burgeoning history of black women, and women of colour. One can look to India, the Middle East and Africa for historical evidence of women's contributions. However, the gaping absence of documented black women's history in Britain seemed to suggest either than black women simply hadn't existed, or that they were completely without importance. Bryan, Scafe and Dadzie's book *The Heart of the Race* (1985) went some way to rectify this omission, and recently a number of books have appeared which deal specifically with black women in Britain since the second world war. However, other than Mary Seacole, it is quite difficult to find documentation about the black women who were here in earlier periods, along with black men. This has consequences for non-racist feminist teaching within the constraints of the British-centred study units. This book tries to counter this bias and to provide suggestions and information about black women who lived in Britain, as well as women abroad, about whom children might learn at both Key Stages.

Class

There was a considerable amount of research about class and education in the 1960s, which tailed off in the 1970s. Although teachers were alerted to the stereotyping of working class children and the effects of a cultural mismatch between largely middle class schooling and working class pupils and their parents, there was little evidence that messages about elitism or bias were applied to the primary history curriculum. History continued to be the history of kings and nobles, of rulers and conquest. If the work of feminist historians has failed to make its way into the primary curriculum, nor has parallel work from socialist historians arguing for a history 'from below', which researches and makes known the experience and contributions of ordinary men and women.

For all periods there is now a growing body of published work, much coming from the members of 'History Workshop' whose *History Workshop Journal* openly testifies to its socialist feminist position. It is as important for primary teachers to know that such material is available, as to be aware of the perspective taken. 'History from below' validates teachers' attempts to make history more relevant to their community of children, and gives academic respectability to work on ordinary people's lives. It is strong on oral history. The issues which it explores include resistance to ruling class and managerial power, working people's organisations, and the culture of a variety of working class communities.

Summary

Recently there have been debates, for instance in *Teaching History* and in the press, about the 'British centredness' of the Study Units, and the way in which world history has been marginalised in the primary years. This is indisputable, but in the concern about territorial history, gender and class have somehow got lost. It's not so much a case of throwing the baby out with the bath water, because in many schools this baby never got near the water anyway. The National Curriculum has opened up a debate about what history should be taught, and I think this is a very good time to widen the debate, beyond the important question of Eurocentrism.

Gender and class, 'race' and ethnicity are frameworks which largely determined lives in the past, just as they determine our lives now. Implicitly, they have influenced how the content of history for children was chosen, what historical questions they were asked to consider, and how it was taught. It is not good enough that these central dimensions remain implicit rather than out in the open. This perspective will be clear in the way I explore the possibilities offered by the history National Curriculum, and in the suggestions and approaches I offer to primary teachers.

Some ethical questions

Conventional 'white', mainstream, male history presents the past as a celebration of progress and does not problematise this 'progress' by taking the exploited, the losers or the conquered into account. For adults, an alternative inclusive history which asks about the poor, the losers, women, black people whose lands were colonised or who were taken into slavery, can prove painful and difficult. This is unavoidable for women and for men, for white and black, or those whose forebears did the exploiting as well as those who were exploited. History may claim and attempt to be objective, but in reality there is no way totally to separate off feeling and knowledge.

An inclusive curriculum for children raises the very same questions about how far historical study can touch raw nerves, render people vulnerable and expose children to anxieties about the future, based on knowledge of an imperfect past. There are important ethical questions about how far we want to protect young children from some of the horrors of history. When is the right time to find out about, say, exploitation of children in coal mines, the fact that Victorian children as young as seven were hanged for theft or deported on prison hulks to Australia, let alone about genocide? Is it preferable to have had a gradual introduction from say, about 7 or 8, acquiring more detail when one is older? Or is it better to know nothing and live in complete innocence till one's teens, only to be deeply shocked and even angry at the amount of information which has been withheld? I would like to offer some personal reflections here, illuminated by African-Caribbeans that I've talked to about this, because although teachers must make up their own minds, some reference points may anchor thinking. It would also be sensible to consult with parents about material that might be too difficult for children to comprehend.

The Holocaust, in which some of my own family must have perished, given my grandparents' origins in Poland and Lithuania, was an unspeakable silence in my childhood. There were hints and allusions about why my family had left Britain hurriedly in 1942; I needed to know the truth. I first learned about the Holocaust when I was about ten, not from my family, but from fiction, searched out and read on my own. Looking back, I seem to have had a self-censoring propensity, and I simply ignored the material I could not handle, which included, at that stage, details about sex or adult lives which was beyond my real understanding. I first learned about the nineteenth century pogroms in Eastern Europe, from which my grandparents' generation had fled, some to America, some to England, some to South Africa, when I was in my early teens.

My parents would not talk about any of this, it now seems to me through misplaced shame and justified fear of continuing antisemitism, from which they were very concerned to protect their children. In the 50s when I was growing up, they were still traumatised, pretending as far as they could not to be Jews — changing a surname was only one symptom. Knowledge of what had happened to the Jews in Europe would, I now think, have helped me understand some of my grandparents' 'difference' and the way they clung to traditions and my parents' defensive behaviour, ambition and attempts to assimilate. It might also have helped make sense of the casual and inexplicable antisemitism I encountered personally, from quite a young age.

Can one — should one — tell young children about the Holocaust, or the Middle Passage? Everyone must come to their own decision about how much horror young children can bear, particularly if it is true, and there is no escape clause that 'this did not really happen' with the adjunct 'and it probably couldn't anyway, it's all just pretend'. There is no doubt that some children who can just cope with fictional horror stories can be haunted by the far more horrific truths of our past. As a child some of my own nightmares did come from history — being accused of witchcraft and drowned, or burned at the stake like Joan of Arc — though I think I knew that these punishments did not date beyond the C17th. But then, I grew up without television or video and who knows what difference that might have made.

Young African-Caribbean people have echoed my feeling that their history was denied them, either in mistaken attempts to protect them, or because the dominant white culture did not feel that their history had any place in the curriculum. Some say they have learned about the history of slavery and exploitation in the West Indies out of school, from family or Saturday Schools; some report the same diffidence that I experienced from my own family; some were only now finding out about both the good and the bad parts of their history, through post-school courses and most are angry at being kept ignorant or only partly informed.

There will probably always be some children in our schools who have themselves come through horrific events; in the 1930s there were children who had escaped from Germany; in the 1950s the few who had survived the camps; in the late 1970s and 1980s there were Vietnamese boat children. Now there are survivors of Bosnia and Somalia. This is not an argument for exposing all children to horror. In my view, it is important for children to know the history of their contemporaries and predecessors, because television and half-understood, overheard stories embellished in the imagination will have given many children partial knowledge, which may be worse than the truth. However, if they are going to know about difficult and painful times, it is essential to know about the resistance and strategies for survival, to avoid a sense of victimisation, the calamitous inevitability of tragedy and a loss of self-esteem. It is, moreover, important in dispelling the ignorance and negative stereotypes held by children who come from a community with no particularly tragic or difficult history. I can't attempt to do more here than open up the debate and point to the existence and value of a few resources, giving one or two examples, in the hope that teachers will feel inspired to think about the issues, and perhaps actively look for and use such material themselves.

I would like to end this section with a long quote from the Non Statutory Guidance, 1991, C18, 10.00 *Equal opportunities and multicultural education.* Though it contains the language of attainment targets which were abandoned by Dearing, it provides a fitting summary to this introductory chapter, and a bridge to the next one, in which I consider possibilities for an inclusive history curriculum with KS 1 children.

10.1. National Curriculum history requires pupils to be taught about the cultural and ethnic diversity of past societies and the experiences of men and women. Through history pupils acquire understanding and respect for other cultures and values. They should develop what the History Working Group called 'the quality of open mindedness which questions assumptions and demands evidence for points of view'.

10.2. The study of history has sometimes concentrated on political at the expense of social, economic and cultural aspects. This has meant the neglect of important groups in past societies. Historical research is helping to put right this situation. Classroom materials are now available which draw on this research and present an accurate view of women and minority groups in past societies.

Attainment targets

10.3 The attainment targets require pupils to think about the limitations of evidence. Pupils might consider why evidence is sometimes unavailable for the history of particular groups.

10.4 ATs 2 and 3 require pupils to study different interpretations of past societies or groups. For example, pupils might study how women were portrayed in late nineteenth century literature and art (AT 3), or explore why textbooks contain few references to the role of black troops in World War 1 (AT 2).

10.5 As pupils' ability to understand interpretations of history develops, they will be able to explore conflicting viewpoints. This will help them identify and thus challenge racial or other forms of prejudice and stereotyping.

Resources

10.6 Resources chosen should allow history to be studied from a variety of perspectives. Pupils should understand that history books reflect the age and culture in which they were written. Many textbooks and other resources carry hidden messages. Pupils should learn how to identify these.

Bibliography

Brown, C., Barnfield, J. and Stone, M. (1991) *Spanner in the Works: education for racial equality and social justice in white schools*, Stoke on Trent, Trentham

Bruner, J. (1990) *Acts of Meaning*, London, Harvard University Press

Bryan, B. Dadzie, S. and Scafe, S. (1985) *The Heart of the Race: black women's lives in Britain*, London, Virago

Epstein, D. and Sealey, A. (1990) *Where it really matters: developing antiracist education in predominantly white primary schools*, Birmingham, Birmingham Development Education Centre

Hatcher, R. and Troyna, B. (1992) *Racism in children's lives: a study of mainly white primary schools*, London, Routledge

Rose, S., Lewontin, R. and Kamin, L. (1984) *Not in our Genes: biology, ideology and human nature*, Harmondsworth, Pelican

Rowbotham, S. (1977) *Hidden from History*, London, Pluto

Stevens, O, 1982, *Children Talking Politics*, Oxford, Martin Robertson

Wright, C. (1992) *Race Relations in the Primary School*, London, David Fulton

Chapter 2

Themes and Topics in Key Stage 1

This chapter explores how history in the infants school can be developed through broad themes, and suggests the kind of resources that can encourage cultural diversity and gender inclusiveness in the curriculum. The use of oral history, which is particularly appropriate for younger children is also considered.

Despite the pressure exerted by the National Curriculum to fragment children's learning into subject areas, many infant teachers are still committed to more holistic, thematic approaches. The criticism in the past was that within such themes some subject areas, particularly history, were marginalised (see for example, the 1989 HMI Report on History and Geography in the Primary School). Ironically, since coherence — at least for pupils — had always been its justification, the 1992 DES Report by the 'Three Wise Men' castigated topic-based teaching as causing subject superficiality and fragmentation.

Though it is not clear how far infant schools are choosing subject specificity rather than cross-curricularity as the vehicle for history, there are good arguments for treating history (and geography) through cross-curricular themes, while being alert to the perils of superficiality. I understand and endorse the necessity of skills-practice in specific subject areas, and recognise that sometimes the best history is done through concentrating on its special concepts and content. That said, it will be apparent to readers of this chapter that this can be achieved while still exploiting the connections between different aspects of learning which are fundamental to young children's growing understanding of their world. This was also the approach taken by the NCC non-statutory guidance of 1993 for Key Stage 1.

An inclusive curriculum for history in Key Stage 1

The Programme of Study for Key Stage 1 history is sufficiently open and non-prescriptive to facilitate rather than frustrate an imaginative teacher wanting to take an inclusive approach. The non-statutory guidance (1991) gave an unambiguous message about content, in a clearly framed statement about the importance and value of history in developing open-mindedness, understanding and respect for others. Disappointingly, when it came to specific ideas to turn these aims and objectives into curriculum plans, the next NCC document (1993, *Teaching History at Key Stage 1*) was remarkably coy. With a few tokenistic exceptions (mention of Florence Nightingale, Divali and Passover and a short section on using Valerie Flournoy's story-book *Patchwork Quilt*), this otherwise sensible and helpful resource is notable for its implicit assumptions and suggested examples that promote a male and Eurocentric content.

This chapter develops some of the ideas outlined in Chapter 1 about inclusivity, current historical thinking beyond the world of school, and children's learning. It also shows that these goals are quite compatible with the requirements and underlying intentions for the infant classroom of NSG 10.0, which concluded Chapter 1. The theoretical basis for history in the infants school has been very poorly articulated. One of my aims is to sketch in some justifications based both on child development and history itself, for ways of working with the youngest children.

Inclusive interpretations of theme work

History can take the lead in cross-curricular themes in some cases, or be part of a theme led by another curriculum area. I focus on three popular child-centred themes, as exemplars of how one might work.

i)   'Ourselves' — which regularly leads into explorations of family history

ii) 'Grandparents and Older People'

iii) 'Moving'.

i)   **Ourselves and Our Families — early work on the history of family and childhood**

This traditional infant theme is relevant to young children's own understanding and also facilitates junior teachers. All the study units in Key Stage 2 emphasise work on lives of men, women and children at different levels of society, and this implies family life and childhood. Juniors will be able to build on the history concepts and skills which infants would develop, honouring the important theory of continuity and progression in children's conceptual learning and knowledge base.

The history of childhood, marginalised and under-researched till quite recently, and the history of family, are increasingly part of serious historical research. A new third level Open University Course is devoted to the history of family. Incidentally, this is not the same as work on family trees, which can provide the data for history of family but which seldom moves beyond personalised amateur research and seldom takes on some of the more complex concepts. Chapter 8, which is about the Victorians, discusses examples of current approaches in historiography to the history of family and childhood, and I recommend that Key Stage 1 teachers turn to pages 131-3 so that they can share the framework of categories and concepts which can be introduced at a foundation level.

Laying down the conceptual framework for history in the early years

Prepared carefully, this project will involve the children's own community and is likely to transcend barriers of class, gender and 'race'. Work on personal time-lines can be the starting point for exploration of many relevant historical themes. Start with the youngest pupils, who will focus on their own lives, for example through looking at artefacts from their own babyhood and making their first attempts at creating time-lines of their own pre-school years. Some people criticise this as being 'pre-history'; however these foundations are as essential to history as much early work with picture books is to learning to read. Work on personal history, over however short a period, is still part of the past, and should establish the basic skills and concepts through appropriate content. The early skills relate to vocabulary, chronology and sequencing. From this base, children start to work with the concept of historical change which they need to distinguish from scientific or mathematical change (all infant teachers are familiar with the notion of learning about physical changes and conservation through manipulating plasticene or playing with water and sand). Historical change and continuity will be introduced with reference to personal issues and in comparison to their peers' experiences. This will lead on to the ideas of historical cause and consequence — again not to be confused with scientific, mechanistic concepts. Science is rule-bound; historical cause is interpretative and open to revision and personal value judgements.

Just by working with material from their own lives and being asked to remember episodes from the past, children will start to understand that the legitimate subject matter of history is human lives and not dinosaurs, fairies, space or plants. Children do not implicitly know that evidence — that is, pictures, artefacts, some of the stories people tell — are the building blocks of history. By working with their own memories and artefacts from their own babyhood they are learning what the nature of evidence is and how it can be used. This is an asset, not a drawback which needs justifying. Study of Vikings or Victorians can be saved till later, when children have started to grasp some of the basic ways in which history is made, how evidence gets interrogated, how the sequential narrative gets put together, using familiar material to interpret and reconstruct the past in the sequence in which events really happened.

The opportunities are obvious for an inclusive curriculum with respect to content. Different communities have different customs and rituals to do with birth, naming and welcoming the new child. Toys, songs, bed-time rhymes and stories have different cultural significance. Different people take important roles in 'parenting' and caring for their young. That said, normative or judgmental attitudes, or targeting some children for particular attention as the captive example of an exotic species, are absolutely unacceptable. Working with young adults as I do, it is distressing to hear how often ethnic minority people have found themselves singled out by insensitive teachers to represent a whole culture, even in the infants school. How diversity is handled is obviously paramount. A true incident told to me years after the event by a student, but not forgotten: 'your family comes from Bangladesh, Fatima, so you can tell us how your people do such and such'. All eyes, greatly unwelcome, on Fatima, who is covered with confusion. Or a personal memory: as a child the embarrassment of being asked publicly in class what we were or weren't allowed to eat during festivals, or as part of Jewish tradition. Since my immediate family were non-practising, and we ate pretty much everything that Christian families did, I really had very little idea. And furthermore, it made me very vulnerable to be labelled as different and 'one of them' among children who were not really getting any positive messages about Jews. It is better to approach parents or speak privately to children if information is wanted, making no assumptions about how far people adhere to conventions and traditions, before going public with assumptions about their families.

Returning to the theme of the historiography of the family, teachers might keep in mind that historians are interested in broad patterns of continuity and change but are just as interested in local diversity. History is not about discovering laws and exceptions to them but about charting the various ways in which people have made personal choices and responded to broader issues. In other words, historians try to create a tapestry, avoiding easy generalisations or stereotypes. By helping children understand the heterogeneity of experience, as well as the broad sweep, teachers will establish appropriate attitudes about the subject.

For some children the immediate family, sometimes but by no means invariably the conventional two-parent nuclear unit, is the extent of their experience. For others, the extended 'family of blood' is very important, with grandparents, aunts and uncles living close by and having a lot to do with the younger children. For some, the boundaries between 'real family' and an extended family of friends who are called aunties and uncles, is quite blurred. Teachers might worry that exploring this information is potentially sensitive. This is true: infant teachers usually understand the importance of confidentiality and may need to consider whether their approach, rather than the topic itself, is exposing some children in a hurtful way. (I know of a teacher who asked each child to draw and write a sentence about their *father* instead of giving a choice — as she easily might have — of a man that they knew quite well, whether their father, big brother, uncle, a family friend or even a male teacher.)

Some teachers start with their own family history, and give their class a first introduction to the power of oral history through telling stories about their own childhood, using pictures or mementoes as supports and encouraging the children to ask them questions. (There is more about oral history on pages 31-33 of this chapter.) When I was first an infant teacher, all my family apart from my brother lived abroad. The children wanted to know how and when my children got to see their grandparents, aunt and cousin which gave opportunities for them to share their own experience. I brought in photos of me and my siblings as children. A favourite showed me and my sister aged about 8 and 6, standing in shorts and bare feet outside the famous and long demolished 'Spotted Dog' Restaurant in Cape Town, built in the shape of a giant Dalmatian. This easily led into discussions and work about how long ago this had been, special memories, family treats and outings (and a time-line, to put it all in chronological perspective). Other adults in the school, for example, dinner supervisors, welfare assistants or kitchen staff who may well come from minority communities, can be asked to come and talk to the children. If they are prepared to lend photographs, these can go on the time-line, and children can certainly write and draw what they have heard about. Teachers who are finding it harder to get personal histories and artefacts from ethnic minority children than from the indigenous white children may need to take a hard look at differences in the nature of their relations with the two sets of parents and try and find out from within the community how they can facilitate the relationships. Perhaps language is a barrier — in which case they might need to think about whose responsibility it is to do something about it.

b)   **A project on mothers and grandmothers**

Seeking to emphasise the role of women in history, some infant teachers have worked with their pupils on the maternal line. They have looked particularly at mothers, aunts, grandmothers, even great-grandmothers (with greater longevity in our generation, there are an increasing number of infant aged children who can get information about this generation). In Ealing in the late 1980s, several infants schools prepared projects for International Women's History Week (International Women's Day is March 8th), in which children found out about and recorded their mothers' and grandmothers' histories. In one school the majority of the community was from the Indian subcontinent. Mothers and grandmothers came into the school and were interviewed by the children, sometimes with the help of another bilingual adult or Section 11 teacher. Photos were brought in of weddings, of visits back to India, and of childhoods spent there. Letters went back to India asking for photos or accounts from an older generation. The process was initially very slow, but the project had begun early in the academic year, was allowed to build up momentum and by March many people had responded and a great deal of work was produced by the children, ready for an exhibition in International Women's Week itself, which then transferred to the local library.

In another infants school with a much more heterogeneous community, a project on Grandmothers unearthed some fascinating life stories. Children who had difficulty finding out about their own relatives could choose to work with another child who had no such problem, or they could find out about a grandmother whom the teacher had identified through her own research and informal chats in the school and with parents/carers. Eventually, as well as people from the community, the project involved women who were schools meals supervisors and kitchen staff, welfare assistants, other members of the teaching staff, and even the Head. These children came to learn about the stories of women who had come originally from Somaliland, Pakistan, Poland, Ireland and the Caribbean. Motivation for moving, continuities and changes, causes and consequences were the recurring themes in this work: courage in the face of hardship, looking for a better life and work, moving as part of the family, the impact of war, birth of children, emerged as the threads which wove the different lives together.

You may not want to focus specifically on women but prefer to interpret the theme of 'generations' more broadly, to include not just fathers and grandfathers but anyone 'older' whose story can be explored. It is likely that this sort of work will bridge class barriers as well as those of nationality, ethnicity or 'race'. In the infant school, the important thing is to ensure that through the hidden and overt curriculum the children are learning in an inclusive way.

In the work I have just described, the presence in the community of a variety of cultures contributed to a multi-textured, rich and fascinating project. Of course not every school has such diversity on its doorstep and the teacher may need to make quite explicit efforts to broaden the children's experience. There are three possible ways to do this and I describe each in some detail on pages 30 onwards.

c)   **A topic on 'Moving'**

This is a popular cross-curricular theme in the infants school, offering obvious opportunities for good work in geography, science, technology and language, as well as history. I first developed the historical aspects of the topic as an advisory teacher working with the Y3 class teacher, in the East End of London (originally reported in *Multiethnic Education Review*, Spring 1983). A few of the children — white indigenous and black British (African and African-Caribbean in origin) — spoke English as a first language. The rest of the class were Vietnamese, Bengali, Sylheti, Pakistani and Moroccan. Some of the children were very recent arrivals who needed considerable support in communicating in English (which wasn't actually available). My intention was that the new arrivals should have a chance to share their history with us, and I chose the title 'Memories' so that everyone would be included. With the help of other children in the school who shared the language, or those parents and adults willing to help, we got all the children working on personal time-lines. It soon turned out that virtually every child in the class had moved at some time in their short life, if only from a smaller to a bigger flat, or down the road in the same area. For many of the children however, the moves were much more dramatic.

Not all the children actually remembered or drew their memories in the correct sequence, but this did not matter since they worked initially on loose sheets of paper. We then joined long strips of cut sugar paper to make concertina booklets, and after discussion about how old they had been, and what else had happened at the same time, before or after a memory, we were able to work out the sequence of events and paste the drawings and brief sentences about them in the right order. Each child's time-line was of course different, in content and length. One child's time-line was about memories of favourite toys and moving from a child-minder to the nursery school. Another recorded the birth of siblings and moving from his cot into a bed in an older brother's room. One Vietnamese boy's time-line recorded different stages of the journey from Vietnam to England with very few words but in pictures of startling and unambiguous clarity. We saw in sequence, soldiers in Vietnam itself, the boat that took the family to Hong Kong, the Vietnamese in the transit camp surrounded by wire in Hong Kong itself, the aeroplane journey to England and the final destination, a tower block near the school. A Moroccan girl drew a picture of the customs officials who had held the family at immigration when they first arrived. Such records revealed the indelible experiences of discrimination that some pupils had suffered in their short lives.

A year or so later, as the class teacher with top infants (Y2) in a different school, I tried the 'Moving' theme again. We worked on the migration of birds, and on moving parts in toys. This time the majority of the children were not immigrants, and their families were reasonably settled members of the community. With children for whom communication in English was not a problem, I designed the history work differently. The children charted moves in their families' lives on a big class time-line (going back into the previous generation). My own moves, first from England to Africa in the war, then back to England as an adult, were recorded too. Instead of individual time-lines, the children made personal books about moves in their own lives or their family's. Children asked at home and discovered why and when a grandparent had come from Ireland, Dominica or Jamaica. One child's book was about moving from Doncaster to London when his mother and father had split up. A moody and unhappy child, this was a bittersweet evocation of a time when he felt he had been happy and had really belonged. In some ways this work was a breakthrough for him and me in a very tricky relationship.

However the most memorable book (of which I still have a copy) again came from a young Vietnamese in my class. She was quiet and reserved and seldom talked about her past. However, she produced a series of stunningly graphic pictures in black and white through which I — and the rest of the class — learned about her and her family's escape from Hanoi. I recorded her story, transcribed it and typed it up. She made this into a book, using her own art work. She kept the original and, with her permission I made several photocopied versions of the whole book for reading corners in other classes as well as our own. Also with her permission, the pictures are now on the front cover of this book.

Here are some excerpts:

> My name is Cu and we didn't like living in Vietnam. My Mum and Dad had to go and work for the soldiers. They had to use an ox to get food. They had to work all day long... The guards were all around the houses. No one could get out. So one night lots of people went and packed their things to run away. ...We took everything except one thing that we couldn't carry. That was a very big Chinese statue... First they went and hid in the woods. My Dad came later. He was carrying me. When we were hiding in the woods we had to wait right through the night. It was a bit miserable. There were lots of sounds, horrible sounds and lots of people hiding and staying close together and they were frightened too. I stayed with my Mum and Dad and held on to them very very tight. My Mum had a stick with a big basket to carry food... There was a short path and lots of water when we got to the boat. If anyone fell in they would be eaten by fish. ...Then we waited for the boat. We got on the boat and we sailed a long way. The boat wasn't so big. It was just as big as this room. About 60 people were on the boat... it was very crowded. There was no room to lie down, only three people could lie down. ... No one didn't want (sic) to go near the edges because they might fall in. There was only a bottle of drink, you got to drink only a little bit, because there wasn't enough and a tin for each person, just for one day you could eat. But the other days you had to starve. ... One boat was going to sink. Some people tried to swim, but the fish [sharks?] ate them up and children too. We were lucky... The guards didn't know. They went to sleep and they forgot about us so we slipped away.

Emotions and confidentiality in family history work

At the beginning of this chapter I mentioned the cognitively-based reasons for cross-curricular work which helps children to make connections and form understandings in a world which does not have subject boundaries round events and material things. There is another sense in which history is cross-curricular: it can involve disclosure and thus move into the realms of personal, social and emotional learning. The point was made in chapter 1 that the subject matter of history is sometimes imbued with strong emotional reactions. Some teachers may themselves have worked on personal time-lines and been startled at the power of the emotions stirred up by charting changes and turning points in their lives. A

'My Mum and Dad had to go and work for the soldiers. They had to use an ox to get food.' (Illustration by Cu San)

theme which draws on children's own lives does run the risk of bringing into the classroom memories which are painful as well as pleasant, as the excerpts from Cu's book illustrate very poignantly.

Margy Burns Knight, an American ESL teacher, has worked with refugees from Cambodia and other countries. Her book *Who belongs here?* based on the true stories of her young pupils, also makes clear that remembering the past can be both painful and cathartic but that it always helps the children feel that their experience is recognised, and certainly can affect other children's ignorance and insensitivity. I always tell children (or adults working on their own time-lines) that they need only reveal what they want to, and decide for themselves who will see their work. Having worked with infants, juniors and adults, my experience has been that giving people the chance to tell others about themselves enormously benefits self-esteem; helps in learning about commonalities and differences; contributes to building respect and awareness of the specialness of other people's lives. But such work must be grounded in a classroom ethos in which trust and mutual respect are well established. For this I have found, as many others have done before and since, that a great deal of preparatory work may be necessary to build self-esteem and collaboration.

Currently, teachers working with Somali refugees or dealing with animosity between young Kurdish and Turkish children may find opening up the curriculum in this way helpful in dispelling ignorance and giving a voice to different experience.

The two books which I describe below were designed as resources for the infant years, to support work on immigration and the disruption caused by war. In Chapter 3 (p.48ff) more story-books which might also be the starting point for work on 'Moving' in the infant classroom, are briefly described.

Exploring History (Liverpool Education Directorate)

Designed for the youngest children, this booklet is based on photographs and lives of real children, and is an example of excellent infant practice. It does not focus particularly on refugee status or immigration, but it is clear that this may be the background of some children in the group or their parents. It contextualises history in a theme about where everyone comes from or has been, rather than targeting particular children. Similarities in the life histories of different communities and families can be drawn out and valued, and space given to the more unusual histories.

New Faces, New Places: learning about people on the move:
a resource for 4-7 year olds, (Save the Children Education Unit)

This little resource pack has a number of 'factional' stories with a mixture of drawings and photographs about children who have had been displaced by war. There are stories about Palestinian children living in a camp in the occupied zone, a Vietnamese family in Hong Kong, Kurds in England, Sudanese and Mocambiquan children displaced within their continent. The authors suggest that the resources could be used as part of a topic on 'Journeys'.

Broadening children's experience

Although one would usually want to start work in history with children's own experiences, this can be limiting and compound disadvantage for children whose lives are not enriched by experiences beyond their immediate environment, as we have seen. Their horizons can, however, be expanded — and such expansion and enrichment is fundamental to the purposes of education — by means of:

- ☐ oral history with specially invited visitors who do not come from the children's families or community

- ☐ written sources, photos and artefacts about real people who the children don't actually know or meet

- ☐ using fiction

Using Oral History

In the adult world, the use of oral history has developed considerably in recent years. Amateur historians, working in local history societies, and professionals are collecting the oral histories of working class women and men, in an attempt to enrich our understanding and knowledge of the past, which generally recorded official and elitist experience.

In South Africa a number of oral history projects are attempting to record aspects of life and resistance under apartheid, by interviewing workers (notably including female domestic workers) and ex-freedom fighters who are unlikely ever to write their stories down themselves. In this country, oral history is well established with the elderly, with minority and local communities and some projects have been televised. One recent programme revealed the tragic fate of people who were locked away for years in mental homes for transgressing moral conventions of the time (e.g. becoming pregnant out of wedlock); another recorded the experience of birth and motherhood in the early years of this century and a third explored the experience of colonisers and colonised under British rule earlier this century.

Oral history is the traditional way of remembering and transmitting the past in many societies, particularly where literacy is recent or not very widespread. Oral history was certainly the main vehicle for history in pre-literate Europe. In many African societies special people were (and still are) entrusted with remembering and recounting the old stories. They develop quite extraordinary memories by the standards of those who have come to rely on modern technologies. It is striking in talking with adult students about oral history (white indigenous as well as from ethnic minorities) how often they say that their knowledge about their own family and community comes from hearing their grandparents — particularly grandmothers — tell them stories about the past.

Oral history in the infant school has received specific endorsement in various non-statutory guidance which has appeared since ERA. The *Oral History Journal* devoted an issue to this methodology in the primary school, and over the past few years there have been a number of articles in the professional journal, *Teaching History*, describing and recommending the advantages of oral history. Increasingly, teachers are realising its potential to bring history alive and make it meaningful for young children — translating abstractions like the past, the passage of time, concepts of change and continuity, and 'evidence' into visible and tangible experience for the children, through narrative. Through oral history young children can start to understand how things and pictures brought in by a visitor can carry a story, and they can start to learn about appropriate questions — that is how to 'interrogate the evidence' — a skill which is essential, particularly when a person who is knowledgeable about the evidence is not there to answer and it is more difficult to corroborate one's hypotheses. Children will need help in learning how to 'interrogate evidence' (in this case the oral history brought into the classroom by a visitor) and examples of the sort of questions they could ask and the answers they might expect. This is why the first person to introduce oral history might best be the teacher, since s/he can slip in and out of role as interviewee and teacher, explaining to the children how and what they are learning. Research with young children has identified the importance of gaining this kind of metacognition, which helps children to reflect on, organise and make sense of new knowledge.

The kinds of questions that apply to oral evidence are similar to those used about artefacts and visual evidence. Here are some examples; you and the children will be able to think of more:

☐ *what* questions — what was it like, what did you do, what has changed or stayed the same, what was it for, what was its value, what is it made of, what happened before that or next, what does this tell us about the past

☐ *why* questions — why did you do that, why was it like that, why has it changed, why did you like or dislike something, why was this made or things done that way

☐ *when* questions — when did you do something, when did you stop, when was it used

☐ *how* questions — how are things the same/different, how did you do things then, how did you feel

☐ *who* questions — who used this, who was there too, who made this, who made you do things, or stopped you.

The important thing is that the person is there to answer, and the children do not have to rely on speculation or further book research, which involve more complex skills.

An inclusive history curriculum means finding people from communities who have been excluded in the mainstream of conventional history. It also means that we counteract simplistic or stereotyped views that everyone experienced the past in the same way. Some adults might talk about their houses and land where they grew up. Some might talk about the work they were expected to do as children, how they spent their leisure time and what kind of education they experienced. This could be compared with children's own contemporary lives. Oral history should be collaborative and interactive, providing scope for children to think about questions they want to ask of their informant, and to question the visitor when she/he is there with them, not just be an opportunity for the visitor to reminisce and 'tell stories'.

People will readily come and talk to infant school children, but should be quite carefully selected, in line with particular aims. Perhaps someone with an interesting past from a minority community can enrich children's understanding and counteract stereotypical or limited perceptions; so can someone whose work was not particularly high status, but nevertheless essential. Or draw on someone known personally (say the mother or father of a friend), or contact Age Concern, a local Old People's group or community group. People could be asked whether they would be willing to be part of a project about Grandparents' lives, or what it was like to be at school in the 30s, 40s or 50s, or talk about their childhood in the war, or life in some other community as a young adult, to compare with other interviewees. The visitor should be carefully briefed before she/he comes to talk to them, and the children properly prepared, perhaps by practising interviewing the teacher or each other. Maggie Hewitt and Annie Harris's booklet *Talking Time* (1992) is a useful teachers' resource with ideas about how to prepare children to interview visitors, and integrate oral history approaches into the general history curriculum.

Equal opportunities for the elderly

Books about oral history often set great store on the personal and therapeutic value to the elderly of taking part in reminiscence work. However, there is another equal opportunities issue: Phil Salmon has written feelingly of the potential for condescension, misunderstanding and exploitation of the elderly through the processes of oral history. She explores how being defined as 'elderly' relegates the person to the past and denies them a stake in contemporary life.

> As the representatives of those far off times, old people themselves become quaint, oddities — museum exhibits — anachronistic, old fashioned, irrelevant. They can hardly be expected to be taken seriously in the modern world.

Their commitment to different ideals might make them seem 'almost unbelievably benighted' in the eyes of their young audience.

How much more might this apply to members of ethnic minority communities whose dress, language or accent might differentiate them from the young children eager to find out about their story. I have argued that multicultural objectives can never be considered as an unproblematic and automatic pathway to harmony and tolerance. The importance of proper preparation for everyone involved, can only underline this point. It's a delicate issue in which one risks the Scylla of patronising or the Charybdis of exposing one's visitors to a stressful experience, neither of which would prove totally positive for the class. The practical difficulties and moral issues should not to be minimised.

One solution might be to interview the person out of school, perhaps take a good photo, ask to borrow photos and artefacts. Discuss how you will tell her/his story and make sure that she/he agrees and understands. Then you can present the story, much as you might that of a historical figure who is genuinely not available.

Some predominantly white rural or suburban schools have liaised with inner city schools and arranged visits after exchanging photos and corresponding. It is more difficult, but not impossible to do a history project collaboratively, in which classes from the two schools actually share their human resources as well as communicating about themselves. This would involve children doing some work about the lives of a few elderly people in their own community and sending this to their partner school — each using the other's work as secondary evidence for further comparisons.

Using pictures, postcards and other artefacts

So ideas for an inclusive history curriculum are not about doing things differently from good practice, but about seeing opportunities to extend the range of children's experience so that they work with resources and people from a variety of cultural backgrounds, and are given opportunities to challenge sex- and class-based stereotypes.

In the primary classroom, as in adult reminiscence workshops, some of the most successful oral history emerges when the visitor has 'props' to talk about, in much the same way as we use props to focus and help carry the action when we tell children stories. Asking visitors to bring artefacts and pictures can help them structure what they will talk about so that it does not become too rambling, give them confidence about their input, and focus the children on the particular nature of the visitor's experience. So, for example, the starting points for some oral history might be to tell the story that goes with a photograph of the visitor as a young girl with her family in the vegetable garden of her childhood home in Guyana, some 50 years before. Or, say, or a piece of jewellery, given as a present to a Bengali woman and brought with her over the seas when she immigrated to England 30 years ago. Or a toy sent from abroad to a child who is now grown up and has saved it as a memento of a loved relative. This is how children can learn that artefacts can vividly recreate the reality of a past life.

It may not be possible for teachers to invite visitors from an ethnic minority community so they might want to find resources which they can use themselves. Mainstream published history resources are seldom strong on including minority experience, even in books about the world wars in which members of the New Commonwealth took an active part, or post war, when they have increasingly been part of the settled community in Britain. However, there are pictures and artefacts to be found. Recently the Ragged School Museum Trust researched the presence of black children in the Barnado's Archives and found photographs and some evidence. The 1993 SATs pack featured a little black boy standing dejectedly with his peers, his label pinned to his coat, in a photograph of children being evacuated from London. Books for older school students (e.g. File and Power (1981), or Elyse Dodgson's *Motherland*, 1983) have photographs which children can work with, without needing to read the text. Community book shops are good sources of pictures and postcards of not just an all-white past. They publish material written by the elderly and adult learners in special workshops, parts of which the teacher might read aloud. These books very often have photographs of advertisements from the time, and common domestic objects. (See particularly the resources list at the end of Chapter 9, Britain since 1930.) The language is usually straightforward and with a bit of help can be understood by older infants.

Just as choosing a visitor to be invited in and interviewed is part of the hidden curriculum, so are the artefacts and images one brings into the classroom. The pictures and artefacts themselves will embody and give value to women's experiences, or an aspect of a working class life, or ethnic minority experience, in an empirical way. Talking about and learning from a picture showing, say, a woman cooking, caring for children, sewing or weaving, fetching water, hoeing the garden, driving a bus in the war, or carefully preserved treasures like wedding shoes, an old quilt or a handknitted baby shawl, tells children that these activities are meaningful, that the people whose work is shown contributed to society and are worth them thinking about and spending time on. And logically, that the life of the person should not be marginalised or ignored as if it were unimportant.

Resourcing topics through artefact collections, photographs, museums and local history libraries

We have explored some specific possibilities for inclusive history within cross-curricular themes. There are many other topics which are used to develop history, for example, transport, shopping, toys or food. Teachers need to think how to avoid biased and partial resourcing in the pictures and artefacts which they bring in to make class museums or for interactive displays. Photographs of the local high street which can be compared with those from an earlier period may be a useful way to reflect the changing ethnicity of the community. The important thing is to focus on change and continuity, noting where newer communities have made their mark, or customs have changed. For this kind of work I have found postcards and reproduction photographs of my area going back to the 1890s in the local history library and local shops. I go out with my camera and take a photograph from the equivalent position.

Children can then work on change and continuity, comparing the contemporary photos with those taken in a previous decade when the community was perhaps relatively homogeneous and monocultural. The chip shop in the 1950s photograph is now the Chinese Take Away. The drapers in the Edwardian photo has become a pizza parlour. Not just the shape of the bus but the ethnicity of some of the passengers and the driver, just visible, have changed. A photo from the end of the Victorian period shows that the market is in the same place, and the same pub is on the corner, but the stalls sell very different goods and the customers once dressed in long dresses, or cloth caps and baggy trousers, wear leggings and t-shirts, baseball caps on backwards, red, gold and green knitted hats over locks, *shalwar kamiz*, or African tie-dyed shirts. A taxi with adverts on its side doors pulls away where a century before there was a horse-drawn cart.

Occasionally a museum mounts a special exhibition which is designed to acknowledge the contribution of immigrants and settlers from abroad to the history of Britain. The Peopling of London exhibition at the Museum of London in 1993-4 was probably the most extensive; but its theme was adopted by many local history museums in smaller exhibitions, for example the Grange Museum in Neasden, and the Newham Local History Museum. Even after the exhibitions end, resources in the form of booklets produced at the time, tapes, and postcards are usually available.

Some books on the history of transport manage to *avoid* including a single photograph of a black person, even in the post-war years, when large numbers of men and women were recruited from the Caribbean to keep a desperately short-staffed infrastructure functioning. The London Transport Museum recently mounted a special exhibition and published a teachers' resource pack to commemorate the essential contribution of Caribbean workers. Similarly, the Imperial War Museum has produced a resource pack commemorating the experience and contribution of Commonwealth soldiers. The newspaper archives in local history libraries have back numbers in which evidence of ethnic minority communities is easily found, if they have lived there. Once you have identified a photograph on the microfilm, there are facilities for enlarging and making a photocopy in one go.

Local history librarians sometimes know of specific photographs in their collection which can be used in a school project. For example, the Southwark Local History Library found me a lithograph of Joseph Lancaster, the man largely responsible for the 'monitorial system' of child apprentice teachers in early nineteenth century English 'National' schools, teaching a large class of children in Jamaica. It appeared he'd perfected his methods there and in India.

Many local education authorities and museums have artefact collections which go out on loan to schools. Boroughs which have identified the needs of their minority communities are usually well resourced. If you are not in an authority with this service, sometimes knowing the sorts of things that other boroughs have collected can give ideas for the second best option, namely a postcard or picture, which might substitute for the real thing. In the section on oral history I sketched the kinds of questions that might be asked about such evidence. Many teachers do encourage children to ask not just what something is made of but where the material or the object came from. Even the youngest children can start to appreciate that British trade connections, and imports of materials that we don't, can't and never have produced ourselves, are central to all our lives.

There is a list of fiction at the end of Chapter 3 and a resource list at the end of Chapter 9. Some books are annotated in Chapter 13, indicated by *[anno]*.

Non fiction referred to in this chapter

Dodgson, Elyse, 1983, *Motherland*, London, Heinemann

File, Nigel and Power, Chris, 1981, *Black Settlers in Britain 1555-1958*, London, Heinemann *[anno]*

Hazareesingh, S. et al, 1994, *Speaking about the past: oral history for 5-7 year olds*, Stoke-on-Trent, Trentham

Hewitt, Maggie and Harris, Annie, 1992, *Talking Time! A guide to oral history for schools*, London, Learning by Design, Tower Hamlets Education

Imperial War Museum, 1995, *Together! the contribution made in the Second World War by African, Asian adn Caribbean men and women*, London, Imperial War Museum Resource Pack

Knight, Margy Burns, 1994, *Who belongs here?* Gardiner, Maine, Tilbury House Publishers

Liverpool Education Directorate, 1993, *Exploring History, KS 1 National Curriculum History*, dual language: English and Somali, Liverpool, Liverpool Education Directorate, Race Equality Management Team

London Transport Museum, 1994, *Sun-a-shine, Rain-a-Fall, London Transport's West Indian workforce: Activities and Resources for Schools*, London, London Transport Museum Education Service *[anno]*

Refugee Council, n.d., *Helping Refugee Children in Schools*, London, The Refugee Council

Rutter, Jill, 1994, *Refugee Children in the Classroom*, Stoke-on-Trent, Trentham

Save the Children Education Unit, 192, *New Faces, New Places: learning about people on the move: a resource for 4-7 year olds*, London, Save the Children Fund

Chapter 3

Using stories to support KS 1 history

This chapter begins with some general discussion about the validity of using fiction to support history in the infants school. The critical word here is 'support'. Even if stories are not themselves historical or 'true', they can be valid and powerful vehicles for working on the concepts of history and introducing multicultural and non-sexist content. We shall see that the shift from story to history is less problematic than some might make out. In addition to new ideas, I return on page 47-49 to specific fictional resources for the grandparents/elderly theme and the theme on 'Moving', which I introduced in the previous chapter.

Using fiction to develop historical skills

To many people's surprise, the 1991 Programme of Study for KS 1 History actually advised using fiction in the infant school. This seemed to fly in the face of beliefs that history is about 'facts' which can be verified.

The NCC Inset Resource, *Teaching History at Key Stage 1*, (1993) cautiously endorsed storytelling as an appropriate method of teaching history to infants, and gave rather ambivalent support to stories which are not actually historical, advising that although they can help children develop a sense of chronology, motivation and the difference between fact and fiction, they should not be used for assessment purposes, since '*they do not contain historical information*' (NCC 1993, p. 33 original emphasis).

Despite this contradictory and limited assessment-led advice, sensible practical suggestions follow, particularly for using stories to explore chronology, cause and sequence (NCC 1993, pp 34-37). This is not an aspect of stories developed here, as it has less relevance to the equal opportunities themes of this book. The 1995 SCAA Order requires that 'stories from different periods and cultures, including stories and eyewitness accounts of historical events' should be the vehicle for children to acquire 'range and depth of historical knowledge and understanding'. This is ambiguous advice — not excluding fiction, but not specifically endorsing it either. In keeping with recent recommendations that teachers use professional judgement in interpreting how to translate the detail of the curriculum through their teaching approaches, I would strongly recommend that teachers look for and include the picture books and fictional accounts which do develop range and depth in the widest sense. In this context, the paragraph which follows discusses the conceptual differences between fact and fiction.

How shall we choose stories as a vehicle for history?

Which stories to choose and use is not always obvious. There are a great many story-books which incorporate historical material. Criteria apply for the choice of any books for children, relating to quality of writing, characterisation, story development, language, production and so on. The quality of books which might develop historical concepts and understanding is variable. Many are poorly written and visually unappealing. Two-dimensional characters, vehicles for swashbuckling bravery or frivolous femininity, are typical. History is reduced to a pantomime of overheated excitement which, although dramatic, can make the lives of people in the past remote, incomprehensible and inaccessible. Such books are unlikely to be helpful, even though they seem, superficially, to be about history.

My other main concern is that through their covert and overt messages about humanity, children should be offered stories which embody equal opportunities principles, which value and respect girls and women, non-European cultures and minority ethnic groups in Britain.

Problems with fact and fiction

The problematic statement of attainment at level 1 (AT 2) of the 1991 Statutory Order, expecting young children to differentiate fact and fiction, has gone from the 1995 History Order, along with the requirements to teach from myths and legends. How myths and legends were supposed to help the youngest children get to grips with history was not explained. However, I would hope that though they are no longer a compulsory part of the programme of study, teachers will not abandon them. They are among the most attractive and powerful morality stories in the culture of every civilisation, usually with deep roots in a pre-literate past, but they are *not history*, as the following quotation makes clear.

> A myth is a sacred story set in a time and place outside history, describing in fictional form the fundamental truths of nature and human life. Mythology gives body to the invisible and eternal factors that are always part of life, but don't appear in a literal, factual story.... Myth reaches beyond the personal to

express an imagery reflective of archetypal issues that shape every human life (Moore, 1992, p.220).

Using myths as a way of learning history in the infant school (as opposed to English) could only have ended up by confusing young children. Nevertheless, they provide plenty of opportunity for comparative multicultural work, whether it be explaining the mysterious beginnings of the world or grappling with moral issues.

As for differentiating fact and fiction, the 1993 NCC Inset Resources on Teaching History at KS 1 quote the child who thought that Jack's mother in Jack and the Beanstalk was real but that the giant was not. The boy's reasoning was illuminating — the woman acted in understandable human ways. This is an important reminder of the post-Piagetian insights we now have about children's need to make sense of the world (see Margaret Donaldson, Jerome Bruner and other child developmentalists). It takes children a long time to come to terms with the difference between fantasy and fact, fiction and fact. Think of the children who believe in Father Christmas, or the tooth fairy — with justification — since the money appears under the pillow, and Father Christmas is to be seen every December in countless stores.

When one reads a story-book one could discuss whether or not it is true, whether there really were people with these names and lives and how we know. It would be tedious and pedantic to do this with every story. The point with infant school history is often: 'could it be true', not 'is it true'. The maturity needed to distinguish between these can only come with considerable experience, and requires testing against the evidence. This sequence of thought is part of the skill underlying successful hypothesising in history (as in science). Some infant school history 'textbooks' actually rely on the blur between fiction and fact, using drawings as well as photographs, and inventing characters in different generations to compare changes and show continuities.

In 1994 two of my Honours students did some small-scale research with reception-aged children on the 'fact and fiction' Statement of Attainment. They confirmed our suspicions that children of this age were confused about whether a story was true or not, even when they had listened to a visitor telling her personal story, supported by photographs! With this in mind, one might be concerned whether using fiction to support history learning could prove a hostage to fortune. However, I think this need not be so. It seems to me perfectly possible to help children work from the internal logic of a story, developing their ideas of chronology and sequence, seeking pictorial, linguistic and motivational evidence to explain their ideas about meanings.

Following the arguments above, one would talk with the children about the story 'not being true', in the sense that it is not about real people who actually lived (or still live) on the earth. Some stories are fairy tales and fantasy (and often anthropomorphic): *Cinderella, Red Riding Hood, The Billy Goats Gruff.* Children sometimes find fairy stories harder to distinguish from fact since they are based on human rather than animal lives and are deeply familiar. Writers such as Bruno Bettelheim have contributed to our understanding of the metaphorical symbolism and 'truth' of such stories, whose currency is not banal or factual detail, but often requires the suspension of reality principles, resonating with our unconscious needs and desires, as we come to terms with the nature of life and chance. I do not want to imply in this chapter that the potential relevance of stories, including fairy stories, for historical work, invalidates or diminishes such psychoanalytic insights. This chapter considers later how fairy tales and traditional stories can contribute to learning historical skills — particularly understanding about different perspectives.

Interesting conversations might develop about how or whether the children know that these stories are 'not true' but I'm concerned here with stories about ordinary fictional people that *might* be true. Very often the author and illustrator actually say they're drawing on their own family, community or experience. The families in *Peepo, Peedie Peebles* and the *Katie Morag* series might well be real people; so might Jamaica and Kristin in *Jamaica's Find.* They behave like real children and the illustrators take particular care to locate them in a recognisable world with objects and surroundings which will be familiar or acceptable as genuine. In other words, what they do makes human sense to children and will be considered seriously in that light.

Another interesting historical question arises when the stories are set in another place and another time, even a decade or so ago. The first step is for children to notice how far the illustrations give clues that the story is not contemporary or that the action takes place beyond their own immediate world, for example in picture books set in rural Suffolk or urban London or a seaside village in St Lucia. This will require them to look carefully at the detail of the pictures and look for similarities and differences with their own experience. They need to ask 'How did the author and illustrator know about the period and place in which the story is set?' Of particular value for history are stories which move between the past and present, where the differences are actually at the heart of the story. You would discuss the fact that there might well have been some real people who did live like the characters in the book, wore such clothes, lived in such houses, did that kind of work. You would know if the book is well written and carefully researched if you could find real people, or books based on true lives, corroborating the fictional evidence. You could check out the detail of clothes, houses, work and so on. This approach has historical authenticity, because it is about checking evidence and interpretations. Because stories are such a familiar and popular medium for children's thinking and learning, you would be working from what they already understand. Thus one would move between fiction and non-fiction, developing and drawing on the historical skills that such work entails.

Learning to 'read pictures' is a skill which is part of 'interrogating' evidence, whether it be artefactual, visual or some other form. A recent book by Pam Baddeley and Chris Eddershaw, *Not so simple picture books*, intended for the English curriculum, explores some psychologically quite demanding ways of working with picture books, going beyond the obvious into the subtleties, ironies and alternative perspectives carried by the illustrations. Such approaches can only reinforce infant teachers' commitment to cross-curricularity and illuminate the advantages to children's learning of fluid subject boundaries.

The previous chapter started from the premise that history would regularly be part of cross-curricular projects in the infant school, and this chapter continues that theme, but with a somewhat different emphasis. Moreover, I argue that using fiction as a starting point for history (whether or not the books are used for other curricular purposes), can introduce ethnic minority, working class and female experience, as well as that of the dominant society, into a curriculum whose history textbooks for this age group do not necessarily take this broad and inclusive perspective.

Learning about artefactual evidence through story-books

Stories based on mysterious evidence from past lives have been around for some time for junior aged and younger secondary readers (for example *The Owl Service* by Alan Garner). Recently a number of children's books for the younger age range have explored this theme, though mostly published in the States rather than in England. These quite explicitly base the story round artefacts found, say, in an attic, or photographs of an earlier childhood or the possessions of a deceased family member. Young children can be introduced to the idea of evidence through learning how old things and pictures carry a story of a past life, waiting to be uncovered, as the following picture books illustrate.

Homeplace

This poetically written and beautifully illustrated book set in the Southern States of America has a white family rambling through the woods and coming across the ruined remains of a house and some buried, broken objects half hidden beneath the trees. The concepts of archaeology and reconstructing lives from detritus and broken fragments are introduced through the powerful medium of fiction. Magically, gradually, the pictures reconstruct the lives of the extended black family who lived there, probably at the turn of the nineteenth century, to judge by their clothes and lifestyle.

The concept of dating the story and how one might surmise and then confirm one's view through checking elsewhere, would be more than incidental to the historical aspects of working with this story. The details about the long dead-and-gone family, their house, the facilities for cooking, washing, sleeping and eating, their clothes, the tools they used as they went about their daily lives are carried in the pictures. It's a story with a tinge of melancholy, even somewhat ghostly, but it conveys the special magic that emanates from ruins and abandoned places, which one knows were once lively and noisy with real people, and suggests the fascination of a mysterious, half-revealed past that motivates many historians.

Kelly in the Mirror

Kelly in the Mirror is another book about a black American family which helps children to think about the way artefacts embody stories of the past. Kelly finds a number of objects in the attic of her house: her mother's discarded clothes, a sewing machine, a brownie camera and, above all, a photograph album with pictures of her mother when she was a child, and other family members now grown up or gone. The story ends with her father taking a photograph of the whole family (with his hi-tech automatic camera) which will itself become a record of that day. What Kelly sees in the old photos is not just evidence of her mother's childhood — in the detail of the clothes, hairstyle, events that were commemorated — but her own identity and family continuity. She finds that she looks like her mother did at her age. Things have changed, but things stay the same. Family history and the concepts of change and continuity are the subtext, with rich potential for development into a class project in which the children's own family histories are explored through artefactual and pictorial evidence.

There are other story-books in which a present or other memento keeps alive or provides evidence of an earlier life, for example a live rabbit, a present from a child's grandfather, in *My Grandad*. You may not be able to go very far in developing historical work from the stories themselves, but they will act as triggers for children to think about how things carry memories for them, and help them to understand that an object can give evidence about the past if you know how to ask the right questions. Books like this can perhaps be the start of a project in which they — and adults — bring in artefacts which carry a story from the past.

My Uncle Max

This gentle story, with its soft pastel drawings, could be part of work on the lives of the elderly. Like *Home Place*, the pictures and main story are set in an earlier period. With its lovely drawings of a treadle sewing machine, people in 30s 'frocks' and furniture from the children's great-grandparents' era, it is an excellent way to get children looking carefully and thinking about the artefacts which were part of ordinary people's lives at an earlier time. Some children may know that their grandparents still have treadle machines and the teacher might even be able to borrow one for a small class museum. Children could think about a time when clothes were not available cheaply off the peg in every high street, when everyone's clothes were home-made or produced by dressmakers who often work in difficult and cramped conditions. In many developing countries, particularly in parts of Africa and the Indian sub-continent, the dressmakers, usually men, sit in open shop fronts with treadle Singer sewing machines and great bolts of cloth. Customers choose their material and the pattern and come back a few days later to try the custom-made garment. Some children's parents may have worn hand-made clothes as a matter of course. The 'High Street Revolution' which brought cheap fashion to everyone, children included, was a phenomenon of the late 1960s and till then making one's children's clothes was much more customary than today. Adults might tell of their mother making their clothes and being dressed identically with a sister. Photographs might show a relative in a well-remembered 'frock', made especially for some occasion.

At the end of *My Uncle Max* we find out that the author — now an adult — is telling his nephews the true story, from his own childhood, about his uncle who lived upstairs. So the bridge is built between fiction and non-fiction, drawing on the genre of family oral history.

Another excellent book that contrasts the present and older people's childhoods is *When I was Little*. A young African-American boy and his grandfather reminisce about the old times before television, before everyone had a car, 'when life was really different'. Black and white pictures interspersed with colour signal the change from the past to the present. Grandfather remembers his childhood in the 30s; the detail in the black and white pictures of artefacts and life-style is careful and accurate.

One could use a book like this to explore the life-styles and the objects of ordinary daily use — 78 rpm. records, gramophones with big horns, sofas, clothes, clocks, washing tubs, cars and early aeroplanes, and what they meant in terms of differences in work and leisure. Though set in America, the similarities with rural England at the same period, as photographs show, are sufficient to give British teachers many worthwhile discussion points about continuity and change. Some children might bring in photographs showing artefacts in their grandparents' childhoods, or the teacher might find some to set alongside the book as part of a display.

In a session I ran recently on using fiction, there was a thought-provoking reaction from a group of African-Caribbean post-graduate students who discussed how they might use this book in an infant classroom. Moreover, since each was the mother of infant-school aged children, they offered a valuable parental perspective. Impressed by its potential, they were also critical of the unproblematic idealised portrait it painted of a black man's life in the 30s, set in the Southern States of America, in a period when Jim Crow laws, discrimination and victimisation of blacks prevailed. They were unanimous that they would have taken the opportunity to tell a class of children — even of infant age — that the book's rosy-tinted view of the past omitted crucial aspects of reality. They felt that such opportunities should not be missed, and that it would be racist by default not to challenge or at least extend the ideas offered in the story.

Many other books draw on inter-generational connections. In an infant classroom one can be 'doing history' in subtle ways at story time and through other curriculum areas, by focusing on the way older people like to reminisce about their own childhoods, by drawing attention to the detail in the pictures, the similarities or differences with the children's own lives and the ways in which the fictional lives might have been similar to those of real people living at the period.

The device of regularly using black and white pictures to denote the past means that young children come to rely on this distinguishing feature. Because they are right nine times out of ten, they may look no further and do not become adept at exploring the detail of the pictures. They have no way of realising that the past was not lived in black and white, or that contemporary pictures can also be in black and white. This misunderstanding is on a par with imagining that something must be new simply because it is shiny. We need to work carefully on the criteria for belonging in a previous period, or being old.

Understanding perspectives, interpretations and bias: the place of fiction

The three Attainment Targets have been replaced by the Key Elements, but their processes are still central in real history. History is not and never can be just a narrative of facts in the right chronological order. In academic history and in school history, selection of what to include and exclude, and different emphases in explanation have always been required. Infant education is continuous with, not fundamentally different to working with older children. The Key Stage 1 Key Elements use the subheadings, *Interpretations of history* and *Historical enquiry* to remind infant teachers not to emphasise information at the expense of teaching concepts of interpretation, perspective and bias. Moreover, these are often the most fascinating and thought-provoking aspects of history. Do we think young children can't cope with the ambivalence and uncertainty that explorations of interpretation and perspective entail? Should we be denying children these insights and real learning experiences?

A brief detour into child development theory: egocentricism and perspective-taking

Despite new research which seriously criticises Piagetian stage theory of childish egocentricism (Burman, 1994), some of his ideas seem very hard to shift. Even adults who have observed very young children trying to comfort a friend who has been hurt, sometimes insist that children can't see someone else's point of view, or show empathy. Yet most of us who work with infants use arguments about why she/he should 'be good' not just to avoid punishment, but on moral grounds to do

46

with being fair, sharing, not hurting others and so on. In other words we are behaving as if the child can and does see another's perspective. There are good arguments for including work on perspective-taking and interpretations in the history curriculum; firstly on the grounds that this is part of doing real history which young children are capable of taking on and, secondly, because such work is a necessary part of children's ongoing social and intellectual development.

In my view there is yet another justification for working on these skills and orientations: namely equal opportunities. Understanding other people's perspectives, being able to empathise and imagine oneself in another person's shoes, is part of an education towards tolerance, mutual respect and understanding. The history curriculum is not the only place for such approaches but it is an important and largely undervalued one.

Fictional stories which children can relate to and understand provide enormous opportunities to develop these historical skills of perspective-taking, which are fundamental within history itself but often quite complex. A bonus of using stories is that the issues and characters are usually starkly simplified (but without danger of a-historicity since they never pretend to be factual). Multicultural and non-sexist contexts are available, and teachers are freed from uneasy pressure to work with historical episodes where the complexity of moral and political issues is perhaps above their pupils' understanding. (Think of the Gunpowder Plot, recommended for Key Stage 1 work, where the real religious, moral and political conflicts are typically trivialised or avoided and the whole episode reduced to an 'exciting story'.)

Fiction about grandmothers, grandfathers and other elderly people

This section takes further the discussion in Chapter 2 about topics on 'Ourselves', or 'Our Family'. The fictional material included here could form part of historical work in a variety of KS 1 projects, for example on toys or school or kitchens.

I suggest two reasons for working from fiction about grandparents and the elderly with infants:

Fiction as the starting point leading into history

First, most infant teachers value and regularly use stories as rich and productive starting points for work with their class. In the area of history, ideas introduced through fiction can then move seamlessly on to the children's personal experience. A story about a loved grandmother is a natural invitation to talk about one's own granny or nan.

Fiction to expand horizons about the known world

Secondly, fiction can supplement experience for a theme the children are already engaged in, and expand their knowledge to include people and places outside their immediate horizons. Working from 'where the child is' should never mean limiting a child to that (possibly narrow) world, but must mean taking them further, helping them get to grips with new knowledge and understandings. The idea of inclusivity is particularly relevant to pupils in relatively monocultural communities, whether indigenous white or ethnic minorities. Some of the books I discuss below will illustrate this theme but first I want to concentrate on the quite substantial 'grandparents' literature (including books about the older generation).

Chapter 1 argued that the absence of children from ethnic minority communities in the school was no excuse for a limited and narrowly focused curriculum. A great deal of material exists to resource schools without a heterogeneous community which they can tap into themselves. It is true that some literature about the elderly is stereotyped and demeaning, particularly when it portrays the old as feeble-minded or risible, or women as witch-like. But there are a number of books which take a positive stance, showing elderly people who are competent, independent, loving and knowledgeable. Valerie Flournoy's *Patchwork Quilt* is justifiably famous for its compassionate message about care and connection between generations and is mentioned as a starting point for work in the NCC INSET Resources (1993, p. 38). Many other story-books can be used to introduce the notion that the lives of elderly people are interesting and to be taken seriously.

Fiction about grandparents seems to me to be one of the most powerful and accessible ways to introduce a range of ideas into the infant classroom, and not just about the past. Fictional stories may be about the diversity of cultures and communities in our world, the commonality of experiences, the emotions that surround ageing and the losing of loved ones. Such stories weave between the children's own experience and different worlds, where the past can be literally 'another country'. ('The past is another country, they do things differently there' as L.P. Hartley says in the opening line of *The Go Between*.)

Work on grandparents can get at the heart of equality issues to do with 'race', class, gender and age and go beyond them, through valuing relationships across generations, taking on issues of connection, acknowledging conflict and necessary change.

Some of the best 'Grandparent' stories I know of deal with just such issues. Take *My Grandpa and the Sea*, set in St Lucia. Grandfather resents and distrusts the new-fangled technology that threatens the ecology of the island and the old ways of making a living from the sea. His granddaughter understands his point of view but argues that progress (which she equates with change) is inevitable. Interestingly, the ability to differentiate change and progress is one of the issues that is highlighted by the Non-Statutory Guidance for History (B5 3.6), though it suggests that this understanding comes at a higher level than infant school. In any event, Grandfather makes his own unique compromise which his young granddaughter accepts.

Look again at *My Uncle Max*. This is set in Brooklyn, New York, in the 1930s to judge from the illustrations. The author tells us that he based it on the true story of his uncle. It would be possible, without stereotyping, to surmise that Max was a refugee (from Germany perhaps?) and that the family is probably Jewish. The book tells the story of a tailor who teaches his nephew how to use his old treadle machine to make a dress for his mother. Here, as in other stories, the story is built round artefacts — the sewing machine, the dress. These give an opportunity to build stories of other lives in other places, to show how artefacts are not just the carriers of memories but that they help us understand the nature of people's working lives.

Grandmother's Tale (dual language) features the Turkish community. The story is centred on the birth of a new baby and the involvement of the older women. Using quite stylised rather than realistic drawings, it vividly depicts village life in Turkey. The vegetables, the market, the babies are common features for all children, even though the setting is foreign.

Mairi Hedderwick's *Katie Morag* stories are excellent for discussing change and continuity, this time in a remote island community in Scotland. As with all good books for young children, the detail is carried in the illustrations as much as the text. Tiny meticulously detailed drawings depict the village shop and post office, the fishing community which depends on boats and sea for its livelihood. A recent book in the series is about building a new pier, allowing large ferries to dock, so replacing the old ferry and bringing the mainland within easy reach of the islanders. The old ways will be changed forever. What better way for young children to reflect on ways of life which still survive but are disappearing fast with the impact of technological 'progress'?

There are also many superb 'grandparent' stories from the States and Canada with which black children could identify, but which can enrich all children's images and ideas about black people. One of the best is *Tell me a Story Mama,* set in America. This is a delicate conversation between a young girl and her mother, who reminisces about her own childhood and her mother and father when they were young people and whom the young child knows now as occasional elderly visitors. This is a real dialogue — almost a duet — with the refrain, 'but you know that darling', 'but tell me again'. For many children this is how family traditions are carried on — through the repetition of much-loved stories about times past, including their own childhoods. A book like this values this tradition and provides an opportunity for children to talk about the way stories are kept alive in their families. When I've talked to students about family traditions, they have sometimes been astonished to realise just how important these have been in their own sense of identity. The links with oral history, discussed in Chapter 2, will be clear.

Using traditional and non-traditional stories to develop understanding about perspectives and bias

Historians accept and work with the idea that there might be more than one version of the past and that personal ideology, bias or perspective inevitably affect what gets remembered and recorded or how an event in the past is explained — both at the time and later on. These ideas underpin interpretations of both primary and secondary evidence. I have found that students in teacher training who have not studied history beyond the lower forms of secondary school have seldom been introduced to these ideas and may initially be quite dismayed that history is not about certainty and memorising incontrovertible facts. Not all are aware that each generation tends to reinterpret the past in the light of its own changing agendas — whether those of women, black people, socialists or revisionists.

Since the introduction of the National Curriculum, junior school children are being asked to become more sensitive to bias and perspective with respect to historical evidence and current interpretations. The chapters dealing with Key Stage 2 refer periodically to how these fundamental ideas can be developed. But it would be wrong to wait for the junior years: the infant school is the right place to start preparing children in these historical concepts. Young children can start to think about how stories get told through the eyes of different interested parties, using material familiar to them and easy to work on. Some of this may be from their own lives, for example different versions of a playground squabble, told not just by the children directly involved but also by onlookers. Or they can listen to different versions of what happened in assembly, or how stories in the class are retold with different emphases and omissions.

As an historian inducting children into the methodology and concepts of history, I want young children to get to grips with the idea that primary evidence — the words from the horse's mouth if you like — may provide only one version of the story. Till you hear the rider's story too, your idea of what happened is bound to be partial. But I have another goal, which could be why I am committed to the honest study of history! I believe that work on perspectives and bias is fundamental to challenging intolerance and stereotypes, not just in history but in the wider contemporary world. Good history is not, and should never be, about indoctrination and propaganda. This means that even the youngest children need to start thinking how a story might be told from another point of view.

The few examples which follow are intended to illustrate how children can work on perspective-taking, develop tolerance for another point of view and demonstrate that the context and content of stories can themselves contribute to an inclusive curriculum.

Traditional stories such as *Red Riding Hood,* the *Three Little Pigs, Goldilocks, Cinderella*

In any such well-known story, the reader is invited to identify with the 'goodie' who outwits or outfaces the 'baddie'. There is not really any dispute about the goodie and the baddie; the moral is clear and the dice are loaded so that the baddie gets his or her comeuppance.

Recently a number of alternative versions of traditional tales have appeared. Some people, particularly those concerned with Freudian or Jungian symbolism, feel strongly that the powerful messages in traditional stories about the triumph of good over evil, or the familiar formulae where lasting happiness is earned through overcoming obstacles, should not be tampered with. Others would say that the stories are sufficiently robust to hold up anyway and that it is rather precious to treat them as sacrosanct.

Alternative versions typically retain the pattern and denouement of the traditional story, but present the villain's behaviour as reasonable — if only you knew their side of the story. For example, the Wolf makes his case for teaching Red Riding Hood some manners. He claims the collusion of 'Granny', who lends him her clothes and hides under the bed, unlike in the usual version where he either kills her or stuffs her in a cupboard. Unfortunately for him, Granny hypocritically backtracks on her support and never tells his side of the story. (See Appendix 1: *Who's afraid of the big bad wolf?* for a version which could be used in Key Stage 1.) In the alternative *Three Little Pigs* (Scieszka), the wolf only wants to borrow a cup of sugar, and an unfortunate fit of sneezing brings the house down. *Goldilocks* is a more ambiguous tale, where it is less clear whether we are expected to take the part of the three bears or Goldilocks. But that is a good question for children — if they were going to be the lawyer representing or prosecuting Goldilocks for trespassing, what would they say?

For those of you who feel interested and confident about telling children stories, rather than reading from a book, an hilarious collection for adults, called *Politically Correct Bedtime Stories: Modern Tales for Our Life and Times* is a wonderful source of ideas. Roald Dahl has also rewritten some of the traditional stories with a typical macabre twist.

I have read, or told, alternative versions of well-known stories and worked with children on the ways in which they think these differ from the traditional tales, how they feel about the new versions; whether they believe the Wolf or feel he had a case to answer. Unlike the traditional versions, the alternative versions are usually written in the first person, this time with the original 'baddie' as the subject, explaining his (her) side of the story. Children can rewrite a variety of stories in this way taking the perspective not just of the baddie but of other minor characters. Baddeley and Eddershaw (1994) include part of a version of *Red Riding Hood* written by junior children. Some schools already encourage collaboration between older and younger pupils, and there are opportunities here for junior children to produce resources for younger pupils. Infants themselves (or juniors who will present their ideas to the infants) can work out and perform little plays or puppet shows which don't need to be written down.

Another strategy which helps children understand about perspectives in secondary evidence, is to try and tell a story as if they were very sympathetic to one or other party. What would they emphasise or embellish — what would they play down or leave out? No matter if the children's productions are quite stereotyped, or the bias unsubtle and unmistakable, since it is a skill they will refine with practice. This is all preparation for work in the junior and secondary years, when they will need to understand that not just the people involved at the time but also historians themselves have a point of view. Examples abound — value judgements on invasions and conquests, those trying to maintain traditions and those working for change in Victorian Britain, royalists or republicans in the Civil War.

For those of you who are uneasy about 'messing with tradition', other possibilities exist, for example identifying similarities and differences in various conventional versions, particularly in the little details. This is a useful historical skill which will serve children well as they move through school.

Using contemporary children's fiction to work on bias, perspectives and interpretations

Although alternative versions of traditional stories are perhaps the most obvious and the easiest starting points for such work a variety of children's stories offer possibilities. Look for stories where the perspective of the main character is obvious but where there are one or more supporting characters from whose position the story could be told instead. Deliberately searching out examples that take on equal opportunities perspectives is equally important, if this kind of work is to meet both the aims that I outlined above (page 47).

I only have space for a few examples, and new children's fiction is published every year (which is bound to make my list out of date) but I think the following books make the point and that teachers will quickly see how this idea can be adapted with their own and the children's favourites.

Crusher is Coming

In this anti-macho story the main character, Peter, completely misinterprets his friend Crusher's attitudes and interests and gradually finds out that the macho behaviour he'd expected is far from Crusher's true nature. Peter's mother and little sister Claire have bit parts in the action and it would be possible to ask children to tell the story from their point of view, as well as from Crusher's himself, whom the author presents through Peter's eyes.

Jamaica's Find

Jamaica's Find is popular for its positive image of the main character, an attractive little Black British girl who finds a toy dog in the park. This is a moral tale in which Jamaica initially doesn't want to give the toy in to the lost property desk, but in doing so makes a new friend in Kristin, the little girl who had lost the toy. What is Kristin's side of the story? What does she think, say and hope for when she finds she's lost her beloved toy? How does she feel about Jamaica?

Dr Xargle and the Earthlets

Some years ago work was published using *But Martin* by June Counsell to support anti-racist teaching. Martin, the green space-creature has a very different perception of the classroom that he finds himself in, than the little English boys and girls of different ethnic backgrounds. Books about space-creatures visiting the earth, or vice versa, can lead into work about the interpretation and misinterpretation of evidence. *But Martin* was criticised for tokenism, a charge which *Dr Xargle's Book of Earthlets* avoids. It's also much wittier and enormously popular with young children and teachers for its hilarious drawings and slapstick humour. Dr Xargle gives his little space pupils a lesson about humans: he explains with pompous conviction — always missing the mark despite some good guesses — how babies are bathed, powder applied to stop them sticking to things, fed through the ears, nose and mouth, and then thrown into the air by their playful parents. He draws attention to the number of arms and legs humans have, and the nature of their 'fur' — observations which would only occur to a non-human.

This is a wonderful opportunity for children to consider how the evidence of their own lives could be misinterpreted, not just by creatures from outer space but by people in some future period or from a completely different cultural background, trying to make sense of our contemporary times by using bits and pieces of evidence and their own perspectives and experience. What for instance might people in the twenty-ninth century make of a baby's dummy or an egg whisk (supposing such objects were miraculously to survive)? The Dr Xargle story depends on real knowledge about the human artefacts and cultural habits, not just to give an edge to the jokes but also to reveal the misunderstandings.

One might follow this up with work on artefacts and evidence left by people from another culture, period or place who are not available in person to correct misconceptions. Books like *History Mysteries*, where children try to work out what objects were for, chiefly from the Victorian period or early C20th and are then shown their function, would be very helpful to introduce such work and take it from the joky 'Dr Xargle' mode into real history. Better still to have in the classroom a collection of mystery objects, some from the dominant British culture — e.g. a Victorian stoneware hot water bottle, a lace-making bobbin or a darning 'mushroom' — but others from abroad — e.g. a tool from the Caribbean for scraping coconut flesh, a thumb piano or a calabash drinking vessel from central Africa. It would be important for the teacher, or a child, to have genuine knowledge about the mystery artefacts so that the children could move from playing games about getting things wrong, to seriously considering not just that we can get things wrong about other people, but in *what specific ways* we might be wrong. One would want to draw lessons from *Dr Xargle* about the importance of cross-checking and trying to find someone or a book which can corroborate one's intelligent detective work.

Another good activity which takes this idea further is to ask children to choose just one or two artefacts which they would like to bury in a time capsule so that people in a future century could work out how they lived. If that was all that was found, what distortions would be inevitable because of partial evidence? If nothing but metal and stone were to survive, what would people know about our own lives?

Using fiction to help young children understand important historical periods, issues and events

In 1986 Little and John published an important booklet, *Historical Fiction in the Classroom*. It emphasised the value of historical fiction for bringing history alive, filling in details of place and character which could make the difference between children coming to love history, believing in and coming to terms with the reality of past lives, or dismissing history as a dead and boring subject where they learned a lot of seemingly irrelevant facts and dates off by heart. Like a recent article about the importance and serious quality of good adult historical fiction (*The Historian,* autumn 1994), they also drew attention to the careful research into authenticity of period that preceded good historical fiction.

Through Whose Eyes (1992) reports Beverley Naidoo's research with young secondary children using historical fiction. She shows how fiction can be used to 'open our hearts and minds' and help children think about issues which might be quite removed from their own personal experience, but which touch on their developing sense of justice and help them talk about their feelings.

Many infant teachers believe that their pupils are too young to think about issues in the news, but they ignore all the evidence of the ways in which television and adult conversation impinges on young sensibilities. *Newsround* is among the most popular programmes watched by infants as well as juniors. Like many other infant class teachers, I sometimes used discussion time in class and assemblies to talk about events in the wider world which were on the news. I found that despite misunderstandings — largely related to the limited experience you would expect from 6 and 7 year olds — children were interested and concerned to discuss issues and know more.

Awareness of children's interest has prompted me to consider how far we might move young children's historical understanding beyond the immediate horizons of their community. The statutory and non-statutory orders do not appear to find this problematic — some of their examples for appropriate work in Y2 not only come from periods well beyond children's possible experience but are also drawn from cultures with which they might have little personal involvement. How are these choices made? It seems to me that, once we have accepted that a conceptual leap in imagination and understanding is required with any historical work that is beyond living memory, and that a major part of the teacher's task is to help children with these understandings, we still need to settle on criteria for selection, rather than operate on hit and miss or personal preference. What follows might appear to conflict with the earlier discussion about not straying into Key Stage 2 territory which is too complex for infant children. My argument is that fiction can act as a bridge or a foundation for ideas which probably are too difficult for infants to study in a truly historical way, but which they can still engage with at a level which is appropriate to their maturity.

The following excerpt from the 1995 Order is the context for this discussion.

> Pupils should be taught about past events of different types, including events from the history of Britain e.g. *notable local and national events, events in other countries, events that have been remembered and commemorated by succeeding generations, such as centenaries, religious festivals, anniversaries, the Gunpowder Plot, the Olympic Games* (Key Stage 1 Programme of Study, SCAA 1995). (Italics in original to indicate non-statutory examples.)

This advice is typically bland and unproblematised. History is conceptualised as celebration, (note 'remembered and commemorated') without any indication that it might depend on whose perspective children were being asked to adopt. Though it was treason, the failure of the Gunpowder Plot and the torture and trial of Fawkes were surely not a celebration for the Catholic community, in England or Ireland, who hoped that the restoration of a Catholic king might change the direction of their history under Protestant monarchs. The commemorations in 1989 of the first settlement of whites in Australia, or the Columbus quincentenary in 1992 were protested, not celebrated, by the indigenous peoples for whom these white settlements had spelled disaster.

This section, and the chapter that follows, make some suggestions for introducing a multicultural history curriculum with infants, not necessarily working from their own community stories but taking on important historical issues in the wider world. In keeping with the title of this chapter, I suggest that fiction may be the happiest medium for such work. Some non-fiction resources which could be used as part of a class theme are also introduced.

Besides the sound pedagogic reasons for working on such issues through fiction, there are currently very few factual history resource books for the youngest children. Those that exist rarely go beyond family and local history or the lives of a few famous British people; a few concentrate on work with artefacts. Most of these date from the late 1980s when the National Curriculum first put history for infants on the publishing agenda and are quite closely tied to it.

Some of the issues from contemporary history which teachers might address will link with some children's own family history; some will deal with the history which explains the presence of certain children in their schools; some will address matters that are in the news. Some will be there because they are important historically, because good resources currently exist and they are interesting and worthwhile for any child to think about. As with all examples offered in this book, they can only reflect what is available as I write and what has come to my attention. I hope that readers will think of this section as a window onto a garden of possibilities, and as more resources are published or come to their notice, they will use their own professional judgement to include them in their planning and practice.

Many of the story-books which take on historical themes and extend children's knowledge about periods and people are American. North Americans have been concerned with inclusive approaches for considerably longer than British educators and publishers and have been more proactive in responding to and resourcing their multicultural history and multi-ethnic communities.

Chapter 1 considered some of the difficulties and controversies that history could entail in the classroom. It is worth remembering that sentimental and romantic notions of childhood innocence are themselves historically short-lived, unrealistic, and often serve the purpose of protecting adult sensibilities. They are usually swiftly punctured by a few sessions in the playground. Nevertheless, there must be sensitivity about infant-aged children's ability to handle 'difficult' material. In the suggestions which follow, I have looked carefully at the writing, illustrations and general approach to painful events, if these are part of the history, in an effort to honour this need for sensitivity.

American and world history

In an earlier chapter I looked at ways in which Valerie Flournoy's book *The Patchwork Quilt* could introduce themes of family history and intergenerational continuity. Designing and making quilts is historically women's work and, like domestic gardening and cooking, part of the heritage of female art and craft, as Alice Walker so memorably wrote in *In Search of Our Mothers' Gardens*. Larkin and Honan (1991) include material on the history of quilt making in their series 'Windows on the World' and show how learning about making quilts can value female talent and skill. Quilts sometimes carry the history of the family they belong to in the very patches of material used. This is the basis for the story in Flournoy's book and is a theme developed in a book by Deborah Hopkinson called *Sweet Clara and the Freedom Quilt.*

Sweet Clara introduces the historical facts of black enslavement in America. It emphasises resistance and the traditions of mutual support which developed in black families during plantation slavery and avoids dwelling on its horrors. Historically this follows the work of eminent American researchers such as Eugene Genovese and Elizabeth Fox Genovese, as well as black American fiction writers such as Toni Morrison and Alice Walker. The story is set in the Southern States of nineteenth century America before the Civil War. A young slave girl, Sweet Clara, hears about and gradually gathers information about the Underground Railway, which was an organised route to freedom from the South through the Northern States into Canada. She makes a quilt which incorporates a map of the route, and leaves this behind for those who will try to follow and also to comfort those who are too old to get their freedom. The story is based on fact, and apparently the real quilt is in a museum in the Southern States.

Like other books I have discussed, *Sweet Clara* is based on careful research and valid historiography. It has the 'feel of truth'. It would be a good book to read and discuss, perhaps in conjunction with another work of fiction, *Aunt Harriet and the Railroad in the Sky* by Faith Ringgold, to introduce the life of Harriet Tubman (see Chapter 13 for resources). Harriet Tubman was a real woman, born into slavery, who led slaves to freedom on the 'Underground Railway' before the American Civil War. It would also be well supported by a recent book for infants about Allen Jay, which tells another true story about the Freedom Railroad from the point of view of a young white boy (*Allen Jay and the Underground Railroad*, by Marlene Targ Brill). Allen Jay was a member of a Quaker family which staffed one of the 'stations' on the railroad. Slaves were hidden and passed on to their next destination. Even the youngest children were implicated and sworn to secrecy. There are interesting issues here about making a stand against injustice which are echoed in our own times. Think about Miep Gies and her husband Henk, the Dutch couple who risked their lives daily for two years to bring food to Anne Frank and her family, who were hidden in the annexe in Prinsengracht. What do young pupils in contemporary infant classes think about this — what would they have been prepared to do? (See Chapter 12 for biographical notes about Miep Gies.)

Starting with works of fiction like *Sweet Clara* or *Aunt Harriet,* the children might move on to learning about Frederick Douglass, who taught himself to write, and escaped to the North with a pass that he had forged himself, or the escape of the famous slave couple, Ellen and William Craft. Ellen disguised herself as a white man, and William as her servant, and they fled from the Southern States to the North. They had to take refuge in England, where they lived and worked for ten years when new laws in America against escaped slaves made their lives unsafe. (See Chapter 12 for short biographies of Ellen and William Craft and Chapter 13 for resources on Douglass.) Lastly, in this genre, *Now Let me Fly: the story of a slave family* (Dolores Johnson, 1993) is another sensitively written and beautifully illustrated picture book, which traces the history of an enslaved family back in time to Africa and forward to freedom.

Tar Beach

Faith Ringgold is a contemporary African-American artist. Parts of the 'Quilt party' on which this book draws, are in the Guggenheim Museum in New York. Set in New York in the 1930s. *Tar Beach* is the story of Cassie and her family. Her father helped build the George Washington Bridge but was banned from the union because he was a 'half breed Indian'. Now the family lives high up in an apartment overlooking the bridge. In this magical story, Cassie dreams of giving back the bridge to her father through her gift of flight. The racism her father experienced is only fleetingly mentioned, but it makes sense of Cassie's dream to empower her family and draws on the potent African-Caribbean symbolism of flight — both physical flight from slavery and metaphorical escape from the humiliations of a material world — already alluded to in other titles. In accordance with the original intention to inspire hope and a sense of spiritual freedom, one would, I think, be content to allow the transcendental, magical quality of the story to work subliminally — much as fairy stories sometimes do. In later years children could return to explore its allegorical meanings.

Talking Walls

This is an inspired picture book featuring the history of a different 'wall' on every double page spread. There are the Mahabalipuram Animal Walls carved into the cliffs near the Bay of Bengal, the Great Wall of China, the Lascaux cave paintings in France, Great Zimbabwe, the Vietnam Veterans Memorial Wall in Washington, the Western Wall in Jerusalem and a decorated wall on an Egyptian house commemorating the owners' pilgrimage to Mecca. The book introduces the idea of artefactual and archaeological evidence in a magnificent, non-tokenistic multi-ethnic context. Some schools might have large public murals in their vicinity, or the remains of ramparts of old city walls. This book could be used alongside study of the local and familiar, to extend children's knowledge — literally — beyond the walls of their own environment. (See illustrations of murals on p. 196 and 198 in Chapter 10.)

The Second World War

In Chapter 1, I reflected on how old children should be before they start to know about the Holocaust, drawing on my own personal history of half-knowledge and misunderstanding. In 1995, as I write, the parallels lie in central Africa and former Yugoslavia. By the time you read this, different places might be in the spotlight. But, sadly, it is unlikely that the whole world will be at peace. If the children we teach know about former Yugoslavia or Rwanda through the television news, then they are already being introduced to the horror of genocide. And if this is so, perhaps they need to be able to talk about their fears rather than have us pretend that they know nothing and have no emotional response.

Rose Blanche

Rose Blanche is described as a book for children aged 7 and up. Only you can gauge, through your knowledge of your pupils and sensitivity to their emotional resilience, whether you feel they can handle this (admittedly beautifully written and delicately illustrated) historical 'faction'. One of my students read it to her 6 year old son, who had noticed and wanted to know about the numbers tattooed on his grandfather's arm. They both cried, but probably that is the appropriate response.

One day, Rose Blanche, a little German child, follows one of the lorries full of pale, quiet people leaving her town. She discovers the nearby concentration camp and sees the starving and frightened people behind the wire. Throughout the freezing winter she brings what she can from her home. Then, as the news of the advancing American army comes to her town and the townspeople load carts and prepare to leave, she runs to the camp to find the wires down and the people gone. Rose Blanche is never seen again. Although it is clear that the people were forcibly removed by an army, and kept in inhuman conditions, there is nothing here about the exterminations. The author's own words on the back of the book tell us that he grew up in the war 'experiencing war without really understanding it' and that he wanted to give a message of simple humanity in the face of horrific events. Rose Blanche is named after the group of young Germans who really did protest against the war, at their peril. Like Allen Jay's story, this book — profoundly anti-war — asks children to think about their own response to injustice.

South Africa

South Africa has been very much in the news this decade and there can be few children who have not heard of Nelson Mandela. He is one of the 'famous men' that one might well want to introduce in Key Stage 1. Television, newspaper and radio featured his walk to freedom from Victor Verster gaol in February 1990 after 27 years incarceration, the miles of voters waiting patiently in line in the historic election of April 1994, and finally, the inauguration of the new black government on the steps of Government House in Pretoria. To contextualise work on Mandela's life, there are a number of works of fiction for young children about South Africa under apartheid, which can help children understand the background to the momentous changes of the 90s. All the books described below offer an opportunity to introduce quite young children to the history of black South Africa, and help them understand what the long struggle for freedom was about. Though it would be quite possible to read any of these stories without giving them a context, I would advocate giving children an explanation which lets them know that the story represents the reality of many black South Africans' lives in a not very distant past and a situation which the new government is trying to redress.

Jafta: The Homecoming

This joyful book about a family reunion, for the youngest children, is set in one of the now defunct, so-called 'Homelands' or 'Bantustans'. These were established on very poor land throughout South Africa by the Nationalist Government from the 1960s onwards. Africans were forcibly removed from areas designated for whites and settled according to their language and ethnic origin in a Homeland. Jafta's father is coming home from working on the mines, after a long separation from his family because, as the text simply states, 'things are changing in our country'. Jafta rehearses the important events at home that his father missed and that he is eager to tell him about. Class work might involve children thinking about memorable events that they would like to tell someone who had been away for a long time.

Teachers might want to amplify on why Jafta's father had to go away to work for extended periods, explaining in language that the children can understand, that the Homelands could not sustain the people deported there. There was no infrastructure of roads, irrigation, industries or viable agriculture. The Homelands became the dumping grounds for women, children and old people, barely subsisting on money sent home from meagre wages earned by men deprived of their livelihoods and forced to become migrant labourers far from home. Many people who disagreed with the government's way of doing things were forced into a long exile abroad, which split families and left children in the care of relatives, but without their fathers and mothers. Mandela and many others were separated throughout the long years of imprisonment from their partners and children. The end of apartheid has seen the return of thousands of exiles, hoping to rebuild their country and their lives.

At the Crossroads

This beautifully illustrated picture book also portrays the time when African men had to go off to work in the mines on ten to eighteen month contracts, leaving their families behind to survive as best they could. This has been the pattern since the mines started 130 years ago, and it still continues. The children in the story wait up the whole night for their fathers and the final page describes and illustrates the reunion.

Charlie's House

In the 1970s and 80s, using army trucks and bulldozers, the ruling white regime attempted several times to demolish the squatter camps outside Cape Town (notoriously Crossroads) and deport the people to the so-called Homelands in the Transkei. The squatter camps were rebuilt by a defiant black population, but some moved to other nearby 'official' townships such as Guguletu and Khayelitsha, where they built themselves shelters from corrugated iron, cardboard, wood and whatever else they could find. These shanty towns are still there (in 1995) awaiting electrification and proper sanitation, as one of the priorities of the new government. This story is set in Guguletu and gives a little of this background, but focuses on Charlie's fantasy to provide his family with a lovely spacious house.

Chapter 2 (pp.26-28) discussed how one might acknowledge the experience of moving from one town to another or one country to another, in many of our pupils' lives, through a topic on 'moving'. I included excerpts from 'Cu's story' dictated to me and illustrated by an 8 year old in my class, who had been a boat child. The topic could bring the history of immigrant and refugee children into the classroom without making them the target of uncomfortable and unwanted attention. The two stories described below might be the way to introduce the human and historical aspects of the theme. Each is about becoming a refugee — one from the perspective of an older person, the other from a child herself.

My Grandmother's Journey

I might have included this book in the 'Grandparents' section above, but for its theme of lives buffeted by war leading to immigration. Like most books of this genre, it is based on a true life story, that of the author's mother-in-law. Her family survived the Bolshevik revolution and the devastation of the Second World War. They were taken into a labour camp by the Nazis and finally able to leave for America, where they made a new life. Despite the underlying theme of the destruction of war, this is a remarkable and tender story of optimism and kindness received even from strangers, and it helps children understand why people might be forced to leave their home country.

Onion Tears

This is an Australian book (for older infants rather than the youngest) about a young Vietnamese refugee called Namh, who has been sent by her family to safety in Sydney. She remembers her life in Vietnam before she was put on a boat by her mother, whom she has left behind. She suffers humiliating teasing about her name and her customs from insensitive peers. Her grandparents with whom she lives can't really help her, beyond conventional advice. The resolution to this unhappy state of affairs comes through Namh 'proving' herself and becoming accepted.

Resources

a) Fiction to support learning historical skills, work about grandparents, historical themes

Brill, Marlene Targ, 1993, *Allen Jay and the Underground Railroad*, Minneapolis, Minnesota, Carolrhoda *[anno]*

Cech, John, 1991, *My Grandmother's Journey*, New York, Bradbury Press

Dragonwagon Crescent, 1993, *Home Place*, New York, Aladdin Books, MacMillan

Flournoy, Valerie, 1985, *The Patchwork Quilt*, London, Bodley

Graham, Bob, 1990, *Crusher is Coming*, London, Picture Lions

Havill, Juanita, 1987, *Jamaica's Find*, London, Heinemann

Hoffman, Mary, 1991, *Amazing Grace*, London, Magi (dual text — a range of languages with English)

Hopkinson, Deborah, 1993, *Sweet Clara and the Freedom Quilt*, New York, Alfred Knopf

Igus, Toyomi, 1992, *When I was Little*, Orange, New Jersey, Just Us Books

Innocenti, Roberto, 1985, *Rose Blanche*, London, Jonathan Cape

Isadora, Rachel, 1991, *At the Crossroads*, London, Julia MacRae

Isherwood, S. 1994, *My Grandad*, Oxford, Oxford Univ. Press

Johnson, A.,1989, *Tell me a story Mama*, New York, Orchard Press

Johnson, O., 1993, *Now let me fly: the story of a slave family*, New York, Macmillan *[anno]*

Kidd, Diana, 1989, *Onion Tears*, London, Viking Kites

Knight, Margy Burns, 1992, *Talking Walls*, Gardiner, Maine, Tilbury House Publishers

Lewin, Hugh, 1992, *Jafta: The Homecoming*, London, Hamish Hamilton

McCroy, Moy, 1989, *Grandmother's Tale*, London, Magi (dual text — a range of languages with English)

Orr, Katherine, 1990, *My Grandpa and the Sea*, Minneapolis, Carolrhoda Books

Ringgold, Faith, 1992, *Aunt Harriet's Underground Railroad in the Sky,* New York, Crown Publishers

Ringgold, Faith, 1988, *Tar Beach*, New York, Crown Publishers

Ringgold, Faith, 1993, *Dinner at Aunt Connie's House,* New York, Hyperion Books for Children

Ross, Tony, 1988, *Dr Xargle's Book of Earthlet*s, London, Andersen Press

Schermbrucker, Reviva, 1989, *Charlie's House*, London, Walker Books

Scieszka, Jon, 1991, *The True Story of the Three Little Pigs*, London, Puffin

Vertreace, M, 1993, *Kelly in the Mirror,* Illinois, Albert Whitman & Co.

b) Adult references

Baddeley, Pam and Eddershaw, Chris, 1994, *Not so simple picture books*, Stoke-on-Trent, Trentham

Burman, Erica, 1994, *Deconstructing Developmental Psychology*, London, Routledge

Development Education Centre, 1991, *Start with a story: supporting young children's exploration of issues*, Birmingham DEC

Garner, J.F., 1994, *Politically correct bedtime stories: modern tales for our life and times*, New York, MacMillan

Larkin, Tom and Honan, Annette, 1991, *Windows on the World*, Book 4, Stories and story telling (for work on patchwork and folklore) Mission Education Department, St Columbans, Navan, County Meath, Ireland

Little, V. and John, T., 1986, *Historical Fiction in the Classroom*, London, Historical Association

MacFarlane, C et al, 1994, *Long ago and far away: activities for using stories for history and geography at Key Stage 1*, Birmingham, Development Education Centre

Moore, T., 1992, *Care of the Soul*, London, Piatkus Press

Naidoo, B., 1992, *Through Whose Eyes? Exploring racism: reader, text and context,* Stoke on Trent, Trentham

Walker, Alice, 1984, *In Search of Our Mothers' Gardens: womanist prose*, London, The Women's Press.

Chapter 4

A place in the hall of fame

Pupils should be taught about the lives of different kinds of famous men and women including personalities drawn from British history, e.g. *rulers, saints, artists, engineers, explorers, pioneers* (Key Stage 1 Programme of Study, 2, p.2).

In contrast to the 1991 Order and the Non Statutory Guidance, the terse and non-prescriptive SCAA Order of 1995 gives absolutely no suggestions about which people should be studied in this part of the Programme of Study. Even the italicised list is not obligatory — as all official advice since Dearing has reiterated several times. This open agenda puts the onus on teachers to develop their own criteria for inclusion or exclusion of individuals. Neither the Areas of Study nor the Key Elements explicitly recommend that Key Stage 1 history include material about social, cultural, religious and ethnic diversity, though the words 'different cultures' and 'other countries' appear as hopeful signs of a more inclusive intention.

The choice of which famous people to include deserves to be thoughtfully made because this area of history can:

i)   extend all children's knowledge beyond the horizons of their own community and give them the opportunity to learn about the contributions of women, and of people from a variety of countries and ethnic groups, whatever their own origin or sex;

ii) improve the self-esteem and knowledge of their own history, for ethnic minority children and for girls.

Choosing a famous person for study

Perhaps we should start by asking these simple questions:

- ☐ Why am a choosing this person?

- ☐ Am I being Eurocentric and sexist in my choices?

- ☐ Am I being Eurocentric and sexist in my presentation and interpretation of this person's contribution?

Teachers might choose a particular famous person for a number of different reasons. You might want to weight these criteria differently, and might extend the list.

- ☐ I know about him/her myself because she/he was part of my own schooling

- ☐ There are lots of resources

- ☐ It fits in with the topic/theme I'm doing

- ☐ She/he exemplifies some qualities which I'd like the children to know about and consider

- ☐ He/she comes from the community where I work, lived round here or made a difference to the part of the country in which we are living and working

- ☐ He/she was significant in some broader historical period and influenced change — e.g. ideas, political, social, technological developments

- ☐ Her/his life exemplified human predicaments, choices and conflicts which are part of the fascination of history and will allow the children really to get under the skin of historical interpretation.

Eurocentrism and sexism

Part of the problem for many of us is that Eurocentricism and sexism were seldom challenged in our own education and few opportunities were offered to look at history from different perspectives. This can make it quite hard to avoid the same traps. However, the recommendations in National Curriculum history to look at interpretations and perspectives on the past is an excellent way for us to think about bias in the choices we make ourselves, as teachers. Something can be done about this, as resources increasingly become available, through mainstream publishers as well as community bookshops (see Chapter 14).

When I ask first year students to write a list of ten 'famous people' that they know about or think would be worth teaching about, the results are fascinating and revealing. When the group consists mostly of young white women or men, the list tends to be dominated by white men, usually royalty or soldiers or sports-stars, justified on the basis that the children will find these people

64

interesting. The students are seldom concerned with criteria other than fame. Mother Theresa and Walt Disney also come up, with little awareness of the current controversies about their personal qualities. The young women quite often include the Queen or another member of the royal family, and sometimes Florence Nightingale. Margaret Thatcher regularly appears, on the grounds that although she was in no way a feminist, she broke the female stereotypes. This is an instance of the oft-noted observation that a woman has to behave like a man to get included in history. Older students and ethnic minority students, on the other hand, regularly include Martin Luther King, Mandela, Malcolm X and occasionally Gandhi.

I use this exercise to explore with students the criteria and the issues that arise from their choices. After some thought, the criteria that are generated usually include something about determination, creativity, dedication to an ideal, moral and physical courage, and quite often the peaceful pursuit of change. Many students appreciate that the choice of a particular individual (for example Gandhi, Anne Frank, Harriet Tubman, Mandela) allows one to introduce and focus on some historical issue of importance.

If I point out that only a small proportion of their list is either female or black, the group usually wants to take some positive action to remedy the imbalance. Students note that the choice of a female or black artist or scientist — a role model — supports work going on elsewhere in the curriculum to counteract stereotypical attitudes about the children's own potential. While there is nothing wrong in teaching children about the lives and contributions of, say Pasteur, Florence Nightingale, Winston Churchill, David Livingstone, the Beatles or the Wright brothers, we need to be aware lest we give children an impression that only white people (and usually males) have made significant contributions and are worth learning about.

There is another aspect of Eurocentric history which needs exposing. The lives and work of the white people who feature in the traditional history curriculum have seldom been unproblematically beneficial to everyone they encountered. The current re-evaluation of the reputations of Albert Schweitzer and Churchill in contemporary historiography is a timely reminder of how perspectives can alter when a wider range of criteria is introduced.

The Inset Resources for KS 1 (1993) included Gandhi, Cleopatra, Mary Seacole, Florence Nightingale, Robert Peel, Queen Elizabeth 1, Columbus, Mary Kingsley, David Livingstone, Amundsen, George Stephenson, Richard Trevithick and St Brendan — an indication, at least, of inclusivity. There are two Victorian explorers in this list and in my view this is problematic — even if Mary Kingsley makes the grade as a positive female role model. Care must be taken not to perpetuate racist, discredited myths about white people in Africa — and thus about black people — through the versions available for teachers to use. Few teachers have access to the original sources which suggest the ambiguities and complexity of the Victorian explorers' views about Africans and Africa. Stanley's violent and unsympathetic attitude to Africans is pretty notorious, but Livingstone was also deeply imbued with the ideology of imperialism, although he was a much more attractive character, gentle and well-loved by Africans. His self-professed mission in Africa was to bring Christianity, commerce and civilisation, a project which was enthusiastically pursued by his successors. It is arguable that the success of British imperialism came through the barrel of a gun, despite such as Livingstone's own peaceful mission.

History is about consequences, not just the events and characters in isolation from motivation, context and outcomes. In my view, Key Stage 1 is not the place to try and treat with the political and moral ambiguities of imperialism. It would be tempting to over-simplify Livingstone's and the other Victorian explorers' agenda of condescension about African ways of life, morality and religions, and the often overt expression of European superiority. This could mean very young children being given a view of the relationship of Africa to Britain which provides the foundation for racism. In contrast, the story of Livingstone's *death* is well worth the telling: a tale of courage, initiative and adventure in which the Africans who were part of Livingstone's devoted party are the heroes. Livingstone's ability to inspire such devotion is central to the story, and thus his memory is honoured. For those teachers who do not know this story and do not have access to the sources, a short outline appears in Chapter 12.

Similar arguments hold for teaching about Columbus, although recent alternative resources offer a more critical perspective on his life. People like Schweitzer and Mother Theresa who have also achieved hagiographic status in the white annals but are viewed with more ambivalence by some people in countries where they established their missions, should also be treated with caution.

While it is good history to learn about human failings and the ways in which personalities represented the attitudes of their time — even attitudes that we no longer hold — these subtleties of approach are unlikely to prevail in the infant school. In my view, it is better not to take the risks of perpetuating racist interpretations and, for infant classes, to choose people about whom there is less ambiguity.

Recognising the hidden agenda in a resource list does not mean that one necessarily knows about alternatives. I have tried to help with this in Chapters 12 and 13. Some areas of Britain are better resourced with Development Centres and bookshops than others. Some teachers may need to rely on catalogues and possibly bookclubs, notably Letterbox Library which specialises in multicultural and non-sexist material for children (see Chapter 14). Some of the material is designed for infants, but you may want to choose a personality for whom resources don't yet exist in a simple enough form. Then you'll need to research pictures and the 'basic story' to work from, adapting material published for older students. This still allows for creative and worthwhile projects in the classroom, where children can dramatise incidents, make their own book or cartoon series — in other words produce resources which others may use. Some of my students, determined to provide a more inclusive curriculum, have prepared booklets themselves to read to children, rewriting stories in simpler form, using resources meant for adults or older children. Children can do the illustrations and the work can be 'published' for the class or school library.

Many publishers of educational resources have series on ethnic minority people and women which they are adding to all the time. These are easily obtained from their publicity departments.

The new order (SCAA 1995) makes no suggestions about individuals to study. The list at the end of this chapter covers all the people who are included in the short biographies in Chapter 12 or in the annotated list of resources in Chapter 13. What follows now is a 'starter list' of suggestions to counter the Eurocentrism and sexism of many mainstream publications. For some of these people you will need to find resources yourself, drawing on your own community and your own and the children's interests.

Nursing and medicine

Mary Seacole, the British-based Jamaican nurse who also worked in the Crimea but had nothing like Nightingale's public support and recognition. Her autobiography, *The Wonderful Adventures of Mrs Seacole in Many Lands* is an easy read for adults and full of delightful human touches. There are plenty of books about her for children from the youngest to older juniors.

Marie Curie, the French scientist who, with her husband Pierre, discovered radium.

Dr Elizabeth Garrett Anderson, Dr Elizabeth Blackwell, Sophia Jex Blake were all Victorian pioneers who challenged sexism in medicine. (For adult information on their campaigns see *Charge of the Parasols* by Catriona Blake.) Sophia Jex Blake had to deal with mudslinging, literally, and was barred from lectures.

Dr Harold Moody, a Jamaican doctor who worked in Peckham in London in the early years of this century.

Lord David Pitt — a Grenadan doctor who had his practice in Marylebone and became a member of the House of Lords.

Edith Cavell, the British nurse who helped British soldiers escape from Belgium during WWI.

'The Arts' — Actors, musicians, dancers

Just a few suggestions which reflect my own interests and knowledge and which you will want to extend — Bob Marley; Diana Ross; Stevie Wonder; Miriam Makeba; Bessie Smith; Josephine Baker ('Ragtime Tumpie'), the black American dancer and singer who settled in France, joined the French resistance, and adopted children from many lands; Paul Robeson; Ravi Shankar; Marian Anderson, the opera singer sponsored by Eleanor Roosevelt who, when banned from the Lincoln Centre, sang on its steps instead; Kiri Te Kanawa.

Political figures — There are simple children's books on the following people, some of which are included in Chapter 13:

Akbar the Great, Mogul of India 1556 — 1605 — a contemporary of Queen Elizabeth I

Olaudah Equiano, who went on speaking tours of Britain in the late C18th and whose account of slavery was part of the British abolition movement;

Toussaint l'Ouverture — the leader of the successful slave uprising in Hispaniola in 1792

Nanny of the Maroons — the Jamaican slave leader

Queen Nzinga of Angola who led resistance against the Portuguese slave traders

King Shaka — the 'Black Napoleon' who forged the Zulu nation in the first quarter of the C19th

The Rhani of Jansi — an Indian female military leader

Sojourner Truth (Ain't I a woman?) — black preacher, feminist and suffragist

Frederick Douglass — black activist in the emancipation and female suffrage movement in the United States, who visited Britain in the late 1840s

Marcus Garvey — who lived in Britain

W. Du Bois, who visited Britain

Rosa Parks — the 'mother' of the American Civil Rights movement

Nelson Mandela — imprisoned for 27 years on Robben Island off the coast of Cape Town, for his opposition to apartheid and belief in democracy for everyone in his country, and is now (1995) president of South Africa

Martin Luther King

Malcolm X

Mahatma Gandhi, who studied law in Britain before going to South Africa in the 1890s and later led the passive resistance movement against the British Raj in India

The Pankhursts — *Emmeline and Christabel* — the leaders of the militant suffragettes, and *Sylvia* — a pacifist who founded the East London Federation; set up a toy making co-operative, a creche and a mothers' food centre during the First World War

Charlotte Despard — suffragist, Irish nationalist and pacifist.

Inventors, explorers, people of courage

The first astronauts — Russians — and the first woman in space, the American *Sally Ride* (1983)

Clare Francis — the first woman to sail single handed round the world

Amelia Earhart, Amy Johnson, Jean Batten — all women aviators

Chief Crazy Horse, (who resisted and defeated General Custer)

Harriet Tubman — the slave who having fled to freedom, ran the 'Underground Railway' which was the route to the North for literally thousands of slaves before emancipation

Sacagawea — a young American Indian girl who guided two explorers (Lewis and Clark) across Canada in the C19th. They took the credit!

Benjamin Banneker — a Black self-taught mathematician and astronomer who invented a telescope, published an almanac in 1792 and became an advisor to the President of the United States

Ida B Wells — a black woman who struggled to be recognised as a journalist at the end of C19th and in the early C20th

Nelly Bly — a white journalist at roughly the same time as Ida Wells, who fought against sexism, exposed social injustice, went round the world to beat Jules Verne's fictional record

Claudia Jones — who lived in England for the last ten years of her life after being expelled from America during the McCarthyite 'witchhunts'; founded the *West Indian Gazette* and the Notting Hill Carnival

Miep Gies — the Dutch woman who was Otto Frank's secretary before the war; she hid, fed and protected the Frank family for two years until they were caught and deported.

Some reminders about work on famous people

1. Avoid Hagiography

Even though the Order suggests Saints as suitable for study, hagiography has no part in history. The word derives from the Greek for 'holy' or 'saint' and is a reminder that biographers can get carried away with the virtues and wonderful accomplishments of their chosen subject. When teaching about famous people it is important to avoid presenting someone in a totally good and saintly light. Realistic evaluations of people's lives are more in the spirit of good history — and the National Curriculum — than sanitised versions. Even the people we admire were real and had human failings. I have already discussed the problems of teaching about people whose ambiguous attitudes or anachronistic ideologies might be too complex to explore with young children.

2. Teach through historical concepts and processes, don't just go for content and chronology

The lives of famous people are usually presented as straightforward narrative and it is tempting to teach about them and forget about the processes and concepts of history. There is seldom any specific encouragement in available resources to consider change and continuity, chronology, sequence, cause and consequence. However all these, and the important concepts of motivation and choice in value-laden situations should be central to well-taught history.

The NCC Inset Resources (1993, pages 36 and 37) actually used the story of Florence Nightingale to illustrate work on chronology, sequence, change, cause and how far characters are central or peripheral to the life story. This is an excellent model and it is easy to see how it could be used without a great deal of adaptation in other life stories. However, no ideas are offered for work on perspective or bias, which are also important concepts for children to start to grasp (see Chapter 3, p.46-7).

When taking on work of this kind, ask yourself:

— can you find different accounts about the same person which offer different perspectives and evaluations of their importance?

— do pictures/portraits/illustrations emphasise different characteristics?

— can children imagine/construct a version that represents a hostile or friendly view of a particular character?

— can children do a role-play of people discussing their character, one of whom approves of her/him, and the other less sure?

Here are two historical examples which could encourage these approaches. Members of the medical profession and students fought to prevent Sophia Jex Blake and her little group of women colleagues from entering the Edinburgh medical school, and once pushed a sheep into a lecture that they were attending, to discourage and humiliate the women.

Crimean soldiers nursed by Mary Seacole gave her a rousing welcome and organised a fund-raising concert in Kennington when she returned to England; in contrast, the *Times* reporter who noted her death was distinctly curt.

3. Do background work into the period and contextualise the study

Work about a famous person should be contextualised, if possible using artefacts, photos, paintings and costumes from the time to help children develop a sense of authenticity. The non-statutory guidance suggested that some work on famous people might be part of a longer historical project, such as exploration, voyages or transport. The context might be a non-historical project about feelings, admirable personal qualities, courage and so on. Many schools involve their children when they develop behaviour policies. Pupils might learn about a person who courageously stood up for their ideals, perhaps facing personal ostracism, or preached a non-violent but principled stance to aggression and injustice. This might provide a broad framework for children to think about avoiding colluding with bad behaviour or challenging unfairness or bullying. One such person was Rosa Parkes, who refused to give up her seat on the bus in segregated Alabama in 1955, was arrested just because she was black and started the bus boycott which is usually considered the beginning of the Civil Rights Movement.

4. **Keep it simple with young children**

Work on famous people in the past does not need to include their whole life story from birth to death. It is much better to focus on an incident which has some drama, or their main contribution to history, with some introductory material and a bit of follow-up about what happened to the person in later life. This still gives room for work on chronology and sequence. One can discuss why and whether they deserve to be remembered, what motivated them, who they influenced and cared about, and who cared about them at the time and now.

5. **Work on interpretations and the interim nature of judgements**

People's judgement at the time, as well as later, is part of evaluating a famous person's life. It is not that one wants children to come down on one side or the other, but rather to become aware that the reputations of the famous are often controversial at the time, and open to review later. Schweitzer and Churchill have already been mentioned. There are other contemporary examples such as Kennedy, Stalin, Mitterand and F.D. Roosevelt. Many other people have not been recognised during their own lifetimes, or in their own countries, and it has taken a historical perspective to establish their reputations.

Young children could think about their responses to Grace Darling's story. In 1838 Grace and her father rowed from their lighthouse through a dangerous storm to rescue the passengers of a shipwrecked paddle steamer. They got there just before the official lifeboat which had struggled from Sunderland through the storm, in even more difficult conditions. Grace was given the substantial reward which the lifeboat crew felt was rightly theirs. Although the public continued to adulate her, Grace suffered accusations from the local people that she had been motivated by selfish egotism and monetary greed. Nowadays her reputation is restored, but the lifeboatmen's courage is forgotten.

Not so long ago the President of South Africa was a prisoner of the very people with whom he now shares the government. His wife Winnie, once adored as the 'Mother of the Nation' is now in disgrace for alleged misconduct and corruption. In the 1920s and 1930s it was by no means generally acceptable for English people openly to support Gandhi's non-violent movement to get the British out of India. Nowadays he is more generally regarded as an heroic figure whose particular methods of protest are approved (though Muslims often have a different perspective on his actions from Hindus).

6.   **'Bringing it all back home'**

I have argued in this chapter for choosing people whose lives have inspired others and are worth remembering. Even young children can think about a person's long term significance to our daily lives and to local or national communities. The Notting Hill Carnival is integral to August Bank holiday weekend for many Londoners, and Europe's largest festival, attracting over a million people. Not many know that Claudia Jones was closely involved in setting it up. Mary Seacole may have been the first well-known black nurse in the nineteenth century but her example has been followed by countless black women, who contribute to keeping the National Health Service functioning. Elizabeth Garrett Anderson, Sophia Jex Blake and others like them opened up medicine in Britain to women, at a period when females were barred from the profession. All those families who have (and prefer to have) a female doctor now are indebted to them.

Through a long campaign that has its roots early in the nineteenth century, the (non-militant) suffragists, and later the (militant) suffragettes were influential in women getting the vote in Britain, something we take for granted now. They might be remembered at those times when primary schools become polling stations! Further from home, Sojourner Truth is a particularly inspiring black American suffragist and campaigner for women's rights, famous for her challenge '..and ain't I a woman?' as she catalogued the trials of her life and her contributions to society, to a patronising man who scoffed that women could not do the same work as men, and therefore should not have an equal say in the running of the country.

Martin Luther King's and Malcolm X's example and messages still inspire pride and self-esteem, different though their ideas might have been. They raise interesting questions about significance — both men's memories have lived on in ways which were probably not foreseeable at the time.

Ways of introducing work on famous people into the curriculum

Two Irish writers, Tom Larkin and Annette Honan, recently published a set of books called *Windows on the World* designed to broaden the curriculum in Irish schools and tackle prejudice and misunderstandings. In Book 3, entitled *Heroes and Heroines*, they have a chapter called 'Becoming a hero/heroine today'. Here they discuss practical ways to explore admirable characteristics and themes of heroism and courage. They suggest very helpful curriculum work in which children are asked to think about why they might admire people and in what circumstances. This provides the introduction to learning about some contemporary and historical characters whose lives have been memorable. There are a variety of life histories included, all simply written in language which is accessible to young children. For example: Saidie Patterson who, in 1918, confronted injustice and violence against a fellow woman worker, when she was only 12. She went on to work for women's rights and the Irish Peace Movement; or Rigoberto Menchu, 1992 Nobel Peace Prize winner, a Guatemalan peasant woman who has organised her people against tyranny and oppression; and Chico Mendes, leader and organiser of the Brazilian rainforest people's resistance against the ranchers who were cutting down the trees to create land for cattle.

Children might work in twos or threes on a simple story about their chosen hero or heroine, ready to present to the whole class what they have found out, and why they would want the person to be remembered. Debriefing discussion about the differences in their choices and criteria would itself be very valuable and thought-provoking, helping to extend their understandings about their peer group and about examples of different heroic or admirable behaviour. Offered a broad spectrum of examples to work from, I can't help wondering whether there would be sex differences in choices and evaluation of heroic qualities, and what relationships to their own ethnicity would emerge.

The Irish material illustrates the value of starting from children's knowledge and experience. If you ask a group of young children whom they admire, be prepared to discuss the significance and qualities of footballers, royals and 'soap' stars. The children's understanding and knowledge can be moved on, starting from their current understanding.

One could develop a good project about famous people in the past, starting with the children thinking about qualities in older people that they admire (for example family friends, their grandparents, people their families talk about). They might also like to think about how they'd like to be remembered themselves. Or begin with people in the news, the celebration of an anniversary or birthday, or someone well known who has recently died. (I have collected useful information and photographs from the obituary columns of daily newspapers!)

Part of a local history project

Cross-curricular topics on 'Where we live' or 'Our Neighbourhood' are sometimes the vehicle for history work on famous local personalities. Perhaps Richard Trevithick and Jemima Nicholas were chosen for the KS 1 history SATs in 1993 because they had lived and worked in areas where the SATs were trialled!

To avoid the elitism and male-centric curriculum which arises if one relies on mainstream resources, look to community bookshops and local history libraries for information about local working people, ethnic minorities and women. White men tend to be very well documented in published anthologies about 'who lived, worked or was buried where'; there are some good books about white women, but very few which include black women or men. Teachers need to research their own locality; a comprehensive list covering every part of the country would be impossible to compile. At the end of Chapter 10 on Local History in the Key Stage 2 curriculum, resources are listed which would also be useful for Key Stage 1 teachers.

Using drama, role-play, 'hot seating'

Drama, role-play and 'first person presentations' are an excellent way for children to think themselves into the life of a person in the past, and background work about the period will help towards authenticity. The idea of 'hotseating' is that children try and find out as much as they can about a character then prepare questions to ask the child or adult who is taking the role in the 'hotseat'.

The teacher or child (perhaps part of a group, with partners who 'shadow') has to do their homework and take on the role, trying to answer the questions as sensibly and seriously as possible. If the questions are inappropriate or the person in the 'hotseat' doesn't know the answer, you can resort to a formula such as 'I can't answer that' or 'I'll come back to that'.

Drama and role-play can also help children take on some of the ideas I have already mentioned and avoid an oversimplistic and perhaps biased evaluation of a person. For example, a 'trial' could be held in which one of the lifeboatmen or a journalist accuses Grace Darling of trying to puff up her image or of having rescued the drowning people simply for the reward. She herself, or her father or sister who stood loyally by her, could come to her defence.

Starting with a work of fiction

The ideas in *Dinner at Aunt Connie's house*, a recent book by Faith Ringgold (whose *Tar Beach* was described briefly on page 57) could be worth adopting. Like Faith Ringgold herself, 'Aunt Connie' in the story is an artist; her niece and nephew have come to see an exhibition she has mounted in her own house, of famous black women in American history. Going through the exhibition on her own, the niece imagines each woman introducing herself and taking part in the family meal. Sojourner Truth and Harriet Tubman, Zora Neale Hurston and Maria Stewart are among the famous women from the nineteenth and twentieth centuries who join the party and briefly say something about their lives. Along these lines, children might choose a person to invite to a dinner party, bringing together the famous from many different periods and places. They could work in small groups to find out something which made their character famous, do their portrait and prepare a short presentation about their chosen hero or heroine — or even — with some props and simple costumes — take on the role themselves at the 'dinner'.

Amazing Grace is another picture book that could lead children to think about people in the past whom they admire. Grace imagines herself in a variety of roles and, like many children, uses whoever or whatever is around as supporting parts and props. Some of the characters she chooses for her games are historical, like Joan of Arc, Dick Whittington or Hannibal, while others, like Ali Baba and Anansi, are fictional. The main story revolves round Grace's desire to play Peter Pan in the school play, needing to overcome her classmates' view that a black girl could not play a white boy.

This book could be used in a number of ways: one would be to find out more about the real and fictional people in the story itself, and extend this to other people the children have heard of but are not sure if they really existed. It is worth noting that in the story, Grace has chosen so many white or male characters. Children definitely need help and information about characters who are female and/or black or from other ethnic minority cultures, who are equally attractive and interesting, if they are to move beyond stereotypes and role models limited by 'race' and gender.

Using fiction and non-fiction together

In the previous chapter I described how a story-book about the Underground Railway could take a project into history, where non-fiction resources are also available. *Aunt Harriet's underground railroad in the sky* is a wonderful fantasy picture book. The fictional elements are easily identifiable — for example children fly through the air (reminiscent of *Tar Beach*). They are combined with authentic detail about the Underground Railroad, which was the route to freedom for slaves from South to North before the Civil War in the States. Used together with a factual 'life story' on Tubman could stimulate discussions about the differences between the two versions, what the children think is fantasy and what is true and corroborated in the factual accounts, and how one tells the difference. (Since this is often a very fuzzy area for adults as well as children, the discussion could be illuminating!) *Aunt Harriet's underground railroad in the sky* has a picture of the centenary quilt made in 1949 to celebrate the Underground Railway and so could connect with other books in which quilts commemorate the past (e.g. *The Patchwork Quilt, My Patchwork Quilt, Sweet Sara and the Freedom Quilt*).

Resources

Children's fiction

Foreman, Michael, 1992, *The boy who sailed with Columbus*, London, Pavilion Press

Hoffman, Mary, 1991, *Amazing Grace*, London, Magi (dual text: a range of languages with English)

Hopkinson, Deborah, 1993, *Sweet Clara and the Freedom Quilt*, New York, Alfred Knopf

Ringgold, Faith, 1992, *Aunt Harriet's underground railroad in the sky*, New York, Crown Publishers

Ringgold, Faith, 1993, *Dinner at Aunt Connie's House*, New York, Hyperion Books for Children

Adult resources

Larkin Tom, and Honan, Annette, 1991, *Windows on the World,* Book 3 Heroes and Heroines, Mission Education Department, St Columbans, Navan, Country Meath, Ireland

File, N. and Power, C., 1981, *Black Settlers in Britain 1555-1958,* Oxford, Heinemann Educational Books *[anno]*

Children's non-fiction and biographies

This is by no means a definitive list of possibilities but shows the people for whom a short biography, or an annotated entry has been included in Chapters 12 and 13. The biographies in Chapter 12 are listed alphabetically by surname; *[biog]* after a name indicates that there are biographical notes in Chapter 12.

All books in Chapter 13 are listed alphabetically, either by title, or by the name of the main person represented; *[anno]* after a name or title indicates an entry in Chapter 13. Many black women and men are included in general books with titles beginning 'African', 'Asian' or 'Black'. Please check these in the annotated lists in Chapter 13.

Aldridge, Ira 1807-1867*[biog]*

Anderson, Elizabeth Garrett 1836-1917 *[biog]*

Archer, John 1863-1931 *[biog]*

Chumah, Susi and Jacob Wainright mid C19th *[biog]*

Coleridge Taylor, Samuel 1875-1912 *[biog; anno]*

Constantine, Lord Learie 1901-1971 *[biog]*

Craft, Ellen 1826-1891 & William 1825-?1891 *[biog]*

Cuffay William 1788-1870 *[biog]*

Cuguano, Ottobah late C18th, exact dates unknown *[biog]*

Davidson, William 1786-1820 *[biog]*

Davies, Emily 1830-1921 *[biog]*

Despard, Charlotte 1844-1939 *[biog]*

Equiano, Olaudah 1745-1797 *[biog]*

Gandhi, Mahatma 1869-1948 *[anno]*

Garvey, Marcus 1887-1964 *[biog; anno]*

Gies, Miep 1909- *[biog]*

Jones, Claudia 1914-1964 *[biog; anno]*

Moody, Dr Harold *[biog]*

Naoroji, Dr Dadabhai *[biog]*

Pitt, David Thomas, Lord Pitt of Hampstead 1913-1994 *[biog]*

Prince, Mary 1788-? (date of death unknown)*[biog]*

Remond, Sarah Parker 1826-1894 *[biog]*

Saklatvala, Shapurji *[biog]*

Sancho, Ignatius 1729-1780 *[biog]*

Seacole, Mary 1805-1881 *[biog; anno]*

Famous people resource list

People included in Chapter 12, and books in the annotated alphabetical list in Chapter 13 are listed below by *category*. Some entries are for books with general titles (e.g. Notable Black Abolitionists) rather than individuals, because the book contains too many names to list individually. Full details of author, title and a brief description of the contents and the reading level are in Chapter 13.

Categories (some names appear in more than one category)

Black Activists

Nursing, Health and Medicine

People of Courage

Inventors and Scientists

Sport

Music, theatre and dance, writers

1. **Black activists**

African Migrations
African Roots in Britain
Baker, Josephine
Bethune, Mary McLeod
Black heroes and heroines
Black Settlers in Britain 1555-1958
Bogle, Paul
Cuguano
Douglass, Frederick
Edwards, Samuel Celestine
Equiano, Olaudah
Famous Campaigners for Change
Gandhi, Mahatma
Garvey, Marcus
Gordon, George William (see Bogle, Paul)
Great Women in the Struggle
Jones, Claudia
King, Martin Luther
Malcolm X
Mandela, Nelson
Nanny of the Maroons
Naoroji, Dadabhai
Notable Black Abolitionists
Notable Black Americans
Parkes, Rosa
Pitt, Lord David
Prince, Mary
Remond, Sarah Parker
Sharpe, Sam
Sojourner Truth
Tacky
Te Whiti
Tubman, Harriet
Wells, Ida B.
Women Leaders in African History

2. **Nursing, Health and Medicine**

Anderson, Elizabeth Garrett
Cavell, Edith
Fry, Elizabeth
Jex-Blake, Sophia
Moody, Dr Harold
Nightingale, Florence
Pawan, Joseph Lennox
Pitt, Lord David
Seacole, Mary

3. **People of courage**

Angelou, Maya
Baker, Josephine
Besant, Grace
Black Heroes and Heroines
Bly, Nellie
Boudicaa
Cavell, Edith
Chuma, Susi and Jacob Wainright
Craft, Ellen and William
Darling, Grace
Earhart, Amelia
Famous Campaigners for Change
Frank, Anne
Gandhi, Mahatma
Gies, Miep
Great Women in the Struggle
Jay, Allen
Johnson, Amy
Keller, Helen
King, Martin Luther
Kingsley, Mary
Mandela, Nelson
Nanny of the Maroons
Pankhurst, Emily
Parkes, Rosa
Remond, Sarah Parker
Ride, Sally
Shelley, Kate
Sojourner Truth
Tubman, Harriet
Wells, Ida B.

4. **Inventors and Scientists**

Banneker, Benjamin
Bi Sheng
Black American Scientists and Inventors
Black Heroes and Heroines
Black Scientists and Inventors
Cai Lun
Carson, Rachel
Curie, Marie
Great Women in the Struggle
Herschel, Caroline
Kinsgley, Mary
Lu Ban
Notable Black Americans
Pawan, Joseph Lennox
Shen Kuo

5. **Sport**

Black Heroes and Heroines
Constantine, Learie
Great Women in the Struggle
Notable Black Americans
Worrell, Sir Frank

6. **Music, theatre and dance, writers**

Aldridge, Ira
Angelou, Maya
Baker, Josephine
Bennett, 'Miss Lou'
Bishop, Isabella Bird
Black Heroes and Heroines
Bly, Nellie
Coleridge-Taylor, Samuel
Fitzgerald, Ella
Henry, Lenny
Marley, Bob
Wells, Ida
Wheatley, Phyllis
Wollstonecraft, Mary

Chapter 5

The Key Stage 2 curriculum

Introduction

The Key Stage 2 curriculum is more prescriptive about content than Key Stage 1, and requires that teachers have much more detailed historical knowledge. Although building on ideas introduced in Part I, I have taken a somewhat different approach. On the one hand, the broad headings introduced in the earlier chapters, namely gender, class and 'race'/ethnicity are used to discuss an inclusive curriculum. I have also tried to reveal and make transparent how subtle messages about taken-for-granted power relationships in society and ideological positions are transmitted through history, and make suggestions about ways to deconstruct or challenge this hegemonic authority.

Not all the statutory units are covered, let alone each of the possible choices within units. From Study Unit 1 I have chosen the Romans as an exemplar of an equal opportunities approach and made only passing reference to the other invaders and settlers — the Anglo-Saxons and Vikings. I have not analysed the possibilities of the Study Unit on the Ancient Greeks, though I think there are immensely valuable ways in which ideas of citizenship, knowledge, democracy and the imposition and maintenance of power can be explored, which are interesting in their own right and have contemporary relevance. From Study Unit 6 I have focused on one option, Benin and discussed broad issues to do with teaching about non-European civilisations. There is a brief history of Benin Empire, and some ideas for work on Benin which I hope will encourage teachers who want to take up the option to work on black African history.

Supporting teachers with historical knowledge and understanding about the Key Stage 2 study units

Most primary teachers find that they do not have the appropriate knowledge and understanding about all the periods in the new history syllabus. This is incidentally also true for science, but a major push through INSET has resourced and supported teachers in primary science. Recognising the problem of inadequate subject knowledge, the DfE's preferred solution has been to encourage subject specialists, who will not only advise their colleagues, but increasingly teach their subject in a discrete way across the school, much as secondary teachers do. I think that this fragmentation of the primary curriculum and the learning experience of young children is problematic, even while I fully support the need for teachers to know more history, in order to teach it effectively and to the highest standard.

To judge from my experience as a teacher, advisory teacher and trainer of teachers, very few of my colleagues have an A level in history, let alone have studied the subject at undergraduate level. The existing constraints of teacher training mean that it is virtually impossible to give trainees anything but the most sketchy and selective overview of the different periods, because the core and the other foundation subjects are all competing for scarce time. Understanding of how to 'do history' and work with historical concepts is improving however, and many teachers have excellent and creative ideas about how to make the content accessible and interesting. However, with little personal background in history, they are forced to rely on the children's resources for content. Sometimes they use books meant for secondary pupils to try and get a grip on issues and facts. Without any real understanding — beyond their own schooling — of what the issues are in each of the periods they have to teach, they cannot judge whether the children's resources are themselves partial, incorrect or based on questionable criteria for selection of content.

This book is an attempt to support those teachers *who want to inform themselves in order to teach history more effectively*. The chapters in Part 2 go into greater depth about history itself than those in Part 1, because I have tried to outline some of the broad historical issues, movements and events that will contextualise the bald statements of required content in the Key Stage 2 units. I have also included in the text possible resources — particularly from autobiography and oral history — because I know that teachers have very limited time for their own research.

Readers should recognise that as an historian I am myself subjective. History is not an objective and unproblematic narrative, 'read off' from existing sources. The chapters reflect my own choices of what to include, my interpretations and — yes — my own perspectives on the past and its significance. Readers may well find themselves challenging my views and noting that other writers might put things differently. This is exactly what real history is about. I will feel that I have achieved at least part of my aim in writing this book if I promote a questioning scepticism and desire to check me against other sources. Best of all would be if teachers then encouraged children to work in just this way, themselves expecting to unpick assumptions and underlying attitudes, and demanding the evidence so that they can reach their own conclusions!

A chronology of multicultural Britain

This book argues for a history curriculum in the primary school which is neither chauvinist nor inward-looking, but recognises that from the earliest times this island has been connected to the wider world. Britain's history has always been 'multicultural', whether in a domestic demographic sense or through important trade, colonial and political connections with other countries and cultures. An attempt to make sense of any particular period or to understand the present in the light of the past has to acknowledge these connections. It is disingenuous and dishonest, and above all unhelpful in support of their growing sense of civic and international understanding, to avoid teaching junior children about these historical connections.

A long time ago, Britain was physically part of the European continent, till it broke away during the Ice Age about half a million years ago. The similarity of the language and culture of the original Britons, the Celts, to the people of Brittany is striking. Immigrants have come to Britain from the beginning of its recorded history. Celts had traded beyond the shores of this island even before the Romans came to settle. The conquest and colonisation by Romans, Anglo-Saxons and Vikings indelibly changed the course of British history in the first millennium AD. One of the main reasons the Romans were interested in Britain was because they knew about the agricultural products and manufactured goods which were part of Iron Age culture. So trade and sea-faring beyond the island coasts were, from the earliest days of recorded history, an important aspect of growth, change and continuity.

The chronological history of Britain weaves back and forth through Key Stage 2 and 3 Programmes of Study. Sometimes there is an overlap of periods designated for study in Key Stage 2 and Key Stage 3, with the stated intention that children's foundation study should be deepened and extended as they get older. This is surely as it should be, in the spirit of Bruner's famous spiral curriculum, which assumes that learning in not just about breadth, but increasing depth of understanding.

Some periods or civilisations are only covered once during the compulsory years of history. The first millennium AD of British history is in Key Stage 2. At Key Stage 3 children learn about the Norman conquest, which had a major impact on domestic history, and also consider how Britain was connected to a wider world, through its membership of the Christian community during the Middle Ages. The Crusades were a major period of Christian proselytisation, involving clashes with another equally committed proselytising religion — Islam — and there is opportunity to work on this in the Key Stage 3 Programme of Study.

Moving on chronologically, both Key Stage 2 and 3 history curricula cover the Tudor period, which witnessed not only the strengthening of the monarchy but also the beginning of competitive international relations, expressed through growing sea power and colonisation of newly discovered territories. The chief expansionist phase of this development was actually under the Stuarts and this period has been removed from Key Stage 2. 'Exploration overseas' is a subheading in Study Unit 2 of Key Stage 2, but not emphasised in the overlapping Key Stage 3 Study Unit 2 — the Making of the United Kingdom 1500-1700. In other words, the only time when the beginning of the first Empire could be treated seriously and in depth is at Key Stage 2, and if it is marginalised, children would have no foundation for Study Unit 3 in Key Stage 3: Britain 1750-circa 1900, where pupils learn about Britain's imperial and colonial expansion.

It is not the primary history teacher's responsibility to fill gaps in understanding that the Key Stage 3 curriculum might create. But it is surely helpful for primary teachers to be aware of what the children will be working on later in their statutory schooling — and also what they won't have a chance to study unless someone arbitrarily decides to teach it. Here then, for primary teachers whose knowledge of this theme is sketchy, is a brief outline of developments and connections with the wider world, from the fifteenth century to our own time.

Expansion and colonialism

Colonisation began under the Tudors, developed through the Stuart period and is a major *leitmotif* of the next two centuries, inextricably linking the island's fortunes with those of other peoples. It is not possible to understand England's changing political status and wealth without knowing something of its political and trade connections to the countries which would in due course become its colonies. Africans from Sierra Leone were transported by Hawkins to the Caribbean to be sold as slaves as early as 1564; in 1579 Native American Indians confronted Francis Drake in San Francisco (which he claimed on Elizabeth 1's behalf as 'Nova Albion'); the East India Company, which had gained its charter at the end of Elizabeth's reign, established one of its 'factories' in Madras in 1639. The beginning of the Indian Empire thus dates from the end of Elizabeth's reign. From the late Tudor period onward, black people in other parts of the world were not just implicated in Britain's fortunes, but were present in increasing numbers in Britain itself.

Throughout the seventeenth and eighteenth centuries (which fall within Key Stage 3 and not primary history), Britain was building its power through increasing its trade abroad and developing stronger links with parts of the world which had been taken over as part of its colonial Empire in the previous century, in India and the Caribbean. International wars and treaties led to the acquisition of new territory in the Caribbean and Canada. Caribbean islands became pawns in European power politics, a foretaste of what was to happen to parts of Africa in the nineteenth century. They were fought over and changed hands as part of wars and diplomatic negotiations between the interested European powers. It should not be forgotten that during this time Britain was developing its financial base through involvement in the slave trade — which had started under Elizabeth. The black population of England was visible in the eighteenth century, even if it was small by today's standards.

By the middle of the nineteenth century British slavery had ended but colonial control had not. The existence of the 'old' colonies and then, in the last quarter of the century, the acquisition of new ones, sometimes through international 'parcelling out', sometimes by force, sometimes through treaties with local chiefs — particularly in Africa — is an inseparable explanatory element in Victorian Britain's struggle to obtain and then maintain international power and industrial hegemony.

Once into the twentieth century, the relationships between Britain and a wider world, forged through many centuries of conquest, colonisation and trade, develop in very different ways. In the two world wars, colonial troops from India, Africa and the Caribbean volunteered and were brought into the fight against the enemy, though without exception they were segregated and in some cases, restricted to support roles and not even armed.

After the Second World War, Britain was short of able bodied workers, and invited members of its South Asian, Irish, Cypriot and Caribbean colonies to supply a labour force for specific service industries. Later, in the face of war and natural disaster, people from the ex-colonies of the Indian sub-continent and East Africa called in the debt and demanded their right to enter Britain as British citizens and members of the Commonwealth. Britain's connections with other people and nations has been formally recognised through membership of the Common Market. (See the chart in Appendix 2 for patterns of immigration and emigration.)

The spiral curriculum and history

We have seen that some periods in the Key Stage 2 curriculum appear again in Key Stage 3. Key Stage 1 teachers are encouraged by the non-statutory guidance to take a flexible approach to introducing junior content in an appropriate form (e.g. through small studies of Victorian school or domestic life). In contrast, although the Key Elements for Key Stage 3 encourage building on primary school study, primary teachers themselves often seem reluctant to look at the next stage in the history curriculum. The overlaps are a positive opportunity to introduce ideas and content which will be studied in greater depth later. This approach is justified in terms of Bruner's ideas of a spiral curriculum and also because the omission of some material might lead young children into erroneous but tenacious assumptions in which Britain is isolated from its international context.

Junior pupils and social issues

A theme of this book is that it is both admissible and advisable to work with young children's interests, to help develop their maturity of judgement, skill in working from evidence and recognising different perspectives. During the junior school years many children become increasingly concerned with a broader social context than their own immediate life and family. A longitudinal study of primary aged children's political attitudes and knowledge (Stevens 1982) revealed the extent to which they were choosing to watch news programmes and documentaries, and were interested and concerned about broad political and social events.

Recent surveys of children's television watching habits make it clear that junior children are, if anything, more likely to watch adult news programmes than they were some years ago. Small- scale work that I have done in a London primary school has confirmed what many adults know: that juniors have views and are concerned about such issues as religious conflict, racism and sexism. It follows that 'cleaning up' or omitting the conflict and dilemmas around these issues from their history curriculum, patronises and underestimates children's interest and intelligence. It also misses the opportunity to do what history is well suited to, namely consider perspectives and encourage serious and dispassionate discussion on controversial contemporary issues, in contexts which are more distant in time and place.

Equality issues and opportunities in the Key Stage 2 curriculum

Naturally, it is not possible to permeate every study unit in Key Stage 2 equally with content which takes account of the history of women or black people, or ordinary members of society. Available academic scholarship determines what is available for younger children. The amount of research done by academic historians on the role of women or the experiences of working people in the Victorian period, far outstrips equivalent scholarship on the contribution of black people. We know a fair amount about individuals who were politically active in Britain in the late eighteenth century and early nineteenth century, including notable personalities like Equiano, Cuguano, William Cuffay, William Davidson, Mary Prince and Robert Wedderburn. There is however, very little material on anything other than isolated figures in the latter part of the nineteenth century, though researchers like Rozina Visram, Sylvia Collicott, and Peter Fryer have done a great deal to try and remedy our ignorance.

Regarding gender in another Key Stage 2 period, the mid-fifteenth to the end of the sixteenth centuries, there is a considerable body of evidence about aristocratic women and the queens, all very accessible to junior children. There is much less about ordinary women's lives, except at quite a generalised level.

Being 'ordinary', their history lacks the drama of skulduggery or sudden death. This could give children a biased view that interesting history is only about elite groups. An inclusive history, and wanting children to study in a rigorous way based on evidence, can be mutually incompatible if the evidence is missing or partial. The NSG (1991) Article 10, which I quoted in full on p.18-19, advised that the hidden agenda and bias of resources be explored with children. Accordingly one should make gaps in evidence the subject of hypothesis and discussion. We should be encouraging pupils to understand that history is not a complete account of the past, and that what we have is the result of earlier historians' selections, the chance nature of what has survived, and also reflects differential technological know-how and power structures within society. These have in turn determined who were in a position to produce and leave the sorts of evidence we find easier to access, and largely rely on.

Even within the National Curriculum, teachers make decisions about inclusion and exclusion all the time, depending partly on what evidence is available and their own preferences. This is encouraged by the 1995 Order, which does not insist on equal time or depth for every element of each study unit. To use Study Unit 2 (Life in Tudor Times) as an example, one could spend more time on, say, Elizabeth and the Armada, and less on court life and the role of a personality such as the Earl of Essex. In making selections for a period, I should like to see equality as one of the determining considerations. However it seems that content choices are being made on behalf of teachers by the providers of published resources, and that teachers who do not have a history background are unsure of what or how to teach in a more inclusive way, even if they wish to do so. The next section considers how the evidence that is available about particular periods might influence choices about a more inclusive curriculum.

Useful evidence and absent evidence

Just as it is sensible to use and teach about archaeology in Study Unit 1, and oral history in Study Unit 3b, so we should choose equality issues for the periods where there is plenty of evidence. Working from strength, we can give children a sense that working women or black people have been part of history and contributed to the story. We can then encourage them to ask why this history is missing for other periods, and cannot be well resourced. Children as well as adults can reflect on the following quotation, and think about how the powerful and the literate have been able to determine what we know about the past:

> Four million Afro-American women were slaves in the years between 1619 and 1865. Of that vast throng, the history books mention only a handful, reporting on their lives with scant detail. What of those faceless, nameless millions who plowed the fields, cooked the meals, nursed the white folks' babies during the long dark years? What did they feel and think? What were their aspirations? How did they view the world around them?

The answers to these questions are hard to come by. Slave women kept no diaries, rarely wrote letters. Even their names were not listed in the census records. Yet here and there, over the centuries, individuals spoke out briefly, took some action, left a mark on the history of their time. (Sterling, 1988, p.3).

In maths we do not expect children to work on area or data handling in every single project, but we do make sure that these feature sufficiently often to teach and reinforce the concepts through the junior years. So for history we need to check that, at various stages across the range of periods and units, we are covering the different issues in a way which honours the evidence and leads to growing understanding.

One might decide that an important focus for nineteenth century study should be women's lives and contributions — both working and middle class — in order to compensate for the male dominance of Study Units 1, 4 and 6. Or, decide that the dearth of evidence about black or ethnic minority experience in domestic Victorian life pushes the forced choice between Study Unit 3a and 3b towards Britain since 1930, where there is plenty of material, and also plenty of possibilities to teach about women, and as many primary schools do, cover the Victorian period through local study.

Organising the curriculum for progression, depth and complexity

Key Stage 3 specifies the order in which units must be studied, but for Key Stage 2 there has always been choice. The reduction from nine to six units over four years has certainly simplified planning, but there is no easy formula for when to do the various Study Units in the junior school. Following the actual chronology of events and periods is not necessarily the best approach. Every Study Unit can potentially be studied in quite a shallow way with the younger children or in greater depth with older children, who are wiser in the ways of the world and capable of handling more complex issues. Foundation work in Britain since 1930 and the Victorians are typically introduced in Key Stage 1 but there are good arguments for leaving these two Study Units to the later junior years. Given the complexity of the Tudor period, there would be an equivalent rationale for undertaking Study Unit 2 as late as possible. If Study Unit 5, Local History, is to develop themes introduced in other units, then it makes sense for it to come quite late in the junior school. The curriculum then ends up totally top-heavy in years 5 and 6, which would become unmanageable!

The non-prescriptive approach taken by the 1995 Order makes it possible to return to a period which was introduced in the earlier years, a planning strategy which child development and learning theory endorse. Some schools are now choosing to do this, giving themselves the opportunity to postpone some issues till the children are older, when they can build on foundation work undertaken earlier. This is not possible for every study unit but worth considering perhaps for Units 2, 3a or 3b, which are potentially very challenging.

British and not just English history

As well as acknowledging and developing the global links in history, and finding ways to include women's history or at least question the absence of evidence or emphasis in textbooks and traditional accounts, there is another concern, namely to respond to the requirement to teach British and not just English history. The boxed introductory paragraph to the Key Stage 2 Programme of Study uses the word '*Britain*' and this is emphasised in the 'British' study units, except for the Tudors. Study Unit 1 reiterates the words 'Britain' and 'British' to remind us that the invasions involved land north, west and beyond the maritime borders of the areas which would later become England. Both Study Units 3a and 3b require that 'pupils be taught about the lives of men, women and children at different levels of society in Britain'.

In the 1991 census, the largest numbers of people in London who were self-designated ethnic minorities came not from the New Commonwealth but from Ireland, Scotland and Wales. Each of the components of the British Isles in fact has its own history curriculum, which suggests ways in which 'English' history might need to scrutinise its assumptions. Welsh, Irish and Scottish history involve very different perspectives from English history. In the chapters that follow, opportunities for a 'British' rather than 'English' stance are indicated, to help children broaden their critical and historical understanding.

Historical Fiction in Key Stage 2

Chapter 3 deals at some length with the use of stories, arguing along the lines of advice from the NCC 1993, that the skills and concepts of history can be taught and reinforced through stories, even if the material is not strictly historical. I discussed how the characters and contexts of picture books could introduce a multicultural and non-sexist agenda. Girls and children from minority ethnic groups could identify with these characters and they could be used to broaden the horizons of children in mainly white areas.

The original 1991 Programme of study for KS 2 allowed that fiction had a role in learning history. Under *Links with attainment targets* (NCC 1991, p. 16), 'films, plays, songs, pageants, models, stories and poems' were all listed as developing the old AT2, Interpretations of History. Support for AT3 (The Use of Historical Sources) could come from 'fictional accounts'. The three Attainment Targets with their statements of attainment have gone, but their processes have reappeared in the Key Elements and level descriptions for the single history attainment target.

Key Element 4 (Historical Enquiry) for Key Stage 2 requires that 'pupils learn how to find out about aspects of the periods studied, from a range of sources of information, including documents and printed sources, artefacts, pictures and photographs, music, and buildings and sites'. To insist that fiction cannot be a possible 'source of information' for children is tantamount to arguing that *Jane Eyre* or *Middlemarch* have no contribution to make to our understanding of nineteenth century middle class mores. There is no justification for self-censorship and good reasons to draw on fiction as a source.

Key Element 5 requires that pupils 'communicate their knowledge and understanding of history in a variety of ways, including structured narratives and descriptions'. This is minimalist, and surely does not exclude the variety of communicative techniques — such as role-play, drama, writing letters from different protagonists, collage, cartoons — through which primary children typically throw themselves into research and representation of their historical understanding. In order to produce high quality work, children need good models. In art and music we introduce children to the best available models to help them recognise excellence and develop their own creativity. For history we regularly ask children to write narrative, produce 'eye witness accounts', imagine that they anxiously await tidings of good fortune or disaster, bring an historical episode to life through poignant poem or punchy prose. When we do this we acknowledge that they must make an imaginative leap, and that the characters they breathe into life may not really have lived, though we demand accuracy in the detail and the context. And yet we limit their resources for such work to textbooks which often provide models of stultifying literary banality, written in lifeless, pedestrian prose. The drama and tension of uncertainty is replaced by smug hindsight. And yet in real life, the best historians are those who translate their gifts for understanding connections, uncovering and pursuing the meanings of evidence, into compelling prose that brings history into the realm of literature. Primary children are too young to read the great contemporary historians who inspire adults — but should we deny them this experience altogether?

I am not suggesting that historical fiction can or should replace the textbooks, but that it should be an indispensable part of the history curriculum in the primary school. Vivienne Little and Trevor John (1986) argued convincingly for historical fiction for junior pupils, to bring history to life, and provide the detail which helps promote understanding that the past was real. So, even though the new slimline Order does not mention stories or fiction, it would be philistine and pedantic to refuse resolutely to consider its value, not just for the reasons given by Little and John, but because children's experience and their own writing could be impoverished.

Teachers might decide to use excerpts from historical fiction as evidence for an incident or because it provides useful detail. Rosemary Sutcliff on Romans in Britain , or Cynthia Harnett on the Tudors, superbly recreate the flavour of their periods with details which can help children to understand how to interpret evidence in a new light. Both authors are quite advanced for any but the most able junior readers, but this does not prevent the teacher from reading excerpts aloud. In the English curriculum, most primary teachers are aware of the power of good prose, and quite regularly choose books which are slightly above the reading level and even vocabulary of some of their class. For example, not all junior children can read Ted Hughes' *The Iron Man* for themselves, nor understand every word, but this does not prevent us from exposing children to its cadences, or to other books of equivalent literary merit. Similarly, many of the children in a Y3 class working on the Victorians would not themselves be able to read Theresa Tomlinson's *Flither Pickers*, Judith O'Neill's *So far from Skye*, or *A Twist of Fate* by Pamela Scobie. But the teacher could choose excerpts to read aloud which vividly portray aspects of early, mid or late Victorian life. The first pages of *A Twist of Fate*, for example, convey the atmosphere of poverty and hope — to be cruelly disappointed by reality — of young children from a workhouse who are being transported north in a cart, to work in a mill, deviously bribed with false promises and a shilling. Railways and cars are still far in the future. So are social security, the Children Act, notions that young children should be in school and not at work. Complicated ideas about the enormous changes, not just in technology but in attitudes, are introduced. Detail and contextualisation in the lives of children with whom the young listeners or readers can identify makes the very different past accessible. One will not necessarily read a whole book aloud or expect children to persevere with a long work of fiction, though some are so well written and exciting that children will be gripped.

Children can use fiction to work on interpretations: they can compare a piece of fictional writing with something from a non-fiction text, looking for differences in emphasis and perspective, deciding whether they would want to cross-check the information offered in both sources, if they conflict. They can choose a short excerpt to dramatise, supplementing fiction with research from non-fiction. They can try writing a fictional piece based on factual research using their history resources, perhaps using figures in a contemporary drawing or photograph as the 'characters' and weaving a short drama from what they know about the issue and the period. What better way for teachers to assess their pupils' real understanding and ability to synthesise and use information. Such work will quickly reveal anachronisms based on lack of knowledge and understanding.

Looking forward to the resources section in Part 3, the historical fiction in Chapter 13 is all appropriate to the junior years although some is more accessible to older and more able readers. Entries in Chapter 13 refer to the Study Units in the Programme of Study for Key Stage 2. However, this is not a comprehensive list of every historical novel that junior children might enjoy and teachers find useful as support material. Like the Key Stage 1 stories, the books listed are generally chosen with a multicultural and non-sexist agenda in mind. They feature girls and women as main characters, or boys and men in non-stereotypical roles, and often introduce a multicultural or non-elitist perspective which might be missing in other resources. I hope, too, that teachers will agree that they meet the prime requisite of good children's books — that they are well written and carry a dramatic narrative about roundly drawn characters.

Using museums, postcards and artefacts for multicultural history work

Chapter 2 explored some of the ways in which multicultural history could be introduced to Key Stage 1 pupils, through making sure that the pictures, people and artefacts that children encountered represented a range of communities and cultures. Specialist museums in London, like the Victoria and Albert, and the Horniman Museum in Forest Hill, curate large collections of valuable artefacts from abroad, including musical instruments, textiles and works of art. The Horniman has a special collection on Benin. Other museums, like the Geffrye Museum in Hackney, make a specific point in their teachers' INSET of drawing attention to the opportunities for multicultural work. For example, they indicate that many of the actual objects in their displays, or the materials they were made from, or the designs, or the craftsworkers came from countries outside Britain. Carpets, which became a feature of wealthy Tudor homes, were not made in Britain, but imported from the Middle East and India. Chinese porcelain and patterns were a terrific vogue more than once in interior design. Even the fashion of the late 1920s and 1930s for neo-Egyptian designs, seen not just in the beautiful Selfridges lift at the Museum of London but in many of the cinemas in our local high streets (often converted into bingo halls), can help children understand international connections. The Egyptian fashion relates of course to the huge interest aroused by the discoveries of the Tutankhamun tombs at the period.

Museum and site visits enrich children's historical understanding, whether of Romans, Anglo-Saxons and Vikings, the Victorians, or the non-European study units. The Key Elements in the Order encourage work with artefacts, for chronology and for interpretations. Museums contain 'the real thing' and there is no doubt that however realistic the replicas, however beautifully produced the postcards, they are never quite the same as contemplating an object which really was used by someone several hundred years ago. This is not to say that postcards and replicas don't have their place in class, both to introduce the interpretation of artefacts and to position on a time-line to help understanding of chronology, change and continuity. Museums are increasingly making use of multi-media interactive techniques; artefacts are displayed in settings which help children to contextualise them in someone's life in a given period, and find much supporting information from paintings, models, documentary evidence, evocative music and sounds.

But there is a special magic which good teachers can evoke from artefacts. Standing in front of an exhibit, closing their eyes, children can be inspired to imagine a Roman tradesman down at the Thames waterfront, heaving the heavy clay wine casks with their pointy base from a boat onto the dock; a Tudor citizen-soldier unstrapping this very leather bottle from his belt, slurping water and passing it round to his mates; a young Victorian seamstress bending in the poor light over the sewing machine, trying to complete the order for someone's ballgown. Museum visits should not be a dreary (or worse, competitive) traipse round the exhibits, filling in pointless closed questions on a worksheet. Much better that children arrive not just prepared about what they will be seeing, but with a purpose to find out something they want to know. This means planning in advance, so that the teachers know what is there and what questions they might ask of the children. I do not have space in this book to discuss museum visits further, but recommend Hazareesingh (1994) and Wilkinson et al (1994) who explore some of the many possibilities.

One may hesitate about or be unable to take children to the museums, but a phone call or letter to the Education Officer will tell you whether they have booklets or postcards which you can buy. I always riffle through the postcard and book stalls when I visit such places, on the off-chance that there will be something I can use later. An attitude of mind about 'thinking inclusive' and an awareness of where the connections are, helps teachers be prepared with resources which they can draw on when the time comes.

References

Hazareesingh, S., et al, 1994, *Speaking about the Past*, Stoke on Trent, Trentham Books

Little, V and John T., 1986, *Historical Fiction in the Primary School*, London, Historical Association

Sterling, D., 1988, *Black Foremothers: three lives,* New York, The Feminist Press

Stevens, O., 1982, *Children Talking Politics,* Oxford, Martin Robertson

Wilkinson, S. et al, 1994, *School Museums and Primary History*, London, Historical Association.

Chapter 6

Study Unit 1: Romans, Anglo-Saxons and Vikings in Britain

Till the lions have their historians,
the stories will always glorify the hunters.
(African Proverb)

Introduction

The 1995 Order requires teachers to broadly outline the first millennium AD of British history and then choose one of the three main settler groups for more detailed study. In this chapter my main focus will be on the Roman invasion and settlement. Some of the ideas, particularly about including women and children, and considering the point of view of the conquered as well as the invaders, apply whichever settler group one chooses for detailed work.

An anecdote neatly summarises the ways in which history can transmit taken-for-granted assumptions. As part of the 'Erasmus' exchange programme, young people from Sweden come as students to Britain. Though they are too tactful to express open dismay, they are amazed at the image of the Viking conquest and life typically held by their British peer group, which they find focuses on ferocity and cruelty rather than energy, enterprise or comparatively legitimate searches for outlets for trade and settlement. Certainly cause for thought for us, so accustomed to considering Vikings in much less positive ways! A few books for children are now becoming available which counteract the one-dimensional image of Vikings as violent and warlike, and provide evidence about domestic and agricultural life in which women are given their rightful place. Both Anglo-Saxons and Vikings had enormously sophisticated artistic skills,

95

publicly recognised in recent exhibitions, for example at the British Museum. Learning about their cultures through work on their extraordinarily beautiful artefacts goes some way to countering the stereotypes of brutal, barbaric 'philistines' (another people with a bad press!). Such work also honours the requirement to consider settlement as well as invasion and helps children understand chronology, since the conquests occupied relatively short periods of time compared with the much longer settled periods.

Study Unit 1 provides an important preparation in thinking critically about invasion and settlement in a period sufficiently removed from the present or any child's personal history not to cause acrimony. Considering what it meant to the indigenous people to be invaded and in many cases enslaved is a precursor to interpreting subsequent periods when the British were in their turn the aggressors. The first millennium AD is rich in opportunities to consider historical perspectives and versions, taking a long view about significance and consequence. While many textbooks present Romans as bringers of peace and civilisation, the Vikings are more likely to be portrayed as destroyers of a (romanticised) Anglo-Saxon heritage. Early Anglo-Saxon depredations are glossed over, and the contribution of Anglo-Saxons (particularly King Alfred) to establishing Christianity, early literacy and the rule of law are emphasised. Since children will now only learn in depth about one of the periods, they could unintentionally get very different messages about how to think about and evaluate invasion, conquest and settlement. The imbalance between treatment of the three major invading groups can reflect judgements about the significance of their contributions. It is interesting to note that in the run up to the English Civil War of the seventeenth century (sometimes called the English Revolution), both sides manipulated Anglo-Saxon 'heritage' history to try and support their own claims for legitimacy. Right now, in 1995 the provenance and authenticity of an important contemporary source on Alfred's 'greatness' — *Asser's Chronicle* — is under dispute by scholars claiming that it actually dates from a much later period than Alfred's own reign, and was written for propaganda purposes.

Whose perspective on the Roman invasion?

Even a cursory look at the available texts for children about the Roman conquest quickly reveals a tendency by authors to present this period through the eyes of the conquerors. Decisions to settle Britain are variously explained through Roman desires to extend their trade links, to get hold of the tin and gold for which Britain was well known before the invasion, and an imperial project to stretch the long arm of Roman suzerainty into far away lands, whose justification is taken for granted. The textbooks describe the importance of roads, the army, the creation of cities as unquestionably progressive features of Roman occupation. Yet the Roman invasion was energetically and consistently resisted by the people already resident in Britain. Could they not appreciate the advantages of Roman technological superiority and government? Is it perhaps the case that from their point of view, the invasion was not 'progress'?

The History order actually requires that the impact of the conquest on the Celtic society be considered. Not everyone who lived, worked and traded in Britain during the period of Roman settlement would have come from abroad, and many Britons would have benefitted from trade and the growth of the new towns which replaced the small settlements. Many British people colluded with the Romans, were rewarded and became 'Romanised'. But many were also enslaved. One would want to be even-handed in assessing the pros and cons from the Celtic point of view. This might be the subject for drama, with small groups of children in role, playing out the advantages or disadvantages to different people.

Primary school textbook interpretations of the Roman invasion and settlement are both traditional and conventional, even if transparently obvious to adult historians. They seldom make clear that the historical account is heavily influenced by the fact that the available sources come, almost without exception, from the Romans themselves, especially the valuable written evidence from Caesar, Tacitus and Suetonius. They are underpinned by an almost unquestioned veneration for Roman civilisation and an assumption that their conquest of relatively primitive people was progressive and 'a good thing'. However, in the spirit of historical work which encourages looking for bias and points of view in both primary and secondary evidence, children should have an opportunity to think about and discuss this overtly pro-Roman perspective. They should be encouraged to consider what the Celts might have made of the conquest; although some of their number colluded with the Romans and got rewarded for doing so (e.g. Casivellaunus BC 54, and Cymbeline, recognised as 'Rex Brittonum' by Rome in 5AD), others resisted. Roman society was a slave-holding society (as was Ancient Greece) and many of the conquered native Celts ended up as slaves to the Roman settlers. Fiction might provide the introduction to these themes: for example, *Catus: a child in Roman Britain,* or Rosemary Sutcliff's classic (if difficult) novel, *Eagle of the Ninth*, which sypathetically and with meticulous detail documents the slave Esca's story, as well as that of his master, the legionnaire Marcus. Even if children can't answer the question, they can speculate about why textbooks about the Roman conquest contain so little about the Celts themselves and concentrate so heavily on the perspectives and history of the invaders. They should also consider why so little was retained of Roman civilisation after the Romans left.

Children might compare the different emphases that different textbooks put on various aspects of the period and be asked to comment not just on the amount of space given to certain issues (for example the role of the army), but about how adjectives, adverbs and the tone of the accounts give different impressions. They should compare the illustrations in different texts, noting where they are offered without citing provenance (i.e. showing where the illustrator got his/her

97

information or where the original artefact was found and is now located). From this, they should be considering how far the author and illustrator are producing a version which should be offered as tentative rather than definite, or perpetrating a version of history without providing the important primary evidence. One example is the illustration of Boudicaa's battle against the Romans produced in the 1960s by Alan Sorrell and reproduced in many subsequent books, without any indication that it is a modern interpretation. There are plenty of examples in history where one historian's interpretation has been taken on by subsequent writers until it acquires the force of incontrovertible 'truth'. Sometimes a major row ensues, with 'revisionist' historians bringing new evidence and inter-pretations, destroying the former certainty and overturning accepted explanations about past events. Battles over interpretations are very much the stuff of real history, and there is no reason to keep this from children (Cf. the comments about *Asser's Chronicle* on p.96).

The resistance of the Welsh, Scots and Celts in Britain

The Welsh, Irish and Scots people were of different stock and pre-dated the taller and fairer Celts who over-ran much of northern Europe, before in turn being subdued by the Romans. Wales was occupied after considerable resistance but, largely for geographical reasons, the Romans never subdued the Scots but were beaten back by Brigantes, Caledonians and Picts. Hadrian's wall, built in the first century AD and renovated in 201 AD by the African-born Emperor, Septimius Severus, was the Roman solution to the raids and rebellions against Roman domination.

One of the ways children might consider the extent of resistance is to look at Hadrian's wall in the North and the military force on the Welsh borders, in terms of military defensive strategy; they could consider why such a huge military presence (estimated at 40,000 soldiers all told) was needed in the three main forts at York, Chester and Caerleon. Where children's textbooks refer to Celtic resistance, there is seldom any suggestion that resentment against foreign occupation might have been just and reasonable or that the outcome for the conquered people might be slavery not just in Britain itself, but also through forced removal to other parts of the Roman Empire. Caractacus' rebellion in the Medway, and the Iceni rebellion led by Boudicaa, in which Colchester, London and St Albans were all destroyed, generally get a mention. However the real reasons for Boudicaa's revolt are sometimes portrayed as an anodyne 'insult' against the queen and her daughters, rather than what seems to have been rape. Here original sources reproduced in Farmer and Ewin (1992) are useful, but it will depend on the age of the children how much this issue is pursued, since Y5 and 6 children are usually considerably more mature than Y3 or 4.

The building of Hadrian's wall in the second century AD is presented as a sensible (if hard and demanding) response to the depredations of uncivilised

'Painted People' and the textbooks tend to concentrate on the technical details of its construction and staffing, thus depoliticising the meaning of the wall. This is as reductionist as referring to the Berlin wall only in terms of its height, length and numbers of soldiers needed to guard it, and neglecting the human tragedy and drama associated with it. The issues and politics are doubtless very different, but analogies with the Berlin wall and with the wall which till 1995 divided Catholic and Protestant areas in Belfast, could help children understand the historical importance and symbolism of Hadrian's wall, and appreciate its different psychological meaning for Scots and Celts on one side and Romans on the other, trying to maintain control of the boundaries they had established.

Multicultural Britain in the first to fourth centuries AD

Although some local Britons agreed to work under and with the Romans, the main administrative posts were occupied by Romans. It was not policy to staff the Roman army with local soldiers, and the military came from elsewhere in the Empire including Syria, North Africa and Greece. A division of 'Moors' is known to have guarded Hadrian's wall in the third century AD; the Libyan-born Emperor Septimius Severus came to Britain in AD 208 to launch a series of campaigns against the Scots. He repaired and restored Hadrian's wall and died shortly afterwards at York, in 211.

There is other artefactual evidence of African connections during the Roman period in the Museum of London: a spoon and a bowl with carved African heads are displayed in their newly refurbished Roman gallery. Illustrations in *The Peopling of London* (Merriman 1993) also provide evidence of the presence of foreigners at the time, for example, inscriptions on tombstones.

Craftsworkers, shopkeepers and labourers came to London from abroad and stayed on. Some household slaves were brought from other parts of the Empire by their Roman owners and, eventually, some were able to buy their freedom. Though some freed slaves would have returned to their home countries, we know from inscriptions on tombstones showing where they were born, that some joined the settled community. Increasingly there was intermarriage and assimilation. This means that for nearly two thousand years Britain has been a multicultural society.

A rubbing and enlargement (x 2) of a denarius minted in Rome in AD 201, and found in England. The coin depicts the head of the African Emperor Septimius Severus. (Fascimile of the coin from the Museum of London shop.)

We tend not even to think how the heritage left by this formidable foreign culture is carried on in our language, long after the Romans themselves abandoned Britain. Not just place names and archaeological ruins but the very words we use on a daily basis are testimony to their influence, though it is also true that many English words with a Latin origin in fact derive from Norman French (very close to Latin) which became the official language of England after 1066. Children might be interested to start a collection of words which have a Latin base as part of their understanding of the antecedents of modern English (for a start: access, adventure, castle, descend, exit....)

Gender

Many teachers see the story of the Iceni Queen, Boudicaa, as an obvious way to counteract the unremitting male-centrism of projects on the Roman army. Farmer and Ewin's (1992) excellent booklet on the Romans, with source material from the writers of the period, includes an account of Boudicaa's rebellion from Tacitus. Children should be encouraged to ask questions about this version and the way it has shaped so many subsequent accounts, pictures and even models of the battle in which the Queen and her Icenian army made a stand against the Romans. They might try to develop a role play — one version purportedly coming from an Icenian sympathiser — emphasising the humiliation that the Queen, her daughters and through them her people suffered at the hands of the arrogant invading force; the other representing the victorious Roman perspective.

A Year 4 child who I talked to recently, assured me that there weren't any women in Britain in Roman times, and when I asked about babies, she conceded that perhaps there might have been a few! This is the ludicrous outcome of the kind of history too many children experience in their primary schools. Too much emphasis on military conquest is bound to marginalise women, who were not part of the army. The order also requires study of the period of settlement, everyday life and the legacy of the Roman settlement. There is plentiful evidence about the daily lives of Roman women who were part of the civic state that was so central to the success of Roman rule, once the native Britons had been suppressed. Much of this is artefactual, retrieved through archaeological digs, and virtually every small local museum has its cases of Roman finds, though they may not compare with the excellent section in the Museum of London at the Barbican, built right on the site of the original Roman city.

If you do not have access to a good museum, there are postcards and pictures available providing evidence of Roman women's daily lifestyle. Teaching packs and books for adults published by the Museum of London and the British Museum are a good source; statues and friezes show the kind of clothes that women wore. Archaeological excavations have yielded up elaborate hair ornaments, bracelets and brooches and cosmetic articles such as tweezers, as well as plenty of domestic artefacts used by women for cooking and serving food. The Museum of London has an excellent permanent exhibition of a kitchen and a living room in a typical Roman villa, with genuine artefacts which have been excavated and reconstructed. Roman women probably spent a lot of their time in rooms like these and pupils can consider what it must have been like to be the lady of the house at this period, or a child, without the labour-saving devices and entertainments we have now. They should also consider the possibility that much of the hard work was done by British female servants and slaves (who were perhaps quite young girls), rather than by Roman women.

Historical Fiction about the Roman settlement

Catus: a child in Roman Britain AD 80 by Teresa Woodbridge, is a well researched, accurate and evidence-based work of fiction that could be used to raise issues about the conquest, avoiding an uncritically pro-Roman stance. Catus, the young hero of the story, is a native Celt who is made a slave by the Roman who builds the villa at Fishbourne and has to decide whether to join a Celtic rebellion. Rosemary Sutcliff's books about the Roman period, *Song for a Dark Queen* — the story of Boudicaa — and *The Eagle of the Ninth*, are quite hard, but thoroughly researched, gripping and well written historical novels for older juniors. *The Silver Branch* and *The Lantern Bearers* continue the story of Roman occupation through the early years of the Saxon invasions. Their telling detail brings the period alive and Sutcliff sensitively picks beneath the grand narratives at some of the human dilemmas and conflicts of the relations between conquered people and their conquerors.

Summary

I have no axe to grind about the outcome of the Roman invasion, but in this short chapter, I have tried to explore the historiography and implicit ideology in conventional interpretations in which the conqueror's perspective is justified and the subject people's defeat is accommodated on the grounds that 'it happened that way'. Children can easily acquire a mind-set which they apply uncritically to the history of invasions, imperial projects and conquests in subsequent periods. Quite subtlely, historical impartiality is undermined and the opportunities are missed for children to learn to think critically about different meanings and perspectives.

On the other hand, starting with this first study unit, children could be considering how the absence of evidence, especially from a defeated people, can lead to marginalisation of their point of view and their history. They can also be presented with the evidence of immigration and multiculturalism dating from the very early history of Britain. If they are old enough, and this has to be the teacher's decision, they can consider the long history of what we now call war crimes against women. What happened to Boudicaa and her daughters was not, it seems, just 'an insult', and her people's desire for revenge suggests how seriously this was taken. All of this is an important part of learning the skills which they will use to evaluate other periods, including contemporary history, and come to understand the words of the African proverb with which this chapter begins.

Resources

Roman Britain

Fiction

Sutcliff, Rosemary, 1980, *Song for a Dark Queen*, London, Hodder and Stoughton

Sutcliff, Rosemary, 1985, *Three Legions,* London, Puffin. *The Eagle of the Ninth*, *The Silver Branch* and *The Lantern Bearers* in one volume.

Woodbridge, Teresa, 1989, *Catus: a child in Roman Britain AD 80*, Tempus Reparatum

Non-fiction for children

Mahoney, C., 1993, *Roman Gallery Resource Pack*, London, Museum of London (Contains A4 cards depicting a number of artefacts, including evidence of foreigners and women's lives, and a teachers' book suggesting how these might be used.)

Wood, Tim, 1994, *What happened here? Roman Palace*, London, A. and C. Black, (Excellent for domestic detail including women.)

Adult Resources

Farmer, A. and Ewin, A., 1992, *Implementing the National Curriculum: The Romans in Britain*, London, Historical Association (Useful primary material for teaching about how evidence represents one perspective and gets interpreted. Contains excerpts from Roman sources about the invasion and settlement.)

Merriman, N., (ed) 1993, *The Peopling of London: fifteen thousand years of settlement from overseas*, London, Museum of London Press (Information about the multicultural nature of Roman Britain.)

Anglo-Saxon England

Fiction

Crossley-Holland, K., 1979, *Sea Stranger, Fire Brother, Earth Father*, London, Piccolo

Hodges, Walter, 1964, *The Namesake*, London, Puffin

Hodges, Walter, 1967, *The Marsh King,* London, Puffin

Keeping, C. and Crossley-Holland, K., 1982, *Beowulf*, Oxford, Oxford Univ. Press

Sutcliff, Rosemary, 1961, *Beowulf: Dragon Slayer,* London, Bodley

Sutcliff, Rosemary, 1959, *The Lantern Bearers*, Oxford, Oxford Univ. Press

Non-fiction for children

Stoppleman, Monica, 1994, *What happened here? Anglo-Saxon Village,* London, A and C Black (Useful for domestic detail and ordinary lives about reconstructed Anglo-Saxon village at West Stow in East Anglia. Very good on using artefactual and archaeological evidence and makes clear that reconstructions are sometimes tentative.)

Adult Resources

Evans, A. Care, 1986, *The Sutton Hoo Ship Burial*, London, British Museum Publications

Webster, L. and Backhouse, J., (eds) 1991, *The Making of England: Anglo-Saxon Art and Culture AD 600-900*, London, British Museum Press

Vikings

Non-fiction

Tolhurst, Marilyn, 1994, *What happened here? Viking Street*, London, A. and C. Black. (Based on reconstruction of the houses at Coppergate in York; domestic detail including women's lives, a useful counterpoise to the macho, horned-and-helmeted, 'rape and pillage' image of the Viking settlement.)

Chapter 7

Study Unit 2: Life in Tudor Times

The Tudors were on the throne for little more than a century but it was a time of turmoil, immense change and complicated politics. Study Unit 2 has been restricted to the sixteenth century (omitting the first Tudor monarch, Henry VII) and the content to a list of six main themes. There are still problems about the depth of understanding that children can achieve. How far they go into different issues will depend partly on the teacher's choice of themes and partly on the age of the children. What you might undertake with Year 4 would not be the same as with Year 6, even allowing for a range of ability in the classes themselves. In Chapter 5 I suggested that it might be sensible to tackle some Units, like this one, twice in the junior years, in two short bursts, postponing study of some of the more complex issues until the children are older.

My intention in this chapter is to provide teachers who are not historians and do not have much to go on beyond the children's textbooks, with some background to amplify or emphasise issues as they see fit. Think of the unit as a many-faceted prism. One could look through only one face of the prism, privileging one perspective. I will be illustrating how one might look through other faces of the prism, exploring connections between Britain and the wider world in the Tudor period, and showing how gender and class can thread through the themes set out in the Order, altering perspectives and countering chauvinism.

Irish, Welsh and Scottish links

In 1485, Henry Tudor, a Welshman flying the red dragon standard, defeated the usurper Richard of Gloucester at Bosworth Fields, and the Tudor dynasty acceded to the throne. The last Tudor, Elizabeth, died in 1603; she was succeeded by James I, King of Scotland, son of the ill-fated Mary Stuart, Queen of Scots. Mary was the granddaughter of Elizabeth's aunt Margaret Tudor (Henry VIII's elder sister) and thus a strong claimant to the throne of England. She was not only Queen of Scots but also closely connected to England's old enemy, France, through marriage to the Dauphin, who had died when Mary was still quite a young woman. She had been brought up in France as a Catholic, and when she returned to Scotland after the Dauphin's death, brought a retinue of French Catholics with her. Bowing to pressure from those who feared conspiracy from Mary's Catholic supporters, Elizabeth had her cousin Mary executed, after keeping her prisoner for nearly twenty years. Scottish history is mingled with English history in the Tudor period, largely through the 'sister Queens', partly through the Scottish response to the Henrician Reformation, Calvinist hostility to Elizabeth's half-sister Mary Tudor and to Elizabeth herself, and partly through Catholic intrigues involving Mary Stuart.

Ireland was conquered by the English in 1171 when Henry II was formally installed as Lord of Ireland. Ireland was ruled as a subordinate kingdom of England from Henry VIII's time through to the Act of Union in 1800. It was Tudor policy to suppress minority languages and culture and neither Celtic nor Gaelic culture was tolerated at the national level. The conquest and subjugation of Ireland dates from Elizabeth's reign and was complete by the time she died, with many bloody rebellions and battles. The indigenous people of Ireland and Wales could only enjoy the rights of free-born Englishmen if they adopted English customs, language and law, and many Welsh and Irish people became bilingual. The establishment of a dominant English culture seems to have been part of an attempt to secure and develop the Tudor state. In 1565 for example, in advocating a plan to subdue Ireland, an English nobleman summarised official policy: 'to augment our tongue, our laws and our religion in that Isle, which three be the true bands of the commonwealth whereby the Romans conquered and kept long time a great part of the world'.

From the 1570s onwards, (when the Pope excommunicated Elizabeth) in the face of real and imagined threats from Catholic Europe and fears of Catholic conspiracy at home, the subjugation of the hostile population of Ireland was seen as a military necessity, lest her enemies use the island as a base for attack on England. A recent children's textbook about the Tudors (Purkis, 1992: *Tudor and Stuart Life*) uses a contemporary engraving of the English army in Ireland to encourage children to work from primary pictorial evidence, but the focus in Purkis is solely on the English weaponry and no information is provided which might help children understand just what the army was doing in Ireland anyway.

Curiously, in the History Order, the Earl of Essex is marked out as a personality whom children might learn about as part of court life. He was sent to Ireland in 1595 to try (yet again) to subdue the rebellious chieftains but returned before his mission was complete, to Elizabeth's great displeasure. It is unclear whether children are expected to learn about this aspect of his life, or whether they are supposed to concentrate on his personal relationship with Elizabeth!

The actual settlement of Ireland by the English dates from the Stuart period, and Ireland was bloodily subdued again under Oliver Cromwell. But it is said that the Elizabethan conquest really ensured that the bulk of Ireland's population would remain Catholic as a last stand against the conquerors. If the descriptions and value judgements about Scottish nobles who became involved in the political manoeuvrings of the sixteenth century are often derogatory, I have been equally struck by the pejorative language used in academic history books by some English historians, to describe the Irish chieftains who resisted Elizabethan subjugation in the late 1500s. It is hardly surprising if this bias is thoughtlessly replicated in the children's texts which draw on such accounts.

Religious conflict in Tudor history and its relevance to contemporary issues

Study of the Henrician Reformation (Henry VIII and the break with Rome) is a statutory element of this Study Unit. There is really no way to teach about the Reformation without considering the deep-seated religious conflicts which mark both the national and international history of the period. Edward VI, Henry's young son who ruled for six years before his premature death in 1553, followed his father's anti-Rome stance and gave sustenance to Protestant refugees. The French Church in Soho Square commemorates the fact that Edward VI offered a safe haven to French Protestants.

During the brief reign of the Catholic Queen Mary Tudor, Protestants were persecuted (again a fact that is sometimes included in children's textbooks). But under Elizabeth, a quarter of a century after Henry VIII's break with Rome, England was once again a refuge for Protestants in Europe who were experiencing religious persecution. Huguenots were welcomed in England after the Massacre of St Bartholomew (in Paris) in 1572. Elizabeth welcomed Dutch Protestants fleeing from Spanish persecution in the Lowlands but then sent them back. Some historians say she was forced to do so by Philip of Spain, others that it was part of her notoriously pragmatic diplomatic behaviour, which always sought to protect England's interest against both French and Spanish interference. The 'Sea Beggars', as they were called, returned to challenge Philip's henchman Alva in the Low Countries and established a small Protestant haven along the coast, under William of Orange. Sixteen years later Elizabeth's continued support for the Dutch Protestants was one of the important motives for Philip's determination to invade and take over the English monarchy with the *Invincible Armada*. Though

The plaque at the entrance to the French Protestant Church in Soho founded in 1550, for Huguenot refugees, commemorates Edward VI's support for Protestants. (Photo Hilary Claire)

Elizabeth attempted to keep excesses of intolerance in check, Catholic priests who came to England to proselytise were often forced into hiding in the so-called 'priest holes', and some were killed. Mary Queen of Scots lost her life because Elizabeth could not turn a blind eye to a Catholic plot. Internationally, the well-founded fear that a foreign king would follow up the Papal excommunication by attempting to bring England back into the Catholic faith, was at the root of allegiances and enmity with Spain which led up to the invasion by the Armada.

The respected German-Catholic theologian Hans Kung argued recently that since the collapse of communism, the greatest threat to world peace comes from the clash between the West and Islam and that 'without peace between religions, there can be no peace at all'. If the study of history can help children make sense of our own times, then Tudor history of national and international conflict linked so tightly to religion has considerable contemporary relevance. The central place of religious conflict in the Tudor period might help children think rationally, at one remove, about analogies in our own time.

Chapters in *Challenging Racism* (ALTARF 1984) and Carrington and Troyna's book, *Children and Controversial Issues* (1988) rightly emphasise the importance of the classroom ethos and strategies which allow the introduction and discussion of such potentially difficult and sensitive material. Religion and ethnicity are closely connected: persecution because of religious affiliation is a tragic aspect of history this century, from the Holocaust to the long-running conflicts in the Middle East and Northern Ireland and, more recently former Yugoslavia and Chechenya. It is important to remember that children in our own schools may themselves have close connections with such places and people. A teacher might decide to use discussion about religious conflict in the Tudor period to help her class understand the long-standing nature of religious intolerance, and think with sensitivity and compassion about the causes and consequences for both sides.

The importance of the cloth trade in Tudor times: acknowledging class, multiculturalism and gender

Nearly seventy years ago the historian Trevelyan wrote that 'the change from mediaeval to modern England might well be written in the form of a social history of the English cloth trade' (Trevelyan, 1926, p. 279). Many late twentieth century historians of early modern England would agree. Another significant feature of fifteenth and sixteenth century society was that it was primarily rural and based on agriculture. The implication for primary school history of the Tudor period is that children should have an opportunity to learn about the tremendous contribution to the economic and social history of Britain of *ordinary* men, women and children in the countryside. Agricultural labourers grew corn, made butter and cheese, and herded sheep. The agricultural and cloth-producing economies in turn depended on a whole gamut of craftsworkers who sheared, spun and wove the wool and took it to market, and metal and woodworkers who produced every kind of tool to support these industries. Weaving was a domestic industry in Tudor times; every member of the family contributed. Lithographs and paintings from the period show women and children busy working in the fields and in their homes, as well as men. This is the sort of pictorial evidence which children should be encouraged to work from, to evaluate the contribution of agricultural and craftsworkers to England's growing wealth and trading power and the role of women and children in the period before 'separate spheres' became the accepted ideology for men and women.

Henry VIII started to develop the British navy which would in due course take trade much further afield. However under Henry VIII and the early part of Elizabeth's reign, cloth merchants concentrated on the European market, avoiding clashes with Spain that intervention in the West Indies would have involved. In the first half of the sixteenth century, the main European port servicing this trade was Antwerp, also the main depot for trade from the East, Africa and the Americas. Via Antwerp, commodities from a wider world entered

Britain, including spices, silk, carpets and glassware. By the third quarter of the sixteenth century, however, the needs of the developing cloth industry inspired Elizabethan merchants to search for more distant markets and were thus an important motive for the explorations which were to lead to British settlement and conquest abroad. Richard Hakluyt, the sixteenth century historian of Tudor sea power, wrote in *The Principall Navigations, Voyages and Discoveries of the English Nation* (1589) '.... our chiefe desire is to find out ample vent of our wollen cloth, the naturall comoditie of this our Realme'. With the South American market under the control of Spain, English explorers concentrated on the Baltic, the Middle East and India, spending many fruitless years trying to find a North West Passage. This was the context for John and Sebastian Cabot's voyages, sponsored by Henry VII.

The contribution of European artists and skilled craftsworkers from the Low Countries and Protestant Europe to English culture

The Plantagenet monarchs who preceded the Tudors had close familial links with the continent and from the early fourteenth century (ie pre-Tudor) Edward III had encouraged Flemish weavers to bring their knowledge and skills to England, to enrich the cloth industry. From the late fifteenth and early sixteenth centuries, when the reformation shook the established church in the low countries and France, many of the people who fled religious persecution in Europe were skilled cloth workers, though the number of refugees included a variety of other tradesworkers and craftsworkers. [In the seventeenth century, large numbers of Huguenot silk weavers fled persecution after the Revocation of the Edict of Nantes (1685) which had protected Protestants in France; many settled in Spitalfields in East London. But that is beyond the remit of the Tudor unit.]

Henry VIII himself was concerned to build up a magnificent court as befitted a European monarch and some of the lavish splendour with which he surrounded himself depended on encouraging European artists and craftsmen to his court. A Dutch artist, Hans Holbein painted the royal portrait; the royal astronomer was German. Elizabeth continued the policy of employing Europeans: in her reign Dutch, Milanese and Venetians set up glass works in London; Dutch engineers who had experience in draining and managing their low-lying land were brought in to help manage the Thames. They were also the main people to develop the brewing industry, and at the end of Elizabeth's reign the Dutch dominated map-making, the manufacture of scientific instruments and line engraving in London (see Merriman, 1993, pp 39-43). There were over 5,000 alien residents in London in 1583 (out of a population of roughly 160,000). Many of these must have been the foreign tradespeople and craftsmen whose particular skills were so welcome and enriched the cult of Gloriana, the Virgin Queen and her court.

Using museums for children's work on multiculturalism in Tudor times

Preparation for a museum visit could introduce children to the multicultural nature of Tudor Britain. Using postcards and pictures from good museum sources, they could look carefully at paintings and engravings showing interiors from the time, noting whether the names of the artists are foreign. They could be asked who they thought designed and made the domestic artefacts and ornaments which were increasingly part of the court and wealthy households. The text describing the provenance of exhibits usually says whether they were made abroad or by foreign craftsworkers living in Britain. A museum visit or resources provided by the teacher would make clear the contribution of foreign craftsworkers, brought specially into the country, as they look at the detail of intricate woven textiles, armoury, fine pottery and glassware and other domestic ware which were used by royalty and aristocracy. Carpets, sometimes called 'Turkeys', were an innovation of late Tudor life. Rush matting was still the norm for the floors, but ownership of an imported Middle Eastern carpet — usually hung on the wall or over a piece of furniture to preserve its beauty, became a status symbol for the wealthy.

As part of their careful examination of artefactual and pictorial evidence, children should be encouraged to move their questions on from 'what is this, what is made of and what is it for?' to

> who made it?
> where did the raw materials or the article itself come from?
> how did the materials or the artefact get to England?
> what does that suggest about trading connections, value and interest in foreign-made goods at the time?

Children can look at the detail in pictures and embroideries, some of which shows the presence of foreigners in Britain. It is not just in the eighteenth century that one starts to see black people represented in paintings or lithographs. The Westminster Tournament Roll (an embroidered cloth which dates from 1511) shows a black trumpeter; a clear illustration in *The Peopling of London* (Merriman 1993) could be photocopied for use in a classroom. The children might be asked to speculate how this musician came to be in England at this early period, several decades before the voyages of exploration which took slavers such as Hawkins to the coast of Africa. One possible explanation is the close connection of England with Spain, and the fact that 'Moors', some of whom were North Africans, had invaded and settled Spain and the Mediterranean coast of France in the Middle Ages. The Moors were expelled from Spain along with the Jews in 1492.

A museum visit might be a kind of treasure hunt to discover just what kind of commodities were imported and from where, or how far foreign craftsworkers were responsible for goods that were used by courtiers or ordinary people. If the children's reading level is not high enough, the teacher or accompanying adult would need to help. In the Tudor Gallery at the Museum of London, for example, children would be able to discover that a ship load from Antwerp in 1567 contained tennis balls, liquorice, silk, warming pans, thimbles and dye for cloth. Glassware from Venice has turned up in archaeological digs in large quantities, suggesting that it was a common import in the early Tudor period. There are clocks from Germany, metalwork from Flanders, Delft tiles which were found in Tudor houses.

Henry VIII brought large numbers of craftsmen from the continent and established them in London, so that goods could be made on the spot and not imported. This was part of the contemporary economic theory that money should not go abroad if possible, and that the country should strive to be self-sufficient. A fair number of hand guns were imported, particularly from Italy and Germany, but Henry established a gun foundry in London and brought in European craftsmen. After the sacking of churches and monasteries, some of the metal from stripped churches was used to make cannons. All this can be discovered from the exhibits on display. By the middle of Elizabeth's reign, there were 5,000 foreigners living in and around London, particularly Spanish, Italians and Dutch, and the latter were not all Protestant refugees. (The total population of London was approximately 50,000 in 1500 and had grown four-fold to 200,000 by the end of the century — opportunities for cross-curricular maths!)

A visit to the National Maritime Museum at Greenwich would provide another opportunity for children to appreciate the importance of global exploration and connections for Tudor Britain. The very maps used by Raleigh when his men established the settlement at Virginia are on display, the original globes and navigational instruments which made the explorations possible, the cannon and other artefacts resurrected from the Mary Rose, which sank because it was overloaded.

Imported foods and tobacco

Children's textbooks often mention that tobacco and sweet potatoes were brought by Sir John Hawkins to England in 1565 as evidence of the early connections with the newly discovered lands of the West Indies and South America. Tomatoes came in 1596. Spanish explorers described potatoes in Peru in 1553 but they were not planted in Britain till the following century. The first coffee seems to have arrived in Europe in the early sixteenth century, from Arabia, and by 1580, Venetian merchants were importing Turkish coffee to Italy. Given the travel connections between Italy and England, it might already have become popular here, though the first coffee houses date from the 1630s. Between them, coffee, tobacco and potatoes would have a major impact on the history of Britain and other countries as they took hold as new essentials in the lifestyles of Europeans.

Sugar, whose import and consumption we take for granted today, is another commodity with important connections to the Tudor period. Children should know that sugar was a scarce luxury in the fifteenth and sixteenth centuries, confined to the richest through its price (a situation which continued through till 1874 when the tax was lifted). Given its cost, the general way to sweeten food in Britain was with honey. However, sugar cane was being cultivated in Spain and Portugal (having been brought by Arab traders from India in the eighth century AD) and though sugar refining for the European trade was centred first in Venice and later in the sixteenth century in Antwerp, there are records of two sugar refineries in London as early as 1544.

Columbus took some sugar canes to Santo Domingo in 1493 and found that the climate of the Caribbean was particularly suited to its growth. This was to be a tragic landmark for the history of Africa and the relationship between European and African people. The increasing demand for labour for the sugar plantations on most Caribbean islands and on parts of the Spanish and Portuguese-held mainland, created and fuelled the trade in African slaves. (Slave labour was also required for the tobacco and cotton plantations but sugar was even more labour intensive.) Even after slavery was abolished on the British-held islands at the beginning of the Victorian period, it continued in Spanish and Portuguese-held territories — notably Cuba and Brazil which were the chief producers and exporters of sugar. So the British people continued to be implicated in slavery, through consumption of slave-produced commodities. On the British-ruled Caribbean islands, and on the sugar plantations of Natal in South Africa (which were established later, after the abolition of slavery) 'coolie labourers', namely indentured East Indians, were brought to do the work which African slaves had done before abolition. Thus European tastes and desires continued to determine the involuntary movement of vast numbers of people across the globe.

Gender issues in the Tudor period: wise women, witches and scolds

Point 2 of the Key Elements of the Key Stage 2 programme of study requires that:

> pupils be taught about the characteristic features of particular periods and societies, including the ideas, beliefs and attitudes of people in the past, and the experiences of men and women; and about the social, cultural, religious and ethnic diversity of the societies studied.

Though sixteenth century Britain was indeed patriarchal and misogynist, many people erroneously believe now that the restrictions on women's lives which actually date largely from the nineteenth century, have a much longer history. In my view it is a helpful aspect of anti-sexist work to make the short-lived nature of some sexist practices apparent, through pointing to the economic and social contribution made by women in the Early Modern period. Earlier in this chapter

I referred to the contribution made by women to agriculture and the cloth industry, apparent in much pictorial evidence which is accessible to children.

The Tudor period was one of uneasy cohabitation of a new form of Christianity (Protestantism and in Elizabethan times early Puritanism) and strongly entrenched beliefs in magic, alchemy and witchcraft. Women had little or no part in the religious hierarchy of either Catholic or Protestant churches. But they did have a very real role in the rituals of magic and folk medicine, particularly to do with birth, marriage and death, where 'wise women' ministered to the sick in body and soul, in the manner of modern psychotherapists and not just doctors. At a period before childbirth became controlled by male medicine, women were midwives, but this meant women were held responsible for things going wrong in the pregnancy or for the infant's deformity or death. In the Tudor period, the boundaries between healing, acceptable superstition and witchcraft sometimes seem very fuzzy to our eyes.

In Europe, witch-hunting took a much more virulent form and was much longer-lasting. In England, Acts were passed in 1542 and again in 1563, making serious acts of witchcraft punishable by death. Witch hunts were at their peak in Elizabeth's reign but few witches were actually executed. (There was another outbreak of witch-hunting at the time of the Civil War, but more witches were prosecuted than were actually hanged.) Witches were often old, helpless and vulnerable widows, frequently the unfortunate scapegoats for accidents and misfortunes which befell a family after they had come begging. Accusations of witchcraft were usually made about a child who had fits, or unexpectedly became ill. The idea that persecution of witches is part of a patriarchal, misogynistic society is only part of the story. Witches were as often prosecuted by other women as by men. Witches were supposed to bear a devils' mark, and other women, particularly midwives, made themselves responsible for discovering these marks.

The association of a 'familiar' with witches, often a cat, dates from Elizabethan times. In much children's fiction, stories about witches hark back to and perpetuate repulsive stereotypes of people who are old, disabled and poor — and female. Sometimes, however, fiction draws on the alternative imagery of good witches, the traditional 'wise' or 'cunning' witch, who had knowledge of spells and magic which brought health and fortune. Interestingly, recent research about 'good witches', suggests that many of them were not women but men!

Witchcraft is emotive and sensational stuff, guaranteed to fascinate even as it arouses tingles of anxiety and horror. Just as the study of Tudor piracy demands a more serious approach which deconstructs the myths, so it is important to move beyond sensationalism in this equally gendered aspect of the past. Sixteenth century Tudor history provides an opportunity for children to understand how ideas of criminality and appropriate punishments change; where both the benevolent and the malevolent ideas about witchcraft originate, how far misogyny, fear and superstition continue to be turned against the elderly and the disabled, particularly if they are unattractive, defenceless women.

It's important to keep a sense of proportion. Children should not be left with the notion that witchcraft was a major social phenomenon, involving large numbers of people. Then, as now, women were much less likely to be accused or convicted of crimes. But this does not mean they were meek and passive. An almost exclusively female offence of the time was 'scolding', meaning making trouble in the community, usually through being hot tempered or argumentative, indulging in brawling or verbal abuse. If found guilty, scolds might be fined or they might be ducked in the local pond or river in a specially constructed ducking stool. There are no records of deaths, and because of the expense of making and maintaining the special stools, which tended to rot, many parishes preferred to fine scolds rather than duck them. Sometimes they were just humiliated by being displayed in a public place, or paraded round the town in a cart followed by people making 'rough music' by banging basins and jeering.

The Queens

The important role of female monarchs and consorts in the Tudor period is perhaps the most obvious way to counter the general male bias of the history syllabus. However, it is quite possible, using the children's material available, for children never to consider the perspective of Henry's unfortunate wives as victims of male manipulation, court intrigue and pawns in his desire for a male heir. Anne Boleyn was the victim of Henry's wrath at her failure to bear him a male heir but she was much more besides. She was clearly a personality in her own right, part of the reforming movement at court, with an entourage of supporters who were, for a while, the predominant faction. Catherine Parr, the only Queen who outlived Henry, was also a reformer. She was a mother substitute to Elizabeth and was responsible for her excellent education. Mary Tudor and Mary Stuart are sometimes reduced to cardboard cutouts, decontextualised from the religious conflict which embroiled England and Europe throughout the century. The different treatment in children's books of Catherine of Aragon (Mary Tudor's mother), the Spanish Catholic whom Henry divorced to marry Anne Boleyn, the two Marys and Lady Jane Grey, can provide a valuable lesson in uncovering bias (see Key Element 3a: pupils should be taught to identify and give reasons for different ways in which the past is represented and interpreted).

Despite anxiety about a female monarch, Elizabeth came to the throne in 1558 amidst widespread jubilation and pageantry which heralded her as a latter day 'Deborah', likening her to the Hebrew Queen who had brought peace to Israel. Looking at the surviving visual evidence, children need to learn about the cult of 'Gloriana' the Virgin Queen, as part of their growing understanding of the attitudes of the period. Some historians have even talked of Elizabeth being 'packaged' by contemporary image makers. Children learning to 'do history' as opposed to indulging in romantic heritage nationalism, need to develop the skills and knowledge to stand back and assess this cult, and the reality of Elizabeth's character as a real person. She seems to have been vain and autocratic, prone to endless prevarication, especially when it came to spending money. She was committed to avoiding international conflict if she could, but she also strung along courtiers and foreign dignitaries with her refusal to commit herself in marriage (which feminists might interpret as a strategy to stay in control of her destiny!). She manipulated the men at her court, and has been accused of treating them like a firm but indulgent nanny treats naughty boys. She believed firmly in the hierarchical Divine Right of Kings.

The defeat of the Armada

In children's textbooks, the defeat of the Spanish Armada is usually described with little or no political context other than the desire of Philip II to put a Catholic monarch (possibly himself) on the throne of England. The involvement of the Pope, who openly supported Philip's enterprise to conquer England, and who proclaimed a crusade against the Protestant Queen, is seldom included. On the other hand, versions which individualise and personalise the history of the period, as if it could be explained simply as some sort of tournament between two rival monarchs, do not really help children to grasp the complexity of historical causes. Elizabeth and Philip were indeed powerful, autocratic monarchs, but to concentrate on individual 'great names' at the expense of more subtle interpretations is part of an outdated historiography which primary schools do not need to perpetuate. Children need to start asking questions about why Philip would want to take over England; why the Pope would be concerned; why Philip ordered Medina Sidonia to the Netherlands, where it was intended that he would take on board a huge army of soldiers to invade England. This would give a context for their understanding of the Armada as part of the major religious and political conflicts of the age.

The classroom texts dealing with the Armada that I have looked at seem to veer from oversimplification to those so suffused with strategic detail about the battle that it is hard to disentangle the overarching historical story. Accounts concentrating on the battle itself — typically beautifully illustrated with old maps and paintings — are usually historically accurate but only tell part of the story. Pupils should be encouraged to move beyond military and naval details and to try to contextualise the Armada in international politics, noting the strategic importance of the Channel with relation to Spanish control of the Netherlands. Philip's concern to strengthen his position in the Netherlands, his growing isolation from the real world around him, his failure to take proper account of the defeat at Corunna are all part of the story of the Armada. A more narrow, ethnocentric, British perspective is likely to concentrate on the development of the new navy under Drake and Hawkins, its superior weaponry and ships, and the rivalry between Admiral Howard and Drake. Medina Sidonia was also a very able commander, hampered by foolish instructions from Philip, and extremely bad luck in the weather. It is not my intention that children should swap one xenophobic version of history for another which is equally biased, but nor is it right that they should adopt uncritically the Elizabethan view that God was on the side of the English. Rather, they need to start to understand the nature of the bias in history which can eventuate in unthinking xenophobia or assumptions about the inferiority of foreigners.

An international context for learning about the Armada — Hawkins, Drake and the Caribbean

The longer term consequences of the defeat of the Armada are seldom highlighted in children's textbooks. The English victory meant that Protestantism and the Reformation in England, Holland and Germany were safeguarded against Catholicism but it did not mean that England had now vanquished her Spanish enemy in Europe or in the New World. The war with Spain continued for another fifteen years in Europe, with Spain intervening in one of the Irish rebellions which plagued Elizabeth's attempts to maintain peace. The Spanish might have been prevented from invading England, but their strength and power in the New World were not affected. The continuing Spanish presence in the Caribbean and South America prevented England from taking over territory there, until the Stuart period and the interregnum (under Cromwell). However, the English navy, the English monarchs and English sea captains were part of the history of what happened not only in that part of the world but in Africa, whence labour for the new colonies would come.

An inclusive approach to Tudor history entails learning about how the English came in contact with black people through explorations at that time and about English people's role in servicing the developing Caribbean-African slave trade. This story is part of the international history which includes the Armada. The following paragraphs briefly contextualise the story of the Armada, to include the role of Drake, Hawkins and long-standing Spanish-English enmity in the Caribbean.

During the late fifteenth century and the sixteenth century Spain and Portugal opened up the sea routes to the great trading regions of India, West Africa and the Americas. (This is the international history which was covered in CSU 6 of the 1991 Order, Explorations and Encounters, and excised from the Key Stage 2 curriculum by Dearing.) In the face of Portuguese and Spanish dominion of the seas, English efforts went into trying to find a North West passage via the Arctic. The Cabots, father and son, who are mentioned for study in the Order, were important personalities in this project. By the middle of the century, English explorers were following the Portuguese down the coast of West Africa, had landed on the Guinea coast and brought back gold. In 1562 John Hawkins sailed from Plymouth with three ships and 100 men and made for Sierra Leone. His ships carried cloth made in England which he would trade on the African coast. There he loaded up with 400 slaves, some captured by himself, some bought from Portuguese middlemen. He sailed on to the Caribbean and the Spanish Main (the north coast of South America) where he sold his cargo. On the way back he collected a consignment of fish to sell back in England. And so began British involvement in the notorious Atlantic triangular trade which was to be the scourge of Africa and the haunting shame of Britain for another 240 years. Hawkins' crest shows the proud face in profile of an African, a rope round his neck and his arms and chest tightly bound with rope.

Elizabeth contributed a naval vessel to Hawkins' voyage and gave him her official backing. In the Caribbean, Hawkins fell foul of the Spanish who had already established their ill-fated outposts, strictly patrolled by their own flotilla and protected by international treaties and licences issued in Seville. In the Spanish colonies, African slaves worked the mines and the newly established plantations to produce wealth for Europe. Elizabeth honoured Hawkins, who does seem by the standards of the day to have been a more humane and scrupulous master of his ship than many others, and financed a ship for his second voyage.

Now Francis Drake, Hawkins' cousin, enters the story. On the third voyage he commanded one of Hawkins' small fleet, the Judith. As before, Hawkins steered the flotilla first to the coast of Africa to collect African slaves, which he would sell to the Spanish in the Caribbean. Caught in a storm on the way back, Hawkins took refuge in a Spanish Mexican port, San Juan. Hawkins and his men were considered pirates and heretics by the Spanish, and despite a promise of safe passage, were attacked and all but two of their ships decimated. The defeat went down in British memory as appalling Spanish treachery. This ignominious battle marked the end of peaceful trade with the Spanish and was the beginning of a period of open piracy on Spanish cities and treasure ships. Drake may be the most renowned Elizabethan pirate, but he was not the only one; all in all, the pirates' activities from then on did nothing for Anglo-Spanish relations.

Drake was determined to avenge the San Juan defeat and spent the next nine years in voyages of exploration and piracy on Spanish treasure ships. In 1581, after a long voyage during which he captured Spanish and Portuguese vessels encountered en route and loaded the Golden Hinde with the stolen booty, Drake returned to England. He was a national hero; he had in fact circumnavigated the world and he was knighted by the Queen. Elizabeth also turned a blind eye to the depredations of the many other fortune seekers who sailed from the South Western ports to try to get hold of the booty being transported in Spanish ships back to Europe. After the treachery and defeat by the Spanish in San Juan in Mexico, Hawkins became professional advisor to the Queen on the reconstruction of the navy. Remember, economic theory of the time proposed that the actual amount of gold or silver in the national coffers determined the country's wealth.

Hawkins believed that the best strategy to weaken the Spanish was to prevent them from bringing supplies of American silver to Europe and that the way to cut the routes was to use the navy. It was this reconstructed navy of fighting ships which would in due course meet and defeat the Armada.

In 1585 Drake was at the head of a fleet of thirty ships, equipped and financed by the Queen, which set out effectively to destroy Spanish power in the West Indies. This put Philip of Spain on the defensive and also complicated his efforts a year or two later to raise loans to finance the great Armada with which he was preparing to invade Britain, intending to put himself on the throne occupied by the 'heretic queen'. (Remember, by this time, Elizabeth had been excommunicated by the Pope.) In 1587 Drake inflicted a second blow on the Spanish near the coastline of Spain itself and delayed the Armada for a year. Still, the Spanish fleet which sailed into the Channel was not that ill-matched with the English fleet. Nevertheless it took a battering when it harboured off Calais and the weather did the rest, driving the remains of the Spanish Armada round the East coast of England, round the north and finally to be shipwrecked off the north west coast.

In 1595, both Drake and Hawkins died of illness in the Caribbean; they were engaged in a raid in which they had planned to repeat the successful plunder of Spanish treasure which had made their names when they were younger men.

English history has mythologised and sanitised the exploits of the Tudor sea adventurers and naval commanders. In children's books, pirates are portrayed as pantomime figures, with black patches and wooden legs, forcing their enemies to walk the plank. Their unprincipled and aggressive actions are translated into curious and heroic adventures on uninhabited islands where they find buried treasure with the aid of rudimentary maps. How much less demeaning of children's intelligence and more historically honest it would be to use these mythological accounts as a springboard to the real history, through work in this unit on the Tudors. The personalities of these famous English adventurers provide opportunities to explore the complexity and ambiguity of human nature, rather than opting for two-dimensional hagiography or dismissing them as totally wicked.

Instead of rather trivial work with fake pirate maps, children can do real history. The necessity of maps to find your way in an uncharted world takes you straight into the fascinating study of cartography; reproductions of the old maps, many of which are in the National Maritime Museum, clearly indicate Early Modern Europeans' misunderstandings and ignorance about the nature of their world, and the people and creatures who lived on it.

I do not want to apologise for the Elizabethan pirate-explorers. But good history demands something other than dismissive judgements made from the comfortable position of hindsight. Drake and Hawkins were pirates and both were indubitably involved in the early slave trade. Hawkins' role in redesigning the navy and Drake's victories against the Spanish at sea contributed to the defeat of the Armada. Both men had many admirable qualities: they were extremely able, talented, single-minded and courageous, as contemporary accounts make clear. There are difficult questions here, which adults as well as children argue over. Their attitudes and behaviour were not untypical of their time: enslavement of black people was accepted and condoned by the Pope and the European monarchs, piracy on behalf of one's own nation and extreme measures against people of the 'enemy' religion — Catholics if you were Protestant, Protestants if you were Catholic — were all normal in times of war. To us, such attitudes and behaviour may not only be anomalous but deeply unacceptable. Yet, in our own times, wars of religion are not unknown. Aggressive international action to capture or protect valuable products (e.g. oil, even sheep) has occurred in the lifetime of junior school children.

Here, then, are opportunities for really thought-provoking educative debate within the context of real events of which we know the outcome, about different perspectives, values and morality. Children need to be made keenly aware that there are two sets of judgements — one from the perspective of the time, in which all kinds of values differ from our own, and a second set, in which one looks back with hindsight and through the lenses of one's contemporary culture. In a class of children there will be different judgements about these Tudor seamen, who certainly affected the history of their times. Children might like to consider how those they regard as heroes of our own time might be judged by future generations.

In the discussion of Key Stage 1 history, the value of role-play and drama in historical study was noted. Through literally putting themselves in another's shoes, children can gain insights into motivation and inevitable bias in perspective about a given situation. The more life-threatening or critical, the more subjectivity is likely to intrude, both on interpretations at the time, and on later versions. The danger presented to Britain by the Spanish Armada is just such an event, as are all the circumstances surrounding Drake's and Hawkins' lives.

Children could hold mock trials, in which they take the stand as Drake or Hawkins, and have to defend their actions against accusations from a fictional twentieth century prosecutor, of piracy and involvement in the slave trade. They could be asked to role-play both sides of the drama — Spanish and English — at San Juan; or put themselves respectively in the shoes of ordinary people in England and in Spain, when they hear the news about the outcome of the historic battle.

The chronology is complicated, but the sequence of events is important in trying to make sense of decisions made at the time and explain cause and consequence afterwards. A time-line is essential. Children could research different aspects and events leading up to the Armada and in the following decade, and put their findings on the time-line. They need to have visual support to see connections and ask questions about the relationship between the monarchs' intentions and the sea captains' quite substantial autonomy of action.

'This is your life', Tudor style, could be a vivid way to bring the period alive, even if various characters really never met. The Queen could knight Drake at Deptford; Medina Sidonia or Alva, a crew member from the Judith scuppered off San Juan, a slave taken from the African coast, could confront Drake or Hawkins and ask them to account for themselves.

Raleigh and the first colonies in America

The Order also suggests that children learn about Raleigh's voyages as part of this unit. I limit myself here to Raleigh's involvement with America, where he established the very first of the English colonies. The story of the beginning of the British Empire is far from heroic. Raleigh was an educated English gentleman, acquainted with the ideas of Richard Hakluyt (whom I mentioned on page 108) about the desirability of colonisation in America to deal with the problems of unemployment, poverty and vagabondage in England. (This view was revived in the nineteenth century for similar reasons.) Tiny though England's population was by contemporary standards, it seems that some Tudors believed the land was overpopulated and that the export of people might solve some of the obvious social problems. There was also the desire to compete with Spain in providing sources of wealth and power, in the form of foreign possessions.

Raleigh did not personally go with the ships dispatched in 1584 to find a promising place for settlement, but he funded the expedition which arrived on Roanoke Island, claimed it in the name of the Queen, and returned with two American Indians. Raleigh called the place Virginia, in honour of his virgin Queen. A drawing in the Maritime Museum at Greenwich and a map records this historic if abortive beginning of English-speaking settlement in North America. A year later a second party of settlers was put down by Sir Richard Greville, but they accepted a passage home in 1586 from Drake, finding the place and the people inhospitable. Greville returned to find the colony deserted; the small force of fifteen left to hold the colony in the queen's name was never seen or heard of again; they were almost certainly murdered by the native inhabitants.

In 1595 Raleigh mounted an expedition to find and claim Eldorado, the source of the fabled gold of South America, for his English Queen. He went a short way up the Orinoco river, lost heart and motivation in that inhospitable territory, and turned back.

Early connections with India

We saw how rivalry with Spain and the necessity to expand English markets led to attempts to find a route to the East through the North West passage, which would avoid going near or through Spanish-controlled territory. Magellan and Drake's journeys were all part of these attempts, though Drake interpreted his mission as an opportunity for piracy on the Spanish main. The end of the Tudor period witnessed another historic voyage of exploration, which was to have a major impact on future international relations and contemporary Britain. For some time London capitalists had been hoping that a direct route through to the rich trading lands of the East would be opened up by British ships. In 1591 the Levant Company, formed in London to develop trade with Turkey and the Near East, financed a fleet under James Lancaster, which got as far as Zanzibar before turning back because of illness.

Meanwhile, an adventurer called Ralph Fitch had travelled overland and into India. When he returned he reported on the great wealth of the Indians and the splendour of the Court of Akbar, the Great Mogul King whom he had visited. Much encouraged, the London merchants applied for a charter for an East India Company to promote this trade. Lancaster now tried the sea route again and this time reached first Sumatra and then Java where he established an English 'factory'. When he returned, the East India Company received its charter from the Queen and thus began the connection with India. The history of British colonisation and imperialism in India belongs in the Stuart, Georgian and Victorian periods. Nevertheless, there is the opportunity here to introduce children to the beginnings of this history. The outcomes for the Indian subcontinent itself were dramatic and a very mixed blessing. For Britain, one of the long-term outcomes is the presence of many citizens of Asian origin.

Black people in Britain in Tudor times

The pages above have, I hope, made it apparent that it would be peculiar and historically suspect to learn about the Tudors within the terms required by the Order without mentioning the early settlement of America and the Caribbean islands and the fact that the transportation of African slaves had started under Elizabeth. There is a notorious proclamation from Elizabeth herself objecting to the numbers of black people in London, 'crept into this realm' since the troubles between her highness and the King of Spain; 'who are fostered and relieved here, to the great annoyance of her own liege people who want the relief which these people consume'. (A facsimile is reproduced in File and Power, 1981.) The actual words of her edict requiring that they be removed have an uncanny resonance with modern objections to a black presence. Elizabeth objects because they are a drain on the Poor Laws, 'in these hard times of dearth' and are not Christians. She requires her subjects to hand over such 'blackamoors' to a certain Caspar van Senden, merchant of Lubeck, who has arranged for their speedy transportation. The names of those who refuse to comply should be certified to Her Majesty who will use her princely wisdom to decide what further action she should take. Elizabeth was dead within two years of her proclamation and it is not clear how successful her order was.

Resources

[anno] after a book indicates that it is included in the annotated lists in Chapter 13.

Children's Fiction

Attley, Alison, 1977, *A traveller in time*, London, Penguin (Period of Mary Queen of Scots.)

Harnett, Cynthia, 1981, *Stars of Fortune*, London, Methuen (Tudor England: Mary Tudor is Queen and Princess Elizabeth living as a virtual prisoner in nearby Woodstock, down the road from the family whose story is told in this novel. Top juniors.)

Harnett, Cynthia , 1951, *The wool pack*, London, Methuen (A novel set in Newbury in 1493.)

Harnett, Cynthia, 1959, *A Load of Unicorn* , London, Puffin *[anno]*

Kaye, Geraldine, 1987, *A Breath of Fresh Air,* London, Andre Deutsch (About the slave trade.)

Manning Sanders, Ruth, 1969, *The Spaniards are Coming*, London, Heinemann (About the Armada.)

Resh Thomas, Jane, 1990, *The Princess in the Pigpen*, London, Collins (Time travel from the Tudor period to the twentieth century.)

Sutton, Harry, 1977, *Fireships Away: the inside story of the Spanish Armada*, Heritage Books, National Trust

Tomlinson, Theresa, 1990, *The Secret Place*, London, Walker Books *[anno]*

Non-fiction

Newbery, Elizabeth, 1994, *What happened here? Tudor Farmhouse.* London, A. and C. Black (Based on the reconstructed farmhouses at the Weald and Downland Open Air Museum. Detail about women's lives and ordinary domestic existence based on archaeological evidence and hypothesising from artefactual evidence.)

File, Nigel and Power, Chris, 1981, *Black Settlers in Britain 1555-1958*, Oxford, Heinemann Educational Books *[anno]*

Mullard, S., 1994, *The British Empire (Beginnings)* Wolf Pack W14, Huntingdon, Cambs., Elm Publications (Resource Pack) *[anno]*

Adult resources and references

Adler, S., Ross, C. and Scadding, H., 1994, *Women in Tudor and Stuart Times, A Resource Pack for Teachers*, Islington Education Service, Isledon Training and Development Centre, London

ALTARF (All London Teachers Against Racism and Fascism), 1984, *Challenging Racism*, London, ALTARF

Carrington, B. and Troyna, B., (eds) 1988, *Children and Controversial Issues,* Lewes, Falmer Press

Kermode, J. and Walker, G., 1994, *Women, Crime and the Courts in Early Modern England*, London, UCL Press

Merriman, N. (ed) 1993, *The Peopling of London: fifteen thousand years of settlement from overseas*, London, Museum of London Press

Trevelyan, G.M., 1926, *Illustrated history of England*, London, Longman, Green and Co.

Chapter 8

Study Unit 3a: Victorian Britain

Good resources for the Victorian Unit are being published now, but many are still bland, over-simplified or stereotyped and appear to be designed for the youngest juniors rather than older children. This is of course a problem with all published material, since its producers cannot know at which age different schools will be teaching a particular Unit. For teachers to evaluate and develop these resources, they need to know something about the history of the period, the issues and controversies that raged, how they were connected, and about the pattern and speed of change. Above all, they need to have a positive intention to look beyond the italicised suggestions in the wording of the Order, for ways to develop the points within each of the suggested themes.

Victoria was born in 1819 and came to the throne in 1837 but these are both very arbitrary dates to use as starting points. It really doesn't make sense to exclude the 1820s and 1830s, when Victoria was princess, not queen, and some historians look to these decades as 'early Victorian' just as they extend their analysis into the first decade of the twentieth century (though technically Edwardian), since there was more continuity than change at that period. It is very important, however, to differentiate between the various periods of the Victorian era. The 1830s and 1840s were as distant in many respects from the 1890s, as the 1930s are from our own times. In the 1820s and 30s the labour of women and children in mines and factories was still unregulated. Canals, still under construction in some areas, were carrying vast quantities of goods, and horse-drawn coaches were the main form of passenger transport. The railways were only just beginning. In the 'hungry forties', depression, cholera, and working class challenge to the established authority — the great Chartist movement —

were key themes. By the middle of the century, Britain celebrated her world industrial supremacy at the Great Exhibition; and in the expanding towns, sometimes characterised by graphic pictures of crowded workhouses and unsanitary and poverty-stricken dwellings, the workers jostled with a prosperous middle class. By the last decades of the century, India and large expanses of Africa had come under Colonial Office control; at home the railway system was fully established; compulsory elementary schooling had changed the lives of children; a new women's campaign to join civic society was under way and the Trade Union Movement was flexing its muscles in strikes and demonstrations..

Gender and class might seem to be the main areas for developing an inclusive curriculum through this study unit and both themes are explored later in this chapter. However, there are opportunities for enormous breadth of study: during the Victorian period major issues of human rights were debated and contested, concerning not just women and children and working class rights but also race. Just as ordinary people in our time do more than go to work or school (or not, as the case may be) and find different ways to fill their lives, so millions of ordinary people were involved in what became a major moral campaign of the time, at least as powerful and broad in its sweep as the current concern for the environment. That movement was the campaign to end slavery, both in the British domains and elsewhere. This is a theme developed further in this chapter, but first I need to set the context.

Trade, the British Empire and Britain as the workshop of the world

The 1995 Order has removed the requirement to teach about trade and the growth of the British Empire from the recommended content for this unit. Unit 3 in Key Stage 3 is now the statutory vehicle for learning about the impact on Britain of its colonial and imperial connections. I have argued earlier (Chapter 5) that a spiral curriculum justifies introducing some of this material in the primary years, even if not at great depth, on grounds that children cannot understand the industrial revolution, and the changes to British society as Britain became the 'workshop of the world', without some understanding of the international economic and political context. The goods produced through mass production in factories were not all consumed at home but were sold on the *world* market, and the raw materials from which they were made were imported.

Victorian history provides opportunities to bring geography and economic and industrial understanding to the support of historical understanding through work on industrialisation (which was interdependent and connected with the wider world) and transport changes in Britain. Although *Curriculum Guidance 4* (Education for Economic and Industrial Understanding) gives an example of how economic understanding can be developed through work on Victorian transport, it fails to explore the much broader possibilities in the period. Excising the 'trade' connections from the Victorian study unit flies in the face of the sound reflection of *Curriculum Guidance 4*, that 'pupils are becoming more aware of the wider world in which they live — for example they are better able to understand the national and *international* implications of economic and industrial activity' (*CG4*, p.20 my italics). A selection of its recommended themes and concepts is reproduced here, to illustrate some of the themes that I now explore:

☐ know that all decisions involve opportunity cost

☐ be aware of some of the costs and benefits of everyday economic choices; recognise that people can have different and conflicting interests

☐ understand what it means to be a consumer and how consumers and producers relate to each other

☐ understand that workplaces are organised in different ways

☐ develop their understanding of the nature of work and its place in people's lives

☐ have some understanding of how goods are produced, distributed and sold

☐ be aware of some effects of new technology and the implications for people and places

☐ appreciate some of the environmental and social issues associated with economic and industrial activity

☐ recognise similarities and differences between economic and industrial activities in different part of the world. (NCC, 1990, *Curriculum Guidance* 4, p.21-24)

In Chapter 7 we looked at ways in which children's understanding of Britain's connections to a wider world could be developed through work on the artefacts and commodities that were increasingly part of Tudor life, particularly in the higher social echelons. Study Unit 3a has similar possibilities, but now the growing and powerful middle classes take the stage. Not just the resources and markets for industrialisation, but the very fabric of middle class home life was tied to Britain's colonial expansion and trade in foreign places. Cotton, coffee and tea, ivory for piano keys, buttons and the handles for fine cultlery, silver and gold for jewellery and tableware, oil for margarine and soap, rubber for bicycle (and later car) tyres, jute for sacks and rope, hardwoods for the fashionable heavy, ornate furniture, cocoa for chocolate manufactured by Cadburys in its model factory at Bournville, none of these was native to Britain. All were imported — chiefly from the old and new colonies, and the trade was managed by British people who established themselves 'abroad'.

Feeding the people in 'the workshop of the world'

The British-global links established in the Tudor period were developed in the intervening centuries, and welded into an even stronger chain in the Victorian era. Britain's industrial supremacy in the mid-nineteenth century was dependent on its trade relationships, in particular favourable connections with countries where the required raw materials were produced, and where its finished products were sold. As the century progressed, Britain became increasingly dependent on the import of food for its burgeoning population, which was growing at the rate of about two million each decade, though the numbers of people who stayed on the land remained roughly constant over the century: the population explosion affected the towns and cities, where people could not and did not grow their own food. Even with agricultural improvements, there was no way that British farmers and agricultural labourers could feed the growing urban millions. Some, but not all, of the countries which provided food were British colonies and part of the growing British Empire. To give an idea of what this means, here are some statistics: they are the sort of figures which junior children might work with on a computer:

Urban and Rural Population of Britain and Grain and Flour imports

The policy of Free Trade was the masthead of the mid-century governments, from the time of the Repeal of the Corn Laws in 1846, which ended protection of British

Year	Approx. Total Population in millions from census — whole of GB incl. Ireland	Percentage Living in the country (England and Wales only)	Percentage living in towns (England and Wales only)	Grain and flour imported (mill hundredweight)
1801	15.8	76	24	
1831	24.1			1.8
1841	26.7	52	48	
1847	(Irish famine years)			46
1851	27.3	46	54	
1871	33.75	35	65	
1874				93
1881	36.1	30	70	
1901	41	22	78	

grown corn and meant that foreign corn could be imported more cheaply for the consumer. However, by the last decades of the century, as protectionism by Britain's competitors undermined Free Trade, an increasingly aggressive policy towards foreign 'possessions' and competitors had developed, and trade in Britain's favour was sometimes established at the barrel of a gun, and maintained only after resistance had been suppressed. So Britain's successful industrial growth at home can only be understood in a world context.

The importance of the cotton industry

When children learn about the factory system and the 'dark satanic mills' that increasingly symbolised industrialisation in the middle of the nineteenth century, they are learning *par excellence* about the cotton textile industry. Just as wool had been the backbone of the British economy under the Tudors, cotton textiles were central to its growth in the mid-nineteenth century. From the 1840s to the end of the century, cotton manufactured goods consistently made up around a third of total exports. This does not mean the amount of cotton produced and exported stayed the same, as the following table shows:

Exports of cotton manufactured goods (figures rounded up to nearest whole number)		
	1840	1874
cotton yarn	200 million lbs.	220.7 million lbs.
cotton piece goods*	790 million yds.	3,600 million yds
All cotton goods: value	£24.6 million	£84 million
* piece goods means cotton material sold by the yard		
Source: Young and Handcock, *English Historical Documents* Vol. VII (1), 1833-1874.		

The popular saying goes that Manchester produced all the cotton goods needed in Britain itself before breakfast and spent the rest of the day producing goods for the world market. Put another way, one fifth of cotton manufacture stayed in the country: four fifths was exported.

Cotton is a tropical plant and it is does not grow anywhere in Britain. In the late eighteenth century when the cotton textile industry was getting established, most of the raw cotton came from the slave plantations of the British West Indies. After the American War of Independence (1775-83), much of the raw cotton needed for the Lancashire mills came from the slave plantations of the Southern States of North America.

The following table could be used to contribute to junior children's understanding of data handling as part of economic history. It shows very clearly the dependence of the British cotton textile industry — and I reiterate that this was *the major* industry at the time — on the slave plantations of the USA. At the beginning of the period, the USA was supplying half the raw cotton needed for the industry. By the 1840s and during the subsequent 20 years until the American Civil War the USA supplied much more than half. During the Civil War (April 1861- April 1865), the supply of cotton dropped suddenly and significantly and created a depression (called the cotton famine) in the cotton area of Britain where people were put out of work; the trade picked up again after the war was over. From the 1830s, as Britain established an increasingly wide network of control over India, cotton goods in a semi-processed form were imported, subjected to further processing, and largely re-exported. The section below on Indian connections takes that story further. After the opening of the Suez Canal in 1869, more cotton started to come in from Egypt and India.

Imports of Raw Cotton into the UK (in millions of lbs.)		
Date	Total imports	Imports from USA
1815	101	54
1830	264	211
1840	592	488
1850	664	493
1860	1,391	1,116
1862	524	14
1865	978	136
1870	1,339	716
1880	1,629	1,224
1890	1,793	1,317
Source: Mitchell, B.R. and Deane, P., 1962, *Abstract of British Historical Statistics*, CUP		

Cotton and India

The beginning of this chapter indicated how India and Britain were connected through cotton. Britain, it is claimed, effectively destroyed the indigenous Indian cotton industry, in order to create and protect the market for cotton cloth produced in England.

Control of the Indian market was not achieved without the establishment of a British presence on that continent and, in due course, military intervention. The Order recommends 'the armed forces' as the subject for study in the Victorian period. This offers a space to consider the First War of Independence of 1857 (or the 'Sepoy Mutiny' in British historiography), when Indians challenged British rule in a bloody rebellion that rocked the country. An editorial in the *Times* in early 1857, shortly after the Delhi uprising, makes no bones about the naked necessity of military conquest:

> We have arrived at that point in our Indian career when the total subjection of the native element and the organisation of all that we have conquered become a matter of necessity.......it is [in] our interest to establish in it [India] a homogeneity which it has never before possessed. There is no reason why the British Government should not attempt to fuse into a solid mass the conglomeration of provinces which is called India. We cannot now refuse our part or change our destiny. To retain power in India we must sweep away every political establishment and every social usage which may prevent our influence from being universal and complete.

A manifesto in the *Delhi Gazette* in September 1857 presents the opposing point of view:

> It is well known to all, that in this age the people of Hindostan, both Hindoos and Mohammedans, are being ruined by the tyranny and oppression of the infidel and treacherous English..... it is plain that the infidel and treacherous British government have monopolised the trade of all the fine and valuable merchandise... leaving only the trade of trifles to the people, and even in this they are not without their share of the profits, which they secure by means of customs and stamp fees..... It is evident that the Europeans, by the introduction of English articles into India, have thrown the weavers, the cotton dressers, the carpenters, the blacksmiths and the shoemakers etc. out of employ, and have engrossed their occupations, so that every description of native artisan has been reduced to beggary...

Comparing the two perspectives would usefully introduce children at Key Stage 2 to the way history habitually comes through interpreted versions, and not as straight 'fact'. But to continue the narrative ...

Fourteen months of bitter fighting ensued before the Indian rebels were defeated. India came under the control of the British government in London. Victoria became Empress of India in 1877, which was soon termed 'the Jewel in her crown'. Thirty years after the failed 1857 uprising, commemorative hand-kerchiefs printed for Victoria's Golden Jubilee in 1887 show her framed by the symbols of her Empire. An Indian elephant fills the bottom left, mounted by a small retinue of turbanned Indians each with his arm raised in deferential greeting;

at the right, a reclining lion and a camel, its African rider holding aloft an ivory tusk; above them, standing as it were on their heads, Australia, Canada and the British Isles are represented by smiling, well-fed men. Curiously, Ireland and the Caribbean are missing from this joyous scene. The details and symbolism of this commemorative artefact would be well worth children's attention, using a postcard of the handkerchief available from the Museum of London shop.

There is another aspect of British history which connects to India, not generally remembered. Drunkenness among the working classes was endemic in the years of developing urbanisation and industrialisation, and recorded in innumerable cartoons and lithographs (e.g. Cruikshank). Through the decades of the nineteenth century when liquor was not regulated, home brewing was as important a source as going to the pub (with consequences for the strength of the liquor) and when there were few outlets for leisure, working people regularly and as a matter of course got drunk to drown their sorrows and cope with tedious and exhausting lives. Only in 1872 was there any official intervention to attempt to control drunkenness but liquor consumption reached its highest point that century in 1875-6. This is the background to all those pictures of women, men and children hop-picking! Meanwhile, the Temperance League and the Band of Hope were set up in an attempt to persuade working people to take the pledge and to relinquish the comforts of liquor. For middle class people, especially 'ladies', trying to set the tone of proper and respectable behaviour, drinking tea, at least in the daytime, increasingly became *de rigeur* in polite society. Increasingly, tea became a necessity among the working class and there are records of poor people begging used tea leaves from neighbours. The new manners did not necessarily get taken up by everyone and beer remained the main beverage for male workers, who believed in the importance of 'putting back the sweat'. Nevertheless, there was an increase in demand for tea, particularly towards the end of the century. It was imported mainly from India and the Far East. When Britain took over direct rule of India after 1858, British entrepreneurs were among those who would go to the sub-continent to buy up and run tea plantations.

Multicultural lives in Victorian Britain

It makes no sense to try and learn about industrialisation and the economic supremacy of Britain in the mid-nineteenth century without contextualising British trade and industry in its world market. We saw how the development of the major industry of the century connects Britain to the Southern States of America and to India. A global framework for understanding about Britain's industrial growth also provides the opportunity for primary school children to learn about historical connections with other countries that became the Commonwealth. In the inner cities, this is likely to be part of pupils' own family history. Outside the cities, such work provides an historical context for children to understand the presence of ethnic minority groups in Britain today.

Theoretically, this understanding is supposed to wait for Key Stage 3, but isn't the secondary school a bit late for children to know something of this aspect of contemporary life?

The wording of the Order — 'children should learn about the lives of men, women and children at different levels of society' — is misleadingly generalised. The inhabitants of Britain in the nineteenth century were not differentiated just by gender, age and class. Britain was already a multicultural society at the beginning of the nineteenth century, as a result of connections with India, Africa and the West Indies, and of well established links with countries on the continent of Europe and the regular movement of people across the Channel. Over the nineteenth century the multicultural nature of British society increased, numerically and in diversity. Connections with her existing and growing colonial Empire (including Ireland) continued to account for some of the new immigrants. But there was a new dimension — the political upheavals in Europe and Russia — which led to the arrival of people who had no direct political connection with Britain.

In teaching about the ordinary lives of men, women and children at work and at home, at prayer, leisure and school, we need to move from portraying general stereotypes of an homogeneous British populace, to showing the variety of people in their different localities. In some areas this would involve learning about the arrival and settlement of Irish (of whom more later), Jews, Poles, Germans, Lithuanians or Italians, all of whom came to England in quite large numbers during the nineteenth century, particularly the latter half. Some groups brought specific skills and crafts and established independent workshops where they continued to carry on their trades. Others joined existing workplaces and were either quickly assimilated, or found themselves in conflict with the indigenous workforce.

People came with their own religious beliefs, chiefly different versions of Christianity and Judaism, and established their own places of worship. Many of these still stand as testimony to the growing heterogeneity of 'ordinary' British society. Some set up their own schools. Many Catholic schools were established in the nineteenth century for the children of Irish immigrants, along with Catholic churches which often date from the period. Detailed study of this aspect of a locality might come into Study Unit 5, the Local History unit, connecting with the community's involvement in a particular event, or illustrating developments taught in another unit (see Chapter 10).

Learning about the lives of men, women and children at different levels of society — working class life

The Victorian journalist Henry Mayhew's classic work about London street life in the 1850s and 1860s, *London Labour and the London Poor* includes fascinating pen sketches of people who lived and worked on the streets, Among these were

Irish, West Indians, Scots, Jews and Germans. The sections on the Jews and Irish betray patronising and somewhat racist attitudes which were probably typical at the time, even of liberal middle class people like him. Despite this, readers not familiar with Mayhew will find his work well worth reading. Vivid detail, drawings of some of the characters that he interviewed, and personal testimony from his informants spring from the page. Here you will find evidence about people who sold ham-sandwiches, ginger beer, pies and cake; child street-sellers, whose slang is carefully recorded; 'mudlarks' who scavenged on the banks of the Thames; 'dustmen' who collected the ashes from coal fires for brickmaking and manure; the child road-crossing sweepers who cleaned up after the horses; chimney sweeps, street entertainers, omnibus drivers and conductors. Women and girls are vividly present in this bustling working society, and it is clear that working class women were no more relegated to domestic life then than now.

Ordinary family life — bridging the gap between Key Stages 1 and 2

Chapter 2, dealing with Key Stage 1, discusses the theme of 'ourselves' at some length. For children who have already done some work on family history and childhood in the infants school, study of domestic life, families and childhood in the Victorian period in Year 3 would help bridge the gap in approach and conceptual complexity that some children experience when they move to the juniors. Key Stage 2 teachers will find the project 'Ourselves and family history' in Chapter 2 useful for ideas and resources. Although these would certainly need extending, they would be equally appropriate to a Year 3 or 4 project, perhaps to remind children of what they had learned before, or perhaps as starting points for children who still need the kind of support that the infant school curriculum provided.

Contemporary historiography of family and childhood

Contemporary history of family and childhood tries to uncover the different patterns of family life, how family size, mortality and fertility have altered and how family and childhood have had different meanings for different cultures and periods. Family history studies patterns of migration, how far members of families have stayed near one another, gone into similar work, maintained traditions and cultural practices and been affected by wider social, political and economic changes.

The history of childhood is concerned with changes and continuities in child-rearing, child labour, the different experiences of boys and girls in families and how class affects childhood; how children are socialised into attitudes about education, work and authority, leisure, future roles in society. Historians of childhood are interested in the rituals, customs and traditions of family life which affected children; for example, how childbirth or illness were managed, how

132

much children knew about birth and death or were kept apart from the adult world, what happened when they broke family rules or societal rules. In the nineteenth century, childhood in the middle or upper class had very different meanings from the working class. 'Childhood', in our modern sense of innocence and lack of responsibility, is relatively new and, certainly in many working class families in Britain till the end of the nineteenth century, there were not the sharp divisions between childhood and adulthood which characterise contemporary British society.

The history of childhood studies children's own historical actions and experiences; for example, resistance or compliance to the demands of schooling or work, how far they contributed to the subsistence economy of their families, the nature of official interventions in their lives, whether through social welfare measures, provision of education and so on, and how children themselves interpreted these measures. Some of this can be found in autobiography and recorded oral history (see for example two books by John Burnett in the bibliography). Autobiographies are very useful sources, from which teachers can take short excerpts to help children get a sense of changes and continuities. Some exemplary passages which teachers might use are quoted at the end of this chapter.

Human rights issues in the Victorian period

Changing Hearts and Minds: The anti-slavery campaigns

For most primary teachers, the campaigns to improve the conditions of children and women drafted into the burgeoning industries and mills of urban Britain epitomise concern for human rights in the Victorian period. The frightful situation of women and children's work is not only very well documented but extremely interesting to primary school pupils, touching nerves of empathy and personal concern. Later in this chapter these campaigns are discussed in more depth.

There is another issue of the period which was equally dramatic and important, and has equivalent potential to involve children's sensitivities and awareness of injustice. In the early and mid-nineteenth century, literally millions of ordinary British men and women were drawn into two great campaigns to do with the relationship of black people and white. The first and largest was the campaign to end British slavery; the second the campaign to emancipate American slaves.

The campaign to end the slave trade and British Caribbean slavery — religious groups and slave rebellions

The role of religion is among the suggested themes for the Victorian unit and could provide the entry point for study of the anti-slavery campaigns. Religious groups played a major role in organising the campaign for emancipation of British slaves in the Caribbean, and then in supporting American anti-slavery campaigns, although it took the American Civil War to finally bring down the institution of slavery in the USA.

The slave *trade* — but not *slavery* — was abolished in the British colonies in 1807, with an Act of Parliament which put an end to more than two centuries of British involvement in the purchase of Africans on the African coast, transportation on the 'Middle Passage' in British ships, and sale in the Caribbean and other slave-owning areas. But slavery on the British-owned Caribbean plantations continued. Anglican Evangelicals, Quakers, Baptists, Unitarians and Methodists from all walks of life publicly condemned the continuation of slavery. They stomped across the country making speeches and collecting signatures for petitions to Parliament. The Quaker faith had instilled notions of equality and the wickedness of slavery. At least in England, Quakers were active and outspoken members of the anti-slavery movement; among them were a number of women, notably Elizabeth Heyrick about whom more in a moment, Elizabeth Pease from Darlington, and Anne Knight from Chelmsford.

Between roughly 1815, when the Napoleonic Wars ended and 1838, when an Act of Parliament finally fully emancipated British slaves (with massive compensation to their owners) the campaign continued, in Britain and in the Caribbean itself. In the Caribbean, rebellions and revolts as well as an ongoing process of resistance by slaves which undermined their owners' authority and sense of security, contributed to the eventual outcome. Women as well as men were part of this resistance. The frequency of rebellion and the news of the vicious reprisals against slave resisters played their part in altering perceptions in England that slavery was acceptable and benign, as its defendants claimed.

Rebellions master-minded by slaves themselves dated from well before the abolition of the trade, and continued in the Caribbean even after 1807. The reprisals by the local white authorities against a (white) London Missionary, the Reverend John Smith, who had supported the slaves in the rebellion of Demerara in 1823, outraged British public opinion. Elizabeth Heyrick, a Quaker from Leicester, was the first person to insist on immediate emancipation of British slaves, in a pamphlet published in 1824, called *On the Reasons for Immediate not Gradual Emancipation: or an inquiry into the shortest, safest and most effectual means of getting rid of West Indian Slavery.* Under the leadership of Wilberforce and his followers, 'gradualism' had been the accepted programme, and Heyrick's pamphlet initiated a new direction for the emancipation campaign, along with the news of rebellion and revolt in the Caribbean itself.

A major revolt in Jamaica in 1831, called the 'Baptist War' after its leader, the black Baptist, Reverend Sam Sharpe, led to immediate action in the British Parliament to end slavery.

Women and the British anti-slavery movement

From the 1820s even quite small provincial towns like Devizes and Colchester had a branch of the Female Negroes Friends Society or the Female Society for the Relief of British Negro Slaves. In larger towns like Sheffield, Norwich,

Manchester, Bristol, Liverpool, Huddersfield and above all Birmingham, women were very active, visiting house to house to persuade women of the injustice of slavery. An interesting and little-known aspect of the anti-slavery campaign in the 1820s and 1830s was the production by the many Ladies' Anti-Slavery Societies of 'workbags' which women embroidered and filled with pamphlets explaining the wickedness of slavery and arguing for boycotts of West Indian slave-grown sugar. Women in some organisations adapted the famous anti-slavery logo 'Am I not a Man and a Brother?' to 'Am I not a Woman and a Sister?' Children might simulate the action of women by preparing a 'workbag', complete with pamphlets, and role-play the doorstep discussions with supporters or those hostile to the cause.

At the time, many people used analogies with working class conditions in the mills and factories of the North of England to support or to undermine the anti-slavery argument. Middle class philanthropists, generally arguing from a religious standpoint about the immorality of treating other humans so cruelly, quite openly exploited concern about the distressing and shameful conditions for English women and children, to argue that West Indian slavery was equivalent and equally unacceptable. Working class people were often quick to use the same arguments to sniff out hypocrisy in those ready to support people far away from home, while turning a blind eye to British workers from whose labour they were personally profiting. This ambiguous morality is the subject of a telling passage in *A Twist of Fate,* a children's novel about early Victorian Britain, mentioned in Chapter 5. A 'do-gooding' middle class woman, deeply involved in anti-slavery work, is portrayed colluding openly with the oppression of workers in her family's factory while urging them to give their support to the campaign.

A very different perspective comes from a contemporary piece by 'Linda Brent', the pseudonym of an American ex-slave, who published her extraordinary and harrowing story *Incidents in the Life of a Slave Girl* in 1861. (This has now been reissued in a simplified version for children but unfortunately leaves out the material about her English visit.) In her book, Linda Brent tells how she spent ten months in England in the 1840s. She had escaped from slavery in South Carolina and was working for a family in New York. When his wife died, her employer Mr Bruce asked her to take his little daughter Mary to relatives in England. They sailed to Liverpool and then journeyed to Steventon in Berkshire, where Linda reports the great poverty of the working people, living 'in the most primitive manner' and earning very low wages. Since at that time, the anti-slavery campaign had transferred its concern with British (Caribbean) to American slavery and frequently compared the condition of English workers with American slaves, it is interesting to read this fugitive slave's comments:

> The people I saw around me were, many of them, among the poorest poor.
> But when I visited them in their little thatched cottages, I felt that the condition

of even the meanest and most ignorant among them was vastly superior to the conditions of the most favoured slaves in America. This ... was because they could still marry and know that their children would be safe with them, they were not slashed and whipped by their overseers and in contrast to the Southern States where a slave was in danger of lashing for learning to read or write, there was even a growing movement to educate the children. (Linda Brent, *Incidents in the life of a slave girl*, p.188-9)

The campaign to free American slaves in the middle of the nineteenth century

The Campaign to emancipate British slaves built up enormous momentum and after the Emancipation Act in 1838 this was channelled into opposing slavery in America. The World Anti- Slavery Convention was held in London in 1840, and here British campaigners met delegates from North America who had come to debate policy and strategy. Among their numbers were free or refugee African-Americans who had joined the campaign. Charles Remond, for example, a free black American who had been on a speaking tour against slavery, had been nominated as the delegate for some women's groups in north west Wales, who were unable to represent themselves. This was the beginning of a connection which continued for the next twenty years, when the Civil War finally ended slavery in the South.

Barbara Bodichon, whose life story has much to offer children, for the many and energetic ways in which she became involved in different issues of the time, particularly women's rights, visited the Southern States in 1857 and returned to report in detail on slave conditions on the plantations. Some refugee slaves were sponsored by English people and came to England when new laws in America made it unsafe to stay even in the North. Among them were Ellen and William Craft, whose life story is summarised in Chapter 12. Frederick Douglass, a leading black abolitionist and supporter of women's suffrage, who had just fled slavery in the Southern States, also visited Britain as a speaker in the 1840s (see entries in Chapter 13).

Black people living in England in the nineteenth century

In Chapter 7, which deals with the Tudor period, the historical context for an early black presence in Britain is outlined. A fair amount of evidence exists for the seventeenth and eighteenth centuries, including paintings, contemporary lithographs and drawings by such as Hogarth, but these are outside Key Stage 2. William Davidson, Robert Wedderburn and the tailor William Cuffay are among the few black people who were prominent political figures in the early part of the nineteenth century, on the side of anti-slavery, workers' rights and social justice. Since it is not always easy to get hold of information about them, I have provided short biographical sketches of Davidson and Cuffay in Chapter 12.

A better-known subject for inclusion is Mary Seacole, the Jamaican nurse who sponsored herself in the Crimea and returned to settle in Britain. So highly thought of by the soldiers whom she nursed was she, that they organised a musical festival to raise money for her after the war. As well as the resources about her for pupils' and teachers' use in schools, Seacole's autobiography, *Wonderful Adventures of Mrs Seacole in many lands*, originally published in 1857, is a very accessible read for junior children.

A black perspective could be introduced into the Victorian curriculum through the stories and writing of women and men who visited and lived in London for a time and were prominent members of the British anti-slavery movement. There is Linda Brent's account of her visit to London in the 1840s. Mary Prince escaped Caribbean slavery and came to London and wrote her autobiography in 1831, which was used for publicity by the anti-slavery society (see Chapter 12). The Crafts went on speaking tours in England, and were involved in bringing the plight of American slaves to the attention of the public, through a carefully orchestrated and publicised promenade through the Great Exhibition at Crystal Palace, on a Saturday when Victoria herself was present. Since the Great Exhibition is mentioned for study in the unit, this might be the context in which their stories are introduced, to remind children not just that there were black people in Britain in the nineteenth century, but also that there was an important anti-slavery movement, even after British slaves were emancipated in 1838, the year in which Victoria was crowned. Sarah Parker Remond, a black woman who lived in London in the 1850s and eventually became a doctor, is another personality whom children might learn about (see Chapter 12).

In Chapter 12 there is an account of how the Africans James Chuma and Susi carried Livingstone's body 1,500 miles through Central Africa to the coast, to be shipped back for burial in Westminster Abbey. An African named Jacob Wainright accompanied the body on board ship and was at the funeral in Westminster Abbey in 1874. Susi and Chuma were brought to England slightly later by the London Missionary Society, to see for themselves where Livingstone was buried, and to receive formal recognition of their heroic action.

Livingstone was one of the most celebrated of all Victorians, both at the time and now, a deeply religious man who in his own way epitomised the values — in an idealised form — of a stratum of Victorian society. His life was originally suggested for study in Key Stage 1 (famous men and women) and then appeared briefly in the now defunct Extension Study D in the Dearing proposals. It is not obvious how this story fits into the given themes of the Victorian unit, if its requirements are met in a minimalist way, but many teachers seem to be taking the encouragement to extend the syllabus to meet their own needs seriously and no doubt those who want to, will find a way to include such material. They might also perhaps work on that other Victorian explorer who appeared and then disappeared from the curriculum, Mary Kingsley. If so, remember the warnings

Mr T.S. Livingstone, Miss Livingstone, James Chuma, Susi and Horace Waller discussing journals, maps and plans of Dr Livingstone, Newstead Abbey, 1874 (photo: Royal Geographic Society Picture Archives)

given in Chapter 4 about avoiding a starry-eyed hagiography of Victorian explorers, which ignores the imperialist dimensions of their projects, and the ways in which they contributed — even if unintentionally — to notions of European superiority and African 'primitiveness'.

Children's biographies have also been written about Ida B Wells, a black journalist whose writing had an impact at the time, and who became a celebrity in Britain at the end of the nineteenth century. Born in 1862 in Mississippi, she made her name in journalism by exposing the horrors of lynching. Her writing was an important catalyst for the anti-lynching campaign in America and Britain. She became internationally known and toured Britain on speaking tours in 1893 and 1894. In the early twentieth century she was involved in women's suffrage and co-founded the NAACP (National Association for the Advancement of Coloured People).

Asian, Chinese and black people in Britain in the Victorian period

It is more difficult to find evidence of ordinary black people in Britain in the Victorian period. A researcher from The Ragged School Museum Trust in Limehouse, East London, has gone through the Barnardo's Archives, and found a number of references to black children and young people who were taken into their care. The Museum has now reproduced some of the photographs as postcards, which children might use as visual evidence alongside the written sources. The case studies suggest that many black people who ended up destitute had come to Britain as seamen and been paid off in British ports such as Liverpool or London. They had tried to make ends meet, but in the inhospitable social and economic climate had to resort to charity. In 1888 for instance, there is an entry for Claudius Tiberius Alexandrinius:

> ... at least as exceptional as his name, and coming as he does from the West Indies, he is as unlike my London waifs in appearance as can well be imagined. At eighteen years of age he found himself in the streets of Liverpool, discharged from the ship in which he had come over, without the least prospect of a livelihood. He tramped to Portsmouth, obtained an engagement there with Sanger's Circus, assisting in pitching tents and the like, for which he received 12s a week, with food and clothing. But this windfall soon came to an end, and then the weary tramp to London began. His clothes in tatters, his dark face against him, the rule of the Strangers' Home forbidding them to receive such cases permanently, unable with his West Indian habit of body to endure our climate of chills and fogs — it was miserable to see the despair in the poor fellow's face. There was not one door in London that would open to him, save the workhouse alone. (From the Barnardo's Archives, Ragged School Museum Trust)

By far the bulk of trade between countries of the Empire was carried on in British ships, but some of their crew came from abroad. Foreign ships also worked the routes and docked at the growing British ports. This meant that not only goods but people from other lands were visiting and in some cases settling in Britain. Sailors from abroad who decided to stay in Britain, or were unable to get return passages, increasingly became part of the settled population. What happened to these men if they were unable or did not wish to continue their life at sea? Many joined the ranks of destitute and homeless Londoners, as the following article from the *Illustrated London Journal* of June 14, 1856, makes clear.

The occasion is the laying of the foundation stone for the 'Strangers' Home' in the West India Dock Road, Limehouse, in the East End of London. A drawing illustrates Prince Albert and a number of Indian dignitaries who, along with the East India Company and English philanthropists, had contributed to funding the home. In the background, two hundred 'Orientals' are visible, assembled 'to testify their interest in the proceedings'. They were given handkerchiefs and bouquets. The accompanying article explains the circumstances:

> The Strangers' Home [is] designed to supply a manifest and long-felt desideratum ... affording all the comforts and advantages of a home to natives

'Be Not Forgetful to Entertain Strangers':'laying the foundation stone for the Strangers' Home in Limehouse
(From the Illustrated London News, *June 14, 1856)*

of India, Arabia, Africa, China, the Straits of Malacca, the Mozambique, and the Islands of the South Pacific, who may require them during their temporary sojourn in London. No man can have walked the streets of our principal seaports without being moved to commiseration by the utterly wretched condition of many of the Lascar seamen and others from kindred climes — friendless, homeless, and destitute — in a country far distant from their own.... The building will be capable of accommodating 230 inmates,... furnished throughout, including lighting, warming, hot and cold baths and lavatories... The object of the directors is to offer to all Oriental strangers who visit England a comfortable and respectable lodging, with wholesome food, at a cost which it is presumed they can afford, and which shall render the institution self-supporting. (*The Illustrated London News*, June 14, 1856)

Twelve years later, the curious picture opposite of the interior of the Strangers' Home, now well established, appeared in the *Illustrated London News*.

*Residents of the Strangers' Home making and serving soup and bread to the
'distressed poor' of the East End, in a period of depression.
(From The Illustrated London News, March 7, 1868)*

At twelve o'clock daily, the African and Asian inmates of the Home served
out soup which they had made themselves, to the poor and destitute of the
neighbourhood. The article gave some statistics: since its opening in June 1857,
2,870 Asiatics, Africans, and South Sea Islanders had been lodged and boarded
for various periods, at their own or their employers' expense; 785 others had been
'sheltered and gratuitously boarded, and provided with employment, or a passage
to their native country'. Beds cost 3d, baths 2d and meals 3d and 5d. Furthermore,
several thousands of Asians and Africans had been visited in hospitals, gaols,
workhouses on board ship in dock and provincial towns in various parts of
England and Scotland.

Rozina Visram (1986, 1987, 1995) has traced the history of South Asian people
in Britain. A surviving photograph of the Ayah's Home in Hackney, run by the
London City Mission, taken in about 1900, provides an interesting bit of evidence
about Asian women left without support in London (see page 142).

The original Ayah's Home was founded in Jewry Street in Aldgate in the 1870s
to provide lodging for the nannies who had been brought back by English families
returning from a stint in India, to look after their children on the journey home.
Often return passages were not provided and some Indian women, unable to find

*Interior of the Ayah's Home in King Edward Road, Hackney, circa 1900
(Photo Hackney Archives Department)*

a family who needed their services for the outward journey, were left stranded. A charity was set up to provide for them; the photograph shows the women sewing — perhaps to contribute to the costs of their keep?

An 1848 *Punch* cartoon of an Indian crossing sweeper in St Paul's churchyard is of a real person, probably a sailor who had jumped ship or got left behind and was trying to make his living. A mission was set up in Limehouse in London for destitute Lascars (sailors) in 1887. A Chinese community of sailors and traders, also grew in the ports. From the middle of the nineteenth century some professional people and merchants came from India to study or set up business connections and there were notable Indian personalities in British public life by the end of the century (see for example, notes on Dr. Naoroji in Chapter 12). Mayhew's *Life and Labour of the London Poor* (1861) contains a number of illustrations which would be excellent visual evidence for children to work with.

Curriculum suggestions for bringing a black perspective to the Victorian unit

Given the depoliticisation of the Victorian unit, it is not obvious just where one might teach about the contribution to British history of the people described here. Perhaps they will be included in Study Unit 3 by secondary teachers, but this is small comfort to teachers looking to an inclusive history curriculum in their pupils' age range. Infant teachers of course have the opportunity for such work in the 'Famous Men and Women' strand of the Key Stage 1 Programme of Study. Chapter 10, Local Study discusses in some detail how black people's history can be studied through the theme of immigration but this scarcely applies to the Victorian era.

Nevertheless, some junior teachers *are* finding ways to incorporate work on black personalities into their curriculum through such broad themes as 'People we admire', possibly as part of general work for assemblies. The pupils in one inner London school, where the majority of the community is African-Caribbean in origin, produced a ring-bound book of notable black people who had lived in Britain in the nineteenth and twentieth century. They used computer technology and photocopied children's artwork, to ensure a high standard for the publication. This book was sold with great pride to parents and children, including infants who were also working on 'famous people'. A book-making project such as this meets criteria outlined for economic understanding and awareness, and could well include aspects of design and technology, as well as fulfilling important objectives in the history curriculum.

Junior classes working on the Victorians might decide upon a straightforward project on 'Multicultural Victorian Britain' or about eminent or interesting people who lived or visited Britain during the Victorian period, without attempting a tortuous justification through the given themes of work, education, leisure, transport and so on. Such a project would come under the broad heading of 'lives of people at different levels of society'. Children could choose someone they would have liked to meet or interview from a selection of thumb-nail sketches resourced by the teacher, and perhaps supplemented by their own research. The children should keep a sense of chronology, and perhaps choose one or two people from different decades, displaying their drawings and written information on a time-line. Such a list would neither exclude nor focus solely on black people but could present an interesting cross-section of all those individuals from different communities who were significant and contributed to Victorian life. People discussed in other sections of this chapter might also figure. The children could work in small groups to prepare interviews for their personality, with one of them taking the role of the chosen person, and others of her/his friends or family. They could develop short dramas about the person, or compile a class book about her/him, with drawings and paintings and written work in a variety of styles, including letters, diary entries or newspaper reports. Another idea is to prepare an imaginary obituary notice which celebrates the person's life, the challenges, trials and triumphs.

Chapter 4 outlined how Faith Ringgold's book *Dinner at Aunt Connie's* could provide a model for work in the infants school on interesting and significant people (see p.74). This approach is equally appropriate with juniors and could be extended along the lines of the TV/Radio game where participants draw up a list of people they would invite to dinner, or want to have on a desert island. They would need to know enough about the individual's life, ideas and work to be able to justify including them, but they would also consider how the various people would get on with each other, and predict possible clashes of ideology and temperament. Next they could write the dialogue, and put on a short drama enacting the conversation round the dinner table, or have a debate, in which these people argued their particular position. Another idea is a public forum or a meeting with a chairperson, who invites each speaker to present their views on a controversial issue of the time. The pupil audience could participate through questions or comments from the floor.

The Irish dimension

Anti-Irish racism is a lamentable feature of English life which goes back to the Tudor period. In Chapter 7 I described the ways in which Irish and English history were linked through subjugation and conquest. Moreover, when England officially became a Protestant country, Ireland remained Catholic, which allied her with the enemy. Negative perceptions of Catholics were officially recognised by the 'Glorious Revolution' of 1689, which prevented a Catholic from becoming monarch in the future. Civil disadvantages associated with Catholicism only ended in England in 1828 and 1829, with the repeal of the 'Test and Corporation Acts' which had prevented Catholics (and non- conformists) from holding public office, and the passing of the 'Catholic Emancipation Act' which allowed them to stand for Parliament — not that dislike and distrust of Catholic people and particularly of working class Irish Catholics disappeared.

The 1840s were years of famine which decimated the population of Ireland. The potato blight first hit the crops in 1845 and one and a half million people died of famine and disease in Ireland in the next six years. (The novel *Under the Hawthorn Tree* by Marita Conlon-McKenna is a powerful fictional account for children about the disaster.) Conventional English-oriented history books often report the devastation wreaked by the potato blight simply as a natural disaster — an Act of God — unconnected to the political or economic policies of the English who ruled Ireland and controlled the import and export of food which could have saved lives. In the face of the famine many Irish emigrated to Britain in the late 1840s looking for work. They encountered open racism, presaging the treatment Jews, Asians and African-Caribbeans would receive later. Contemporary cartoons in *Punch* and the *Illustrated London News* provide evidence of the prevailing disparaging attitudes. Henry Mayhew's book *London Life and the London Poor* (1862) contains several portraits of Irish people living and working in London, and descriptions of the crowded and unsanitary Irish quarter off Charing Cross Road, which some have interpreted as subtlely racist in tone.

Including Irish history in the Victorian Unit through study of changes in industry and transport

How and where might an Irish dimension enter the Victorian study unit? One possible way would be through the recommendations to work on developing transport and industry and changing living conditions. Irish 'navvies', working in gangs, formed a large part of the labour force which built the canals — still expanding and developing in the first half of the nineteenth century. The canals carried more goods than the railways in the mid-1840s. The Irish were also an important part of the workforce which built the railways with their massive bridges, earthworks and viaducts which transformed Victorian transport (see Terry Coleman's *The Railway Navvies* for a fascinating account). The word 'navvies' is an abbreviation of 'navigators', the word used for the canal workers.

Road building went alongside the developing railways system, and again Irish labour was employed. The families of the Irish labourers who were building the transport infrastructure settled in English cities, particularly Liverpool and London. The census figures, which become increasingly accurate from the middle of the century, show large groups of Irish-born people living in the towns at periods which coincide with the great transport revolution.

The Irish contributed not just to the transport revolution of the nineteenth century: in the 1840s there was a mass influx of Irish workers into the labour force in the factories and mills of Northern England and the Midlands, usually for unskilled jobs. The 1840s, called the hungry forties, were difficult, tense years in England. While Irish labour would contribute to the industrial boom in the 1850s, their presence was by no means unproblematic. There was open and violent hostility against the Irish immigrants during the 1840s, 50s and 60s, increasingly anti-Catholic over the period, but accompanied also by accusations that the Irish kept wages down. It is clear from the censuses that Irish people concentrated in 'Irish areas' in many towns, possibly as a response to hostility. Further evidence for the lives of Irish people in England, the contribution of the Irish factory workers and the navvies can be found in engravings from the middle of the century and later from photographs. Many Irish women became domestic servants to the middle class families who were benefiting financially from industrialisation; some Irish were artisans and professionals but the majority were labourers. Writing in the early 1860s, Henry Mayhew estimated that about one third of the costermongers (street sellers) in London were Irish. Many were amongst the poorest in the community, as contemporary illustrations of largely Irish areas like the Rookery in St Giles, central London, show.

Scottish dimensions

Possibly the most potent history of Scotland in that period that is accessible to children, is the forced emigration associated with the Highland Clearances. As sheep became a better financial bet than people on land owned by aristocrats (typically absentee English rather than Scottish themselves) so plans were made to remove the 'surplus population' to Australia and Canada. Schemes of sponsored emigration provided passages and some financial support, but the choice to stay was not an option (see Gunn and Spankie (1994) *The Highland Clearances*).

Here, to show how fiction can provide the graphic detail which brings such history to life, and carries potential for curriculum work through drama, art or writing, is a passage from *So Far from Skye* by Judith O'Neill. This children's novel is set in the 1840s. A community of crofters from Skye are leaving their land to go to Victoria (named for the Queen). Their departure is sponsored through the Emigration Society — and is very much against their will. The ship which will take them to Australia docks at Greenock, where cholera rages among the poverty-stricken inhabitants.

> The stench in Greenock was terrible. The narrow streets were choked with mud and filth. Foul, stinking rubbish thrown out from the houses overnight, still lay in heaps up every alley. Soon Morag's bare feet were black with slime. Long lines of haggard women, shawls over their heads, waited outside the pawnbroker's shops, each one of them clutching a pair of shoes, a blunt knife or a chipped brown teapot to exchange over the counter for a few pennies. 'They get their things back on pay-day,' explained Jimmy. 'They need the money now for food. Or for the drink. Everyone lives like that here. It's the only way'......... Suddenly, without warning, a terrible roaring and whistling filled the air. The buildings around them seemed to shake. Morag clutched at Jimmy's arm. 'What is it?' she gasped, her voice muffled by the cloth around her mouth. 'That's just the blower for twelve o'clock,' said Jimmy. 'All the mills let off their hooters at noon. Now the men who're lucky enough to have work go home to eat some bread and swallow some whisky before they start on the afternoon shift.' In an instant the streets were packed tighter still by the men rushing home from the mills and the docks, their pinched white faces streaked with grease... (Judith O'Neill, *So Far from Skye*, p 42-43)

Gender and Class in Victorian England

The very wording of the Victorian study unit draws attention to the disparities of class and gender, requiring study of the lives of people in town and country *at different levels of society*. Of all the ways in which one's life experience could be determined by forces beyond one's control in the Victorian period, gender and class were the most powerful. Change and continuity, the two fundamental concepts of historical study, provide the framework for considering how far attitudes in our own society still affect and determine different people's potential, according to gender and class.

Most primary teachers are aware of the enormous *class* differences in Victorian Britain and children's textbooks also make much of the way in which working class people's lives diverged from those of the upper and middle classes. However, many teachers tend to be less clear about the domination of *gender,* which cut across class. Working class women had very different experience and opportunities from their men folk, and these differences became more exaggerated as the century progressed, influenced by middle class obsessions with 'separate spheres' for men and women.

The early years of Victoria's reign (pre-1850) saw the height of the movement to get women and children out of the mines, and to reform factory labour. After 1842, it became illegal to employ women and children underground, but work at the pitheads continued right through to the twentieth century. If pupils are shown the now notorious pictures of girls pulling carts full of coal along underground passages or being let down into the pits, a time-line must show that this phenomenon ended by the mid-1840s.

The recommendation to look at working lives, including factory life and reform and the work of Lord Shaftesbury creates opportunities to explore these issues. Lord Shaftesbury was *not* a saint, although some of the material produced for children seems to suggest that he was single-handedly responsible for all the major reforms to working children's lives in the century. This is simplistic, a-historical, elitist history and it is false. Moreover, it diminishes the contribution of people in the Ten Hours Movement, whose names have been generally forgotten because they were not members of the aristocracy, or public speakers and in Parliament. Radical reformers from the working and middle classes were also part of the movement to improve working conditions for women and children. It would be like attributing the abolition of slavery to Wilberforce alone, ignoring the resistance of the slaves themselves, and disregarding all the people who tramped the country, petitioning and building up the groundswell of public opinion through pamphlets and meetings.

The situation was complex. Although there was considerable justified anxiety about the labour of women and children, much of that anxiety now strikes us as patronising to women and lacking in understanding about economic realities. There is plenty of evidence that working people were unhappy about the harshness of their children's lives, but were forced through economic necessity to have them earning wages as soon as possible. As already noted, the concept of childhood that we now take for granted is a construction of the West in the twentieth century, not a natural phenomenon.

Philanthropic concern about long hours and inhumane working conditions, also focused on the immorality of women and young girls working alongside men, on lewd behaviour and neglected children. The men rode, so to speak, on the backs of this gendered attitude about women at work, and were able to exploit it to obtain improved conditions for themselves. 'Sweated labour' and domestic work — where women and children were also exploited — were never subject to the controls of legislation and inspection, possibly because concern about them was minimal as long as they were safely tucked away in the domestic sphere.

Working class men and women increasingly did different work as the century progressed. At around 30% of the total workforce, women were an important (and politicised) part of labour from the middle to the end of the century. It is likely that the actual numbers of working women stayed constant from the previous century; in other words, industrialisation did not suddenly bring women who had not been working into the labour force. It was the *nature* of their work that changed. About 45% of working women were in the textile mills of the North of England. The other main occupation was domestic service, where girls as young as nine might find themselves working long hours, isolated from their own family. They were excluded from the new transport revolution and from the increasingly mechanised heavy industries on which late Victorian economy was based: ship building, coal, iron works. In the countryside women and children worked in agricultural gangs — photographs and lithographs show women alongside men and children. Oral testimonies survive of the hardship of long hours tramping to and fro and working in mud and frost — witness this one from Mrs Burrows of Croyland, Lincolnshire, writing about the 1850s:

> On the day that I was eight years of age, I left school, and began to work fourteen hours a day in the fields, with from forty to fifty other children of whom, even at that early age, I was the eldest. We were followed all day long by an old man carrying a long whip in his hand which he did not forget to use. A great many of the children were only five years of age. You will think that I am exaggerating, but I am not; it is as true as the Gospel. (Burrows, in Llewellyn Davies, 1977, p 109)

In 1866 a Royal Commission enquiring into agriculture showed concern with female morals, working conditions and the hardships of these women's lives, which eventually led to improvements.

In the towns the great source of work for married women and children, and very occasionally for men, was sweated labour — that is piece-work carried out in the family's own home (or shared room if that was all they had). Women stitched sacks, sewed buttonholes and seamed trousers by the thousand. They made matchboxes and put pins onto cards. Women and children spent hours by poor light producing the knicknacks and finery that would adorn the more prosperous and fashionable classes, the covered buttons, the intricate lace, the

148

artificial flowers, the belts and buckles and elaborate hats, without which no self-respecting lady would be seen in public. Many working women were employed making the fine dresses that Victorian ladies paraded in their drawing rooms.

Much earlier in this book, I discussed the pitfalls of 'whiggish' history, which emphasises improvements and progress, and avoids or denies continuing lamentable conditions. Time-lines are the best way to show that though the Factory Acts improved conditions in mines and factories from the early 40s, women and children continued to labour in the fields and to work their fingers to the bone in dimly lit workrooms for many decades after. Pictorial evidence is the best source for such understanding and from the middle of the century, as photography developed, this becomes an increasingly available source. Children can set copies of photographs and contemporary drawings out on a time-line, illustrating how late in the century such conditions prevailed. If it is well used, and children are encouraged to ask searching questions about the possible lives and livelihoods of people, pictorial evidence can be an important source for understanding class differences and divisions, as well as the impact of gender.

Gender and education in Victorian Britain

As well as work, education, too, was affected by gender. Until the Forster Act of 1870 and the subsequent implementation in various authorities of anti-truancy measures, there were always fewer girls than boys in schools in working class communities. Girls were needed at home to mind babies and help their mothers. Girls' education was taken less seriously. When girls did go to school, they were likely to receive a different curriculum, concentrating on the skills they would need to make a living (eg lace making, straw plaiting, sewing and knitting) and often missed out on arithmetic and even writing, which their brothers were likely to learn. After 1870, when national and compulsory education for all children up to the age of ten became available, gender differentiations in the curriculum were reinforced. Written evidence describes, and photographs show, girls learning needlework and domestic science, and boys doing woodwork, metalwork and technical skills.

This short excerpt from the autobiography of Charles Cooper, who was born in 1872, describes his schooling at Walton National School in the West Riding. (This and other extremely interesting first-hand accounts about schooling in the nineteenth century, including a very early one from James Bonwick, who attended the Borough Road School, Southwark, London from 1823, are to be found in John Burnett's book *Destiny Obscure*.)

> Opposite the school, across the road, was a laundry used for training poor and needy girls. Behind the laundry was a drying ground and the Head Master had his rose garden and a small greenhouse. A part of the laundry was used by the Infants. Here the Infants and Standard 1 were taught by a Mistress, assisted by a girl from the Orphanage. The big school consisted of one large

room, with no partition or classrooms, in which upwards of a hundred boys and girls were taught in Standards 2, 3, 4, 5, 6 and 7 by the Head Master and two Pupil Teachers, in mixed classes. The girls were taken in needlework in the afternoons by the lady who was really responsible for the school, and the older girls were taken in cookery and housework in a house near the school under her supervision. (Charles Cooper, in Burnett, 1982, p.193 -195)

In the next few pages Cooper describes in considerable detail the morning work in the three Rs, for both boys and girls. He gives a graphic account of the harsh treatment meted out to boys and girls and their fear of the cane. The next part makes clear that the boys' academic education (of a kind!) continued while girls sewed: '...in the afternoons when the girls were sewing, the boys would work from cards. There were many packs of cards in the cupboard for each class...' Apparently, the arithmetic cards in some elementary schools were even marked 'For girls' and 'For boys', with more difficult sums on the latter!

Middle class girls also had different educational opportunities than their brothers. Destined for wifehood and motherhood, they were generally educated by governesses at home when they were quite young, and might then go to a private school where they received an 'ornamental education' in music, flower arrangement and other accomplishments to fit them for their future. Meanwhile their brothers went to grammar or endowed schools to be educated for the professions and a place in civic and industrial society.

The following short extract from Sylvia Pankhurst's autobiography describes her early education. Elementary education was available to all working class children but anxiety about mixing with such children kept many middle class children out of the Board Schools. The Pankhursts were middle-class enlightened parents, for whom a liberal education was extremely important, but it is clear from Sylvia's account that their daughters' early education was fragmented and not always appropriate and that the little girls were largely dependent on their own initiative, which included trying to teach one another. [At the time Sylvia and Christabel were aged five and seven respectively.]

A Miss Pearson was now engaged as a daily governess for Christabel and me, but after a short time she habitually sent her sister, 'Miss Annie' as a substitute. Coming in as a stopgap, Miss Annie made little attempt at teaching, but read aloud to us the novels of Dickens, Thackeray, Scott and George Eliot. The murder of Nancy by Bill Sikes made an indelible impression of horror upon me: for years I was haunted by visions of her beautiful face of agony and fear, confronting his brutal strength... (Sylvia Pankhurst, *The Suffragette Movement*, p 84)

Shortly afterwards a Miss Cecil Sowerby became the children's governess and Sylvia writes: 'She gave us no lessons, but read to us and took us to museums and places of interest. Much of our time was spent in the British Museum, where my greatest enthusiasm was for the Egyptian section' (ibid p 107). Their father wanted to send them to school, but their mother objected that they were too highly strung. Their maid told them that 'if we went to a Board School, we should catch 'things in our heads' and all sorts of illnesses, that the children would be 'rough' and the teachers would use the cane' (ibid p. 108). They were finally sent to school together in 1892, when Sylvia was ten and Christabel twelve, the age when working class children would be leaving formal schooling.

Using fiction to understand working class life in the nineteenth century

The importance of narrative in making sense of the past, in providing a structure for thinking about chronology, motivation, context, cause and change has already been discussed. History is not a series of facts but an interpretation of the past, an attempt to explain what happened, and why people behaved as they did. For this interpretation, the narrative forms of fiction are a very powerful vehicle and we saw how children's novels can provide graphic support for work on certain issues like the Famine in Ireland, and the Highland Clearances. In this next section short extracts from a variety of children's historical novels are used to illuminate just how fiction can recreate detail and atmosphere of a period and give children a model in words for describing and interpreting what they see in visual evidence or in somewhat opaque documentary evidence.

First, a short passage from *The Rope Carrier* by Theresa Tomlinson. The book is about working class childhood, family life and work in Derbyshire and Sheffield in the early nineteenth century. Fourteen year old Minnie, who has spent her life so far as a ropemaker in the cave village above Derby, has gone to live in Sheffield, in a tiny one-up-one-down with her heavily pregnant and ill sister, her brother-in-law, their children, his mother (whose bed she has to share) and his father, who is dying of a disease caused by working with iron filings. A book like this is important because it shows continuity from the previous century and counteracts the erroneous idea that industrialisation was a sudden event, as if everyone 'changed trains' at one and the same moment. Industrialisation and the move to the factory system were much slower, with much overlap in old and newer working methods and technologies. The first few decades of the century can be understood not just as inexorable 'progress' of modern technology (creating hardships for working people) but also in terms of the resistance to change (for example through Luddism and the Swing Riots), in the face of decaying possibilities for making a living from home-based crafts and trades such as handloom weaving and spinning. In the first half of the nineteenth century, not all children worked in factories. Some worked within a family economy at home, where each member, including children, contributed.

More able pupils might read the whole of *The Rope Carrier*, or work from passages chosen to give further information about domestic life and work in the early nineteenth century. There are excellent passages illustrating the themes of public health and medicine (the grandfather, the baby and her pregnant mother all suffer illness during the novel), sanitation (lining up to fetch water from the well; a vivid description of how the roads were flooded once a week, washing away everything in the water's path in an indiscriminate system of public cleansing); and most poignant of all, the incarceration of the young father, Minnie's brother-in-law, in the debtor's prison when he cannot fulfil his orders.

> Minnie spent the rest of the day running back and forth to Dame Eyre's orders, seeing to the children, carrying drinks to the sick man, cooking and cleaning and keeping the fire going. At least she'd not been asked to make another visit to the well. By dusk she was fit to drop and ready for her bed no matter whom she was to share it with. Josh's mother was pulling out the spinning wheel, moving it towards the fireside and asking her if she could spin a decent thread. Minnie was torn between weariness and fury at the insult of anyone asking her, a ropemaker's daughter, if she could spin, when they heard thumping and crying coming from upstairs. (Theresa Tomlinson, *The Rope Carrier,* p 69 -70)

A *Twist of Fate* (mentioned earlier in connection with the British anti-slavery campaign), is set in the late 1830s, a little later than *The Rope Carrier.* Workhouse children are the main labour force in a cotton textile mill in a fictitious place in the Midlands, called 'Hanbury'. It's an exciting adventure story which manages to incorporate a vast amount of authentic historical detail about working conditions and attitudes of the period. Here is a short excerpt early in the book, where ten year old Evelyn, previously resident in Saint Mary Magdalene workhouse in London, is being inducted into her new life.

> Evelyn became aware of Rose, crouched on the floor watching the underneath of a machine. Just as she had said, the part called the carriage was moving backwards and forwards, backwards and forwards. Rose was looking at something. A bobbin had rolled under the machine. She waited for her moment then launched herself forward on hands and knees, her chin almost grazing the ground. Hot oil from the moving parts splashed down on her. The floor was thick with white dust. She groped for the bobbin. Then the carriage started to rattle back towards her. Just as Evelyn thought she must be dashed to pieces, she snatched up the bobbin, wriggled out backwards faster than a rat faced with a terrier and jumped to her feet, waving her trophy aloft. 'That's a good girl!' grinned Thacker. 'Speed and efficiency. You'll all get to have a try at it soon enough. And all that 'fly' down on the floor there, that has to be swept up, and at dinner times you have to oil everything. Speed and efficiency.

Remember, if you get your arm ripped off, we ain't got a doctor.' (Pamela Scobie, *A Twist of Fate*, p 45)

In some schools, the older juniors write 'reading books' for the younger children. If you teach the younger juniors, you might collaborate with a colleague to get summaries of parts of historical fiction or non-fictional lives prepared by older children as part of their work in English. For example, children might rewrite passages from *A Strong and Willing Girl,* a book about a servant girl in Edwardian England, which is very accessible to older juniors, or from *Grace — a novel*, or they could prepare an easy version of the life of a notable Victorian.

Autobiography and oral evidence

There is not only pictorial evidence and fiction for Victorian working class lives towards the end of the century, but also autobiography and records of oral history. I included part of Charles Cooper's autobiography in the section about education. Autobiography provides graphic and accessible material about human lives, and creative teachers will see how they can develop activities based on drama, role-play, 'trials', or 'This is your Life' formats based on autobiographical sources. Some books are not outside the reach of good readers in the primary school, as this excerpt from Hannah Mitchell's autobiography, *The Hard Way Up* indicates. Hannah was one of six children born in 1871 to a poor farming family in a remote part of the Peak District. She became a socialist and an early member of the ILP. Later she joined the Pankhursts' suffrage movement and became a suffragette. After the war she was a Labour Party Campaigner and a public figure in Manchester. At fourteen Hannah ran away from home to escape the vicious tongue and bullying of her mother. She was taken in by her sister-in-law and her story continues...

> That very night my sister-in-law found a neighbour who wanted some plain sewing done. It was a working class district where many women worked in the cotton mills, and were glad of some help in their homes, and I soon found it possible to earn enough to keep myself. Eventually I obtained a situation as maid in a schoolmasters' family at a wage of four shillings a week — poor wages indeed but I had a comfortable bed and plenty of good food. The work did not seem particularly hard after my strenuous upbringing, and I was not unhappy, especially as my mistress made me free of a well filled book case.....
> There were six to wash and cook for, and a six roomed house to keep clean, which left little free time. I had an afternoon out once a fortnight from two o'clock until nine. (Hannah Mitchell, *The Hard Way Up*, p.67-68)

An excerpt from Alice Foley's autobiography, *A Bolton Childhood* gives a different picture, equally vivid, that can help children gain an insight into the similarities and the differences between a child's life now and a century ago. Alice was born in 1891, and she is describing impecunious but respectable working class life before the end of the century:

> On autumn afternoons, whilst mother starched and ironed piles of shirts and collars (for she took in other people's washing) I played by the window, breathing on the glass and watching eagerly for the approach of the lamplighter. He carried a long pole and as the minute points of light began to twinkle in the street opposite, they looked so pretty and friendly that I was loath to drop the curtain and let mother pull down the blind....

> Each Monday morning, after brushing and sorting out the Sunday clothes, such as they were, a big parcel was made up; mother carried this whilst I, clutching her skirt, trotted along quite joyfully. Walking quickly down the back street, we nipped smartly in at the side door of the 'Golden Balls' at the corner of Punch Street. The pawnshop was owned by a big jovial man who I later knew as 'Bill'..... As mother was a regular customer he never opened her parcel, but placed it in one of the cubicles just above his head, and then slipped some silver coins to her under the grill.... In these early days we lived frugally and austerely. I recall that we had no cups and saucers; just blue and white ringed basins. Our diet was mainly milk, porridge, potatoes and butties of bread and treacle with a little meat at weekends. (Alice Foley, *A Bolton Childhood*, p 7-8)

Some of the writing is too difficult for children but some passages could be read aloud. Alice tried to avoid part-time work in a factory, and went into shop work at the age of twelve, but she was fired and ended up, like all her classmates from school, at the mill.

> I quickly learned how hateful it was having to get up at five o'clock each morning, especially in winter. As a young child I had often lain in bed anticipating the tap-tap of our knocker-up on the window panes, but now that I, too, had to roll out into the cold darkness I dreaded his approach. Dragging on my clothes and washing at the kitchen slop stone, then crouching before the fire in a dull stupor, I tried to dry myself on our one damp towel. (Alice Foley, *A Bolton Childhood*, p 53)

The contrast between middle class and working class women related not only to prosperity but to leisure, although, for sure, some middle and upper working class women worked hard physically to keep up appearances, unable to afford the number of servants that made for a comfortable life.

Leisure is a theme suggested in the Study Unit. At the end of the century, cycling became increasingly popular. Alice Foley saved her pennies and bought a second hand bike for 25 shillings. She finally learned to ride the thing and joined the local *Clarion* cycling club, going out at weekends with the group. The cycling clubs had been founded by the Socialist journalist Robert Blatchford, who also produced and edited a popular weekly journal called the *Clarion*. Large numbers of young working class people mixed politics with pleasure in the clubs, and learned about socialism and female suffrage through the *Clarion's* pages.

> In merry company we slogged up long hills and free-wheeled joyously down them thrilling to the beauty and excitement of a countryside as yet unspoiled by the advent of motor transport. Not only did we use our bikes for healthy exercise and jolly fellowship, but we followed in the wake of the missionary Clarion Van travelling the highways and byways of the neighbouring counties. The Van itself, in charge of a 'lone scout' was a relic of Liverpool's soup kitchen used in the days of mass unemployment and the horse attached had acquired the reputation of being 'as quiet as a lamb but a devil to go'. Where the Van halted we cyclists loyally dismounted and, grouped together, formed the nucleus of a gathering for the speakers; we distributed literature at wayside corners and on village greens disturbed the sabbath quiet with our socialist hustings. (Alice Foley, *A Bolton Childhood,* p 72-73)

Class and Gender: the middle classes

Earlier in this chapter I refered to the idea of 'separate spheres' — that women's proper place was in the home, with her husband as breadwinner — and suggested how this ideology permeated philanthropic notions about women at work. Despite these attitudes, it was possible, albeit a struggle, for a working class woman to support herself. However, this was a much more difficult option for middle class women. They were literally the property of first their fathers and then their husbands. They could not own anything and had no legal rights because it was assumed that their fathers or husbands acted legally for them. Adult spinsters and widows had more rights than married women, but might find themselves without livelihood or means of support. Moreover, in the middle of the century, there were about one million more women than men, with obvious consequences for the numbers of unmarried women. It was not considered respectable for middle class women to do paid work; this was seen as reflecting badly on men generally, and undermining the husband's role. Desperate for a real role in society beyond domesticity, many middle class women involved themselves in charity, particularly those motivated by strongly felt religious convictions. This was considered respectable and womanly. Some became prison visitors (like Elizabeth Fry) and workhouse 'guardians' and, from the 1880s, 'visitors' and rent collectors for the new 'buildings' put up to house working people, which involved supervising the tenants' personal lives as well. Women like Octavia Hill and Beatrice Potter (later Webb) were involved in this kind of charitable work. Some women were able to become Poor Law Guardians and members of School Boards when the restrictions on women were lifted and they exerted an influence in the public domain.

Part of the middle class women's struggle in the mid and late nineteenth century was to be allowed to work in occupations and professions which were closed to females. Being a governess in a well-to-do family (like the fictional Jane Eyre) or a writer (like the real life author of that novel, Charlotte Bronte) were among the few paid occupations open to middle class women. But governesses were poorly paid and exploited. Many women writers were extremely successful and prolific, but those who wanted to express unconventional views for the time usually took a male pseudonym. Working in printing and publishing, as opposed to staying at home producing text, was not open to women.

Emily Faithfull's Victory Press, which printed much of the journalism produced by the growing first wave women's movement. was set up in 1859 by Barbara Bodichon and Bessie Parkes' 'Society for the Employment of Women', precisely because women found it difficult to get work in printing, due to restrictions operated by the male guilds and unions. The Society for the Employment of Women tried to find work for women in a variety of areas, such as law copying, commerce and business, telegraph work, nursing, cooking. Barbara Bodichon's group of friends, who met and campaigned from their offices in 19 Langham Place London W.1, were also crucial in opening up opportunities for women to qualify and work in medicine.

The first women's movement: great women reformers of the nineteenth century

The first wave women's movement was largely a campaign conducted by middle class women *on their own behalf*, for rights of property, custody over their own children in divorce cases, and for employment and education. The suffrage movement grew out these concerns, as women increasingly realised that without the vote their power to change discriminatory law was completely dependent on male support. Working women were certainly involved in the struggle for the vote, but the working class women's movement at the end of the nineteenth century reflected their own pressing concerns for rights within the industrial workplace and trade unions, where many of them cut their political teeth.

Between 1858 and 1865, Barbara Bodichon and Bessie Rayner Parkes published a magazine called *The English Woman's Journal* which became for a while the main mouthpiece for feminist debates and ideas, reprinting speeches that women made at national conferences, as well as specially written articles. The major middle class feminists of the time contributed to it, and it was probably widely read in these circles. Women wrote about the need for education, for proper jobs for women, why they should be allowed to become doctors, about the problem of surplus women and emigration, about the dreadful consequences of being literally the property of a man — whether father or husband — and on the importance of the vote for women. As part of their work on Victorian middle class women, pupils might produce a 'commemorative issue' of the magazine.

In my view there should be no difficulty with including notable women in the unit, using the categories outlined in the Order. Elizabeth Fry was involved in workhouse and prison reform in the 1820s and is the subject of good biographies for children. Work on the armed forces in the Crimea should include Mary Seacole as well as Florence Nightingale. During the Boer War (at the end of Victoria's reign), Emily Hobhouse went to South Africa to inspect the concentration camps set up by Lord Roberts to contain Boer women and children whose homesteads had been burnt in the (ultimately successful) attempt to subdue the Afrikaners. Her scathing reports and revelations about the appalling conditions in the camps horrified the British public and led to improvements. Mary Kingsley, more well known for her travels in West Africa, also went to South Africa during the Boer War. She died of typhus at the naval base in Simonstown and was buried at sea.

Studies of public health and medicine might include not just the contribution of the great reformer Chadwick but also the first women doctors, Elizabeth Blackwell (who was a close friend of Florence Nightingale), Elizabeth Garrett Anderson and Sophia Jex-Blake (see Blake, 1990, for more information). Most of us know about Florence Nightingale, but the Victorian women's campaign to enter medicine also deserves a place in history. This struggle focused on the moral as well as medical reasons why females should be treated by women doctors. If you have a woman doctor now, thank the women who broke down the barriers to entering the profession! A contemporary woman doctor, a women and children's hospital in your area (even if derelict) or even a dispensary could be the starting point for children to learn about this specific Victorian campaign against discrimination. Barred from qualifying or working in male-dominated hospitals and medical schools, women often opened dispensaries, particularly in working class areas. Elizabeth Garrett Anderson's first hospital in Seymour Place in Marylebonewas in fact a dispensary for the diseases of women and children.

The women's campaign to enter medicine provides wonderful potential for drama. In 1870 male medical students at Edinburgh University rioted to try and prevent Sophia Jex-Blake attending lectures. Children might take roles as the *opposite sex,* or you could hold a 'mock trial', setting up the court with judge and jury, counsels for the defence and prosecution.

While work on education and schooling might deal with Ragged Schools and Board Schools, and perhaps take in the reformers of public schools such as Matthew Arnold, it could also encompass the lives and work of the women who fought for higher education for girls. From the 1860s, feminists became increasingly convinced that the route to a more fulfilling life was education. A number of women were notable for their contribution to girls' education, Barbara Bodichon, Emily Davies, Miss Buss and Miss Beale among them. Many girls' grammar schools date from the late nineteenth century, testimony to this

This hospital, established in 1889, stands on the site of Elizabeth Garrett Anderson's original dispensary and Free Hospital for Women and Children, on the corner of Seymour Place and Marylebone Road, London.
(Photo Hilary Claire)

particular struggle by 'strong-minded women' to ensure a decent education for middle class girls so that they could equip themselves for something other than ornamenting their husbands' drawing rooms, and take their place in the world of professional work.

It is not possible to include material here about all the eminent women who might be included in the Victorian unit. Please look at the lists below, and then for more detail, at Chapters 12 and 13.

Resources

Children's Fiction

[anno] after a title indicates that there are fuller notes in Chapter 13 about this publication.

Avi, 1990, *The true confessions of Charlotte Doyle*, Orchard Books *[anno]*

Bawden, Nina, 1973, *The Peppermint Pig,* London, Penguin (Children in Norfolk in Edwardian England)

Conlon-McKenna, Marita, 1990, *Under the Hawthorn Tree: Children of the Famine*, London, Viking *[anno]*

Coppard, Audrey, 1973, *Nancy of Nottingham*, London, Heinemann (About the Luddites: early C19th)

Darke, Marjorie, 1989, *A question of courage,* London, Collins *[anno]*

Edwards, Dorothy, 1982, *A Strong and Willing Girl,* London, Magnet (A young girl finds work as a domestic servant in an Edwardian house)

Gibbons, Alan, 1992, *Dagger in the Sky*, London, Dent *[anno]*

Leeson, Robert, 1983, *Bess,* London, Armada (set in Edwardian England)

Lively, Penelope, 1983, *Fanny and the Monsters*, London, Mammoth, Heinemann *[anno]*

Lively, Penelope, 1986, *A stitch in time*, London, Puffin *[anno]*

O'Neill, Judith, 1992, *So far from Skye*, London, Hamish Hamilton *[anno]*

Park, Ruth, 1982, *Playing Beatie Bow*, London, Penguin *[anno]*

Pearce, Phillipa, 1968, *The Children of the House*, London, Puffin

Ringgold, Faith, 1993, *Dinner at Aunt Connie's House*, New York, Hyperion Books for Children (see Chapter 4, p.74)

Scobie, Pamela, 1991, *School Strike,* Oxford, Oxford University Press, (based on the true story of the children's strike at Burston School, Norfolk)

Scobie, Pamela, 1992, *A Twist of Fate*, Oxford, Oxford University Press

Tomlinson, Theresa, 1987, *The Flither Pickers*, London, Walker Books

Tomlinson, Theresa, 1991, *The Rope Carrier,* London, Julia MacRae

Tomlinson, Theresa, 1994, *The Herring Girls*, London, Julia MacRae

Walsh, Jill Paton, 1986, *The Butty Boy*, London, Penguin (Set in 1880)

Walsh, Jill Paton, 1991, *Grace — a novel*, London, Viking *[anno]*

Children's non-fiction

Adams, C., 1982, *Ordinary lives a hundred years ago*, London, Virago

Birkett, D., 1991, *Women and Travel,* Hove, Wayland *[anno]*

Chandler, Clare, 1994, Victorians, Hove, Wayward *[anno]*

Gunn, Donald and Spankie, Mari, 1994, *The Highland Clearances*, Hove, Wayland with BBC (Education) Scotland

Kramer, A., 1988, *Women in Politics*, Hove, Wayland *[anno]*

Lyons, Mary, 1993, *Letters from a Slave Girl. The story of Harriet Jacobs*, New York, MacMillan, Charles Scribner's Sons for Young Readers (Based on the 1861 autobiography of 'Linda Brent')

Visram, Rozina, 1987, *Indians in Britain*, London, Batsford *[anno]*

Visram, Rozina, 1995, *The History of the Asian Community Britain*, Hove, Wayward *[anno]*

Warner, Rachel, 1994, *Indian Migrations,* Hove, Wayland *[anno]*

Woodhouse, J. and Wilson, V., 1994, *The Victorians*, London, BBC Fact Finders *[anno]*

Worsnop, R., 1994, *The British Empire (Expansion)* Wolf Pack W15, Huntingdon, Cambs, Elm Publications (Resource pack) *[anno]*

Adult resources

Beddoe, Deirdre, 1983, *Discovering Women's History*, London, Pandora (Useful on where to find and how to use primary evidence)

Bell, Florence, 1985, *At the Works, a study of a manufacturing town* (original 1907) London, Virago (A study of Middlesborough)

Blackburn, Geoff, 1994, *The Children's Friend Society*, Access Press, Northbridge, Western Australia (The story of the 2,000 children 'rescued' from the streets of London in the 1830s and sent to Canada, South Africa, Australia and Mauritius)

Blake, Catriona, 1990, *The Charge of the Parasols: Women's Entry to the Medical Profession*, London, Women's Press

Brent, Linda, 1973, *Incidents in the life of a slave girl* (original 1861), London, Harcourt Brace Jovanovich

Burnett, John, (ed) 1974, *Useful Toil: autobiographies of working people from the 1820s to the 1920s*, London, Allen Lane

Burnett, John, (ed) 1984, *Destiny Obscure: autobiographies of childhood, education and family from the 1820s to the 1920s*, London, Penguin

Coleman, Terry, 1968 (2nd ed), *The Railway Navvies*, London, Penguin

Dayus, Kathleen, 1982, *Her People, Volume 1 of her autobiography*, London, Virago.

Dove, Iris, 1988, *Yours in the Cause: suffragettes in Lewisham, Greenwich and Woolwich*, Lewisham and Greenwich Library Services

Ferguson, Moira, (ed) 1987, *The history of Mary Prince by herself*, London, Pandora

File, Nigel and Power, Chris, 1981, *Black Settlers in Britain 1555-1958*, Oxford, Heinemann Educational Books *[anno]*

Foley, Alice, 1973, *A Bolton Childhood* (autobiography), Manchester, Manchester University Extra-Mural Department

Fryer, Peter, 1984, *Staying Power: The history of black people in Britain*, London, Pluto Press

Kingsley, Mary, 1993, (ed E. Huxley) *Travels in West Africa*, (original 1897) London, Everyman

Lacey, C.A., (ed) 1987, *Barbara Leigh Smith Bodichon and the Langham Place Group*, London, Routledge Kegan Paul

Liddington, Jill and Norris, Jill, 1978, *One Hand Tied Behind Us: The Rise of the Women's Suffrage Movement*, London, Virago

Liddington, Jill, 1989, *The Long Road to Greenham: feminism and anti-militarism in Britain since 1820*, London, Virago.

Llewelyn Davies, Margaret (ed), 1977, *Life as we have known it by co -operative working women* (original 1930) London, Virago

Mayhew, Henry, (1985) *London Labour and the London Poor*, (original 1851-2, second enlarged edition 1862) London, Penguin Classics

Midgley, Clare, 1992, *Women against slavery: the British campaigners, 1780-1870*, London, Routledge

Mitchell, Hannah, 1977, *The Hard Way Up: the autobiography of Hannah Mitchell, Suffragette and Rebel*, London, Virago.

Pankhurst, S., 1977, *The Suffragette Movement*, London, Virago

Seacole, Mary, 1984, *The Wonderful Adventures of Mrs Seacole in many lands*, (ed Ziggi, Alexander and Audrey Dewjee, original 1857), Bristol, Falling Wall Press

Sterling, Dorothy, 1988, *Black Foremothers: three lives*, New York, The Feminist Press, City University of New York.

Visram, Rozina, 1986, *Ayahs, Lascars and Princes*, London, Pluto Press

Ware, Vron, 1992, *Beyond the Pale: white women, racism and history*, London, Verso Press

Victorians included in short bibliographies and annotated lists in Chapters 12 and 13

Aldridge, Ira 1807-1867 *[biog; anno]*

Anderson, Elizabeth Garrett 1836-1917 *[biog]*

Archer, John 1863-1931 *[biog; anno]*

Besant, Annie 1847-1933 *[biog; anno]*

Bishop, Isabella Bird 1831-1904 *[anno]*

Bly, Nellie 1868-1922 *[anno]*

Bodichon (Leigh Smith), Barbara 1827-1891 *[biog]*

Bogle, Paul *[anno]*

Cavell, Edith 1865-1915 *[anno]*

Chuma, Susi and Jacob Wainright (mid C19th) *[biog]*

Coleridge Taylor, Samuel 1875-1912 *[biog; anno]*

Craft, Ellen 1826-1891 and William 1825-?1891 *[biog]*

Cuffay, William 1788-1870 *[biog]*

Darling, Grace *[anno]* (see *Grace — a novel*)

Davidson, William 1786-1820 *[biog]*

Davies, Emily 1830-1921 *[biog]*

Despard, Charlotte 1844-1939 *[biog]*

Douglass, Frederick 1818-1895 *[anno]*

Edwards, Samuel Celestine 1858-1894 *[biog]*

Fry, Elizabeth 1780-1845 *[anno]*

Gandhi, Mahatma 1869-1948 *[anno]*

Herschel, Caroline 1750-1848 *[anno]*

Hobhouse, Emily 1860-1926 *[biog}*

Keller, Helen (1880-1968) *[anno]*

Kingsley, Mary (1862-1900) *[biog}*

Naoroji, Dadabhai 1825-1916 *[biog; anno]*

Nightingale, Florence 1820-1910 *[anno]*

Pankhurst, Emily 1858-1928 *[anno]*

Pankhurst, Sylvia 1882-1860 *[biog]*

Prince, Mary 1788-? *[biog]*

Remond, Sarah Parker 1826-1894 *[biog]*

Saklatvala, Shapurji *[biog]*

Seacole, Mary 1805-1881 *[biog; anno]*

Sharpe, Sam *[anno]*

Swanwick, Helena 1864-1939 *[biog]*

Te Whiti *[anno]*

Wells, Ida B 1862-1931 *[anno]*

Chapter 9

Study Unit 3b: Britain since 1930

The study of different periods in history, as we have seen, encourages the use of specific kinds of evidence. For example, archaeological evidence is particularly appropriate for studying Ancient Greece, the British invasions of the first millennium, or the civilisations in the 'Non-European' Study Unit. Of all the study units, *Britain since 1930* is the most appropriate for oral evidence. Oral history — with its own techniques and methodology — has increasingly been exploited by social historians — particularly socialists and those who take a black/feminist perspective — for the wealth of information about experience, perspectives and attitudes seldom included in documentary and more formal evidence.

The contribution of oral history to children's learning

Readers who skipped Part 1 of this book because they don't teach Key Stage 1, should turn back to Chapter 2 p. 31-34, for the discussion of oral evidence and a warning against exploiting the elderly. For Key Stage 2 pupils, oral history can be used with greater sophistication than at Key Stage 1. Children can compare the different perspectives of interviewees with one another, and with published or pictorial material. Working with different versions of the past, brought into the classroom by people who are still alive, makes explicit the variety of experience from the same period and can counteract tendencies to overgeneralise. Children could use the insights they acquire to think about earlier periods and about how much one can ever really know about ordinary lives in times and places for which the evidence is quite scant.

Upper juniors can consider the methodological problems of oral history — the ways in which self-presentation distorts the account, the tendency towards selective memory, and to romanticise 'the good old days' or dwell on harsh memories which bias the information. One of the best ways to evaluate the nature of personal evidence would be for children to consider critically their own and each other's oral accounts of events in which they were involved, whether a playground argument, a presentation in assembly, or participation in a group activity. The human tendency to privilege our own perspective, participation and contribution in such accounts is often transparent, and the ways in which we present ourselves in a favourable light — through humour, irony and so on — is also worth noticing.

Much current research about learning suggests that this 'metacognitive position', in which children are encouraged to stand back and reflect on their own learning, is fundamental to cognitive development. In other words the skills involved in learning to evaluate oral evidence are part of more general aims of education. Many of the problems of oral history are, of course, common to other forms of evidence, and children could consider the similarities. Children should also be reminded that written evidence (particularly autobiography) has also at some point been affected by the perspective and intentions of the writer and the conventions of the genre. In oral evidence and in autobiography we make a story, providing contexts, purpose and meanings for the benefit of the audience and for ourselves. In doing so we might make unjustified assumptions about the listeners' knowledge and prior understandings, or with hindsight, explain events differently from how we did at the time. These assumptions and modifications are precisely what make historical interpretation necessary — and fascinating.

Bringing history alive in the classroom through oral history

Oral history might well be one of the most fruitful resources for bringing the real life history of working class people, women or members of ethnic minority communities into the classroom. The medium will be the message, whatever the content of the study. Pensioners, i.e. those now in their sixties, seventies or eighties, usually have vivid personal stories about the pre-war period and can recall small details about their working lives, family traditions, clothes, shopping, holidays and days out which fascinate children. People who are now in their late fifties and grew up in England, will remember the war itself. Some will have been evacuated; they will certainly recall the post-war years, the gaping holes between buildings from bomb craters, filling up with wild flowers. They will remember the end of rationing and the Festival of Britain, launched in the centenary year of the Great Exhibition of 1851, Teddy Boys, Mods and Rockers, full skirts starched with sugar-water, elastic waist nippers, the first Carnivals, Elvis Presley and the Beatles. Then the 'swinging sixties' — years of full employment and fun after deprivation — that are part of the memories of the pupils' grandparents' generation. People who were born abroad can be asked about their lives there during the war years as well as their experience of moving to Britain, and the post-war years. There were food shortages abroad during the war as well as in England; fathers went away to fight; some lives were irreparably altered. All the Commonwealth countries celebrated D-day and VE-day with flags and mugs and holidays from school.

Oral history and the war

The myth that the war was purely a white British affair needs to be counteracted by inviting elderly men and women from the New Commonwealth to talk about their participation in the war effort. Special regiments were formed and staffed by men and women from India, the Caribbean and the African colonies — although it is a telling indication of attitudes of the time to discover that segregation was the order of the day, and few if any black or Asian soldiers were promoted to higher ranks. The Imperial War Museum in London recently published a resource pack about the black Commonwealth contribution to the Second World War. The community itself is likely to be the richest source of such evidence, and only those schools where there are very few African-Caribbean or Asian people would have to rely on published resources. (See Chapter 13 for extensive material to support these themes.)

Children whose parents or grandparents were immigrants in the last forty years might tell you that members of their family were part of the war effort. One of my students, who had come as a young adult from India in the early 1970s said that her father had fought in a special regiment of Asian soldiers during the war, and she had photographs of him in uniform in her family album. Janice Ryder, a primary teacher in Ealing, produced a booklet for primary children recording the story of Connie Mark. Connie, a Jamaican woman now settled in Hammersmith, was a corporal in the British army in Kingston and had a great many photos and souvenirs — as well as an excellent memory. Janice used a simple desktop publishing package and a photocopier — techniques available to people interested in producing their own resources based on people in the local community. Even if one doesn't want to go to the effort of producing fairly permanent material like this, one can certainly look in the community that the children come from for this kind of information.

Oral history and the effects of fascism

Oral history or autobiographical writing might be the way to help children to begin to understand the traumatic effect of European fascism on many people's lives. World Jewish Relief brought 723 boys and girls who were survivors of the camps to England just after the war. Two of their accounts, simply told, without emphasising the tragedy and the horror, are reproduced in a booklet printed by Tower Hamlets Arts Project. Other children were sent by their families before the war started. I spoke to John Adamson (not his real name), who came to England with his sister from Austria as a ten year old child, and was settled in Glasgow. John wrote out his answers to my questions, and they are reproduced here:

Hilary: *What was life like in Austria just before you left?*

John: Anti-semitism was rife but tolerable and not violent, more a kind of snobbishness that we were complacent about. We happily shared other Austrian prejudices against Slavs, English hypocrisy etc. Public life was run on Catholic and masonic networks, but also on personal relations. Personally we were a first generation bourgeois family with business and property, only superficially Jewish in upbringing and as Austrian in sentiment as neighbours and schoolfriends. I wasn't aware who was or was not Jewish.

Hilary: *Why did your parents decide to send you abroad and how was this arranged?*

John: After the annexation my governess took me to see Hitler drive through Vienna, but the crowds were too thick for me to see him. When the SS came on 9th November 1938 (Kristalnacht) they asked to see any Jewish males and were contemptuous when I, as a ten year old, was all that could be produced. All my male relatives who were in Jewish homes were taken. It was time to go. Many routes were explored, businesses grew up to cater for this exploration, although only one in the end was possible.

Hilary: *Did you come to England alone or with other members of your family, or with other children from your town?*

John: I came with my sister and we were put in a sealed railway carriage with about fifty other Viennese Jewish children, and corrugated paper so that we could sleep on the floor, with perhaps two adults from some Jewish organisation, who had to return to Vienna.

Hilary: *Can you tell me briefly about your memories of arriving and being sent up to Glasgow?*

John: My sister and I spent the night in London with a very English family (hotwater-bottles and bacon and eggs for breakfast) and then to Glasgow by train, to be welcomed by a children's party with kissing games — perhaps the worst experience of all — unless it was seeing oranges eaten in halves instead of by segments!

Hilary: *Could you tell me something about the family who took you in?*

John: My sister and I were taken by two different Jewish families in different parts of Glasgow. My family pluckily concealed their disappointment that I was four years younger than their only son, for whom I was intended to be a playmate.

Hilary: *Were you ever able to contact your family after the war?*

John: No. They had all perished.

Judith Kerr's autobiographical novel for the junior age group, *When Hitler Stole Pink Rabbit*, tells the story of a family who escaped from Germany at the same period. Like John's story, this could be used to widen the narrow theme of evacuation from British cities, to an understanding of the wholesale disruption of lives for people in many parts of the world, as a consequence of the build-up and the war itself.

My own family has stories which must be typical of any Jewish family's. One of my uncles by marriage, a Jewish German, got out of Germany before the war started and joined the British army. After the war, in the sixties, he and my aunt went back to his birthplace to see where he had grown up, and to try and find the business that his father and mother had run. They were devastated to find that there was absolutely no sign that this had once been a Jewish quarter. Every Jewish name on every shop or business had changed. My uncle received financial compensation from the German government for the family business, which had been seized and given to a gentile family by the Nazis, but this could never wipe away the psychological pain.

My mother tells a story of spending an idyllic summer in 1933 in Budapest, as a German language exchange student and guest of a wealthy and cultured Jewish family, who wanted their children to practise English with a native speaker. Already it was not considered safe for a young Jewish woman to go to Germany itself. She went back the following year, and maintained a correspondence with Bela, one of the sons. Sometime early in 1938 she received in the post a large album of valuable stamps — a collectors' item — with a letter asking her to keep it till Bela got back in touch. A little while later another parcel arrived. This time there was no letter. Inside the padding, she found a carefully wrapped glass jar of tomato puree, not a common commodity, but not unknown. Hidden in the puree was a diamond ring. Guessing its source she had the ring valued and put it in safe deposit with the stamp album. Two or three years passed and she heard nothing. Then out of the blue she received a letter from Australia. Poland had fallen to the German army; Hungary was next. Bela had got out just in time before the Germans invaded. Not so the rest of his family, nor any of the young Jewish friends she had made that lovely summer. All had disappeared in the Holocaust. Yes, she sent him the ring and the album that she had kept safe. They continued to correspond for a time, then she and my father emigrated to South Africa and she lost his address. Nearly sixty years later in 1994, given the opportunity to visit Budapest, she booked her ticket and found she could not bring herself to go. The memories of the friends she had lost were still too raw.

The fiftieth anniversary in 1995 of Anne Frank's death, was the occasion for the publication of many children's books about her life and new versions of her Diary. Some primary schools contextualised work on her life and death within the History Study Unit on *Britain since 1930*. Children could also consider, through role-play and drama, the huge moral dilemma of whether or not to hide Jews and risk one's own life — as Miep Gies and others like her did.

My own research with junior children has revealed misconceptions and enormous gaps in children's knowledge about what WWII (and other wars) were about. One of my students successfully started her project with Y6 pupils on the war years with the question: 'Why did Britain enter the war?' This helped the children make sense of the history in relation to the rise of Nazism in Europe in the 30s, allowed them to find out about the protests and demonstrations against the Blackshirts in Britain before the war (e.g. Edinburgh, 1934; Cable Street, London, 1936) and opened up debates about their attitudes to militancy, appeasement and pacifism.

The forties and fifties — gender

A study of the forties and fifties is possibly one of the best ways to put into perspective and understand 'race' and gender within contemporary society. The following paragraphs explore how changes in gender roles might be a theme, and then discuss 'race'. People who were young in the fifties can usually vividly recall the ways in which one's gender seemed to determine one's life chances, in ways which are more reminiscent of Edwardian attitudes forty years earlier, than those which are prevalent today. As we approach the end of the century, it could be very enlightening for children (and teachers who were children of the sixties and seventies) to place the 1950s on a time-line half way through the century and move backwards and forwards in time from that decade, considering major issues like communications, transport, population, clothes, jobs, the nature of city and country, and, of course, the roles of women and men.

Unit 3b is the only unit that refers specifically to the changing roles of women and men but, curiously, includes this under the heading 'At home', where possibly the fewest changes occurred. The war years had a great impact on gender roles, as in the First World War. During the war itself women were extensively involved in work outside the home but expected also to maintain the home as part of doing their bit for Britain. Some wonderful adverts from the war years are reproduced in *What did you do in the War Mum?* (Schweitzer 1993), which would give children a sense of how gender roles get manipulated, and put our own decade in an historical context.

Along with unsubtle pressure to keep the home fires burning, women were subjected to equally propagandistic calls to enter the public realm and do their bit for Britain while the men were away fighting. They were urged to dig for victory, make munitions in the factories and run the transport service. These aspects of women's lives, as well as their participation in the armed forces, are well resourced and many primary teachers already teach about them. But if children take a long view of changes over three or four decades, from the thirties through to the seventies or eighties, they can get a much better sense of the see-saw nature of change and realise that 'two steps forward and one step back' is often what really happens.

The late forties and the fifties were notable for the swift reversal to pre-war attitudes and curtailment of the opportunities for women created by the war. The significant feature of post-war women's history is how they were pushed *back* into their conventional roles in the home as wives and mothers. This is a well documented and fascinating area of history. Children can see the similarity in material from the thirties and the fifties. In both decades advertisements, magazine articles and official material on bringing up babies, cleaning and cooking, bombarded women with a message about their 'rightful place' in society, suggesting that hoovering carpets, getting washing whiter than white, smilingly producing a meal for your man and bathing babies was exciting and fulfilling. (These images are currently being recycled by advertisers with an ironical feminist twist.) Anyone familiar with the extensive research on gender roles in the home would probably argue that change not associated with the war effort only got underway in the 1970s with the advent of the second women's movement.

'Race' and ethnicity

There is room in this Unit to work on the contribution and impact of new communities through an inclusive interpretation of all three of the highlighted issues: 'Changes in technology and transport', 'Britons at War' and 'Lives of people in different parts of Britain at different levels of society'. The Dearing proposals gave the opportunity for a 'long study' on immigration and emigration, but this has been transmuted into a recommendation in Unit 3b to include emigration and immigration as part of study of the lives of people at different levels of society.

Immigration and emigration are major economic, social and political markers of change and continuity. Taking immigration and emigration as a theme entails asking big historical questions like *why? how?* and *what then?* It leads to study of the way people's lives have to alter and adapt, how they carry on or modify traditions in a new place, and how established communities adapt to the arrival of newcomers. Britain has been a multicultural country from its earliest days, a country of immigrants. Large numbers of people in most communities are themselves first or second generation immigrants, or descended from immigrants in earlier periods, whether refugees or citizens of the Colonies and Commonwealth. Even the smallest towns in rural England and Wales have some recent immigrants, as can be seen from the Indian and Chinese restaurants. Many British people have relatives who immigrated to the Commonwealth countries or to America, particularly in the nineteenth century, because of the condition of the British economy.

Possibilities for work on immigration and emigration

History Study Unit 3b is not the only possible vehicle for teaching about emigration and immigration. It could also be the unifying theme for cross-curricular work, with obvious possibilities for geography, English and maths. Another way to work on emigration and immigration might be through the NCC (non-compulsory) cross-curricular themes of citizenship, or economic awareness and understanding (as suggested in Chapter 6, for Study Unit 2, on the Tudors).

Another facet of this theme could be personal, social and emotional education. Officially recognised in the secondary school and allocated timetabled periods, it is more often relegated to the unofficial agenda of primary schools, with their packed compulsory curriculum. A project on emigration and immigration in the primary years needs to acknowledge and work with the possibilities for emotional growth, not avoid or deny them. Within the theme of movement into or out of this island, children can gain general insights and understandings of what immigration and emigration means in human terms. A work of fiction like *Kezzie* (by Theresa Breslin) about a Scottish child sent to Canada in the 1930s by the 'welfare', or *Hope leaves Jamaica* by Kate Ernest, can illuminate such themes. However, with this kind of emphasis it is best to start from the children's own lives. Chapter 2 illustrated how a cross-curricular topic for infants on 'Moving' can bring every child's personal history, however mundane, into the classroom and still allow space for the more dramatic stories of immigrants and refugees. I noted that some of the work I have done with infants has revealed hidden lives to me and other children, but has also apparently been deeply cathartic for the children themselves. This is where fact and feeling cannot be separated. (See Chapter 2, p.28-29 for Cu's story, which a young Vietnamese refugee wrote for me and made into a book, when I was her class teacher.)

The following section draws on a number of sources, including discussions with my friends and members of my family who moved as children or adults from one country to another and are still sometimes bewildered by feelings of 'unbelonging' and ambivalence about identity. I have tried to offer a framework for classroom study which recognises not just the political, economic and social dimensions, but also emotion-laden aspects of such work.

The broad explanatory categories

Historically, emigration and immigration are usually explained in terms of 'push' and 'pull', pain and promise. People leave because they are pushed out, whether by war or poverty or famine. They choose a new place because it is possible to enter, because there is a prospect of work and a better life, a promise of safety among friends. Sometimes people have had no choice — convicts or press-ganged crews, deportees or slaves have been forcibly removed. Some people choose to follow a partner or go where their children have gone. Marxist interpretations of emigration and immigration emphasise the benefits to capitalist

economies of highly motivated cheap labour and new skills; liberal interpretations concentrate more on choices and self-determination in the search for
a better life. Children can start to understand these explanations, becoming
familiar with life stories around them and by evaluating the evidence offered
them. Personal case studies are probably the best of all — but children will still
need help in recognising the concepts of 'push and pull' in the individual stories.
However, generalisations of social science (at times reductionist) must be
avoided. In history, children need to get a sense of human differences and
motivation, the idiosyncratic and the atypical, and to explore the personal
experience which generalising inevitably condenses or overlooks.

The human dimensions of emigration and immigration

Once arrived in the new country, people's lives take different paths. Some are
welcomed and assimilated into the prevailing social and economic structures.
Others might be invited in to fill job vacancies but still meet local prejudice. Some
people, perhaps coming to terms with a painful wrench from their home country,
feeling less confident about their welcome and worried about loss of identity,
meet indifference or hostility by withdrawing into tight, familiar communities.

Junior schools might initially approach emigration and immigration as a theme
within the Study Unit 'Britain since 1930' by exploring some of the psychological
experiences undergone by immigrants. Pupils could begin by brainstorming some
of the situations and accompanying emotions that are within their own frame of
reference as 'newcomers'.

Here are some starting points for children to take forward:

- ☐ going to a new school, playground or club or even someone's house
  where everyone but you knows everyone else and what's expected

- ☐ getting reprimanded for doing what seems natural, and not quite
  understanding what the unspoken rules are

- ☐ not fitting in or being picked on for what seem like quite arbitrary
  reasons

- ☐ being singled out for special treatment although you would prefer to
  be left alone or treated like everyone else

- ☐ having qualities or characteristics attributed to you and certain things
  expected of you (i.e. being stereotyped)

- ☐ having to deal with expectations that you will share your parents' and
  previous generations' values and customs, appropriate in their time
  and place, even when you don't

- ☐ being patronised because of people's stereotypes and assumptions
  about your identity and language

- [ ] being insulted or laughed at, or overhearing ridicule against members of your community

- [ ] missing familiar friends and ways of doing things from your old home

- [ ] being embarrassed by the obvious differences between your family and the other children's.

Work on psychological responses to moving could lead to exploring the reasons why people move, again drawing on the experiences of the children and their families. In a project on this theme with Y3 (8-9 year olds), children found out about their grandparents and even earlier generations, and were able to bring into the classroom case histories which exemplified some of the 'push-pull' causal factors outlined on p.170-1. For example, one boy who knew that his family was Irish in origin, although both parents were born in England, found out that his paternal grandfather had come to find work in the 1920s but that his maternal great-great-grandparents had come in the middle of the nineteenth century because of the famine. This was part of the family lore which he had never made much sense of, until then. Two children who had come from the North of England and Scotland knew that their families had been driven by the need to find work in a period when unemployment and industrial recession affected regions differentially. Several children in the class were African or African-Caribbean; one girl's father had come from Sierra Leone for higher education, and another's father had come from Nigeria because of the political instability. This linked with a Vietnamese child whose family had fled from the war.

It was important that the children realised that though there were commonalities the reasons for migration differed, and that for many families migration had been triggered by more than one cause. We collated this information along with the reasons why other children's families had migrated, and also put it all on a time-line, to help children generalise causes. The time-line helped give a sense of different issues related to politics and economics taking precedence at different periods. Approaching the topic like this seems to exemplify the ideas raised in Chapter 1 about how history might be instrumental in developing children's analytic reasoning, helping them to categorise evidence in a coherent way, working with human subtleties and complexities rather than only with scientific 'facts'. Starting with the children's own histories leads naturally into a broader national context in which one might work chrono-logically. For this the chart in Appendix 2 might be useful.

A chronology of immigration and emigration since the 1930s

All Britain's major cities have communities from the New Commonwealth, most of whom have come since the war. In London, a quarter of the population defined itself as belonging to an ethnic minority group in the 1991 census, though not all originate in the New Commonwealth.

A little potted history sets the scene for this Unit. The years leading up the war brought communities of Europeans fleeing from Nazi persecution, particularly Jews, Communists and left-wing radicals from Germany. During the war, Polish naval and air force units were based in England and the military headquarters for the Polish resistance was near Victoria Station in London. Unlike members of the French resistance under De Gaulle, whose headquarters were also in London, many Poles wished to stay on after the war, when their country was taken over by a Communist regime.

Other groups have come since to Britain since the war, because of political or economic difficulties or disasters in their own countries (East African Asians, Cypriots — both Greek and Turkish — Bangladeshis, Pakistanis, Indians, Vietnamese, Zairians, Somalis, Kurds and Bosnians). Many of them came to Britain because of Commonwealth connections established mainly in the nineteenth century.

The experience of the New Commonwealth communities

The majority of African-Caribbeans came shortly after the war and were specifically recruited to help Britain to staff its vital infrastructures depleted by the war. The London Transport Museum publication, *Sun a-shine, Rain a-fall* (1995) includes primary evidence about the recruitment of labour in the Caribbean and records and celebrates the history of the West Indian contribution to London transport. *Motherland* (by Elyse Dodgson) documents through oral history the experience of Caribbean women, and makes clear how recruitment to the new National Health Service acted as a powerful inducement to come to Britain.

Claudia Jones, the Trinidadian editor of the *West Indian Gazette*, wrote the following in 1964, in a piece called 'The Caribbean Community in Britain':

> Throughout Britain, the West Indian contribution to its economy is undoubted. As building workers, carpenters, as nurses, doctors and on hospital staffs, in factories, on transportation system (sic) and railway depots and stations, West Indians are easily evidenced. (Claudia Jones, in Johnson, p 145)

Housing conditions for immigrant groups when they first arrived in the 50s and 60s is an area of investigation in its own right, and even teachers working in mainly white areas may want to introduce their pupils to this history, the run up to the Nottingham and Notting Hill Riots of 1958. African-Caribbean and South Asian men usually came on their own, saving up enough to bring their families later.

The same piece by Claudia Jones describes the housing conditions for immigrant communities:

Excluded from skilled jobs and forced into lower paid ones, still another disability must be faced in the field of housing accommodation. In addition to the problems occasioned from the general housing shortage, the West Indian immigrant and other coloured Commonwealth citizens are widely rejected as tenants of advertised flats and lodgings on the basis of a colour bar, and are obliged to pay higher rents even than white tenants. 'So sorry, No Coloured, No children', 'European Only', 'White Only', signs dot the pages of advertised flats and lodgings. A 'colour-tax' meets the West Indian purchaser of property, often inferior lease-hold ones. No wonder estate agents, some of them coloured themselves, have not been averse to exploiting for huge profits this housing shortage. (Claudia Jones, in Johnson, p.148)

Oral history recorded by Age Exchange in a number of publications is another rich source of first-hand evidence about housing conditions experienced by some newly arrived immigrants shortly after the war. Here is part of a transcript from *A Place to Stay* (Schweitzer, 1984) recorded by a Caribbean woman who joined her husband in Leeds in the 1950s:

When I came, he was very sad he didn't have a proper house to put me into. The landlady had said we couldn't walk through the front door.... He bought a right big basin and said 'this is where you have to wash cos they are not going to let you use the bathroom'. (Schweitzer, 1984, p.28)

Books like this, in which ordinary people tell their life stories, provide the evidence so often missing from mainstream books about the black contribution to the war, work or home life and experience in Britain. They usually include photographs and sometimes advertisements or newspaper articles from the time, and these are particularly useful sources for primary school children.

The Order suggests work on new technologies. It was often to industries such as food processing, plastics, man-made textiles and rubber that South Asians were recruited, through newspaper advertisements placed in Indian papers by British firms. South Asians (particularly Punjabi Sikhs) came also because they were recruited for post-war reconstruction and the growing economy of the 1960s. Irish people were also recruited to support the economy, in the 1930s and again in the 1950s. In the post-war years the major work for men from Ireland has been in the construction industries, and for women, nursing. (See *Across the Water* by Lennon for Irish memories.)

Summary

When we look at economic changes and developments — whether in industry, transport or health — it is impossible to ignore the new settlers. They have become part of the economy, as workers, tradespeople or professionals. In certain cities, workers from ethnic minority communities are the major labour force in factories producing goods for export as well as home consumption. In the decade leading up to the war, and over the past forty-five years or so, consideration of changes in the economy, housing, home life, diet and health, work and leisure cannot ignore the experience, presence and contribution of the new communities. They have introduced ideas, products, foods and lifestyles which have changed the face of British culture.

Class and consumerism

Initially mass-produced items were imported from the United States but in the 1930s mass production of motor cars and other 'mod cons' took off in Britain. The first people to own the labour-saving devices which would replace servants were upper and middle class. Few households boasted a car before the war. In 1938 there were 39 passenger cars per 1,000 people, (the top six names being Morris, Austin, Ford, Vauxhall, Rootes and Standard. Where are they all now!). Even after the war, when labour-saving devices, a refrigerator, a vacuum cleaner, a radio and gramophone became more common in the home, very few working people owned a car. In 1967 there were still only 167 cars per 1,000 people.

James Hardie was one of the lucky ones. He was interviewed by Steve Humphries and Pamela Gordon for a television programme and book about the inter-war years. He was 28 in 1938, working in a local dairy, when he bought his first car, an Austin Seven. It was a great novelty and everyone in the family was very excited and wanted to go for a drive. This excerpt comes from the transcript of his interview:

> Of course they weren't as reliable as they are now. You had one windscreen wiper in the middle and you pulled a little lever out and then it went, but sometimes if it conked out we'd fall back on the old remedy of a potato. You cut it in slices to get the moisture of the potato and rubbed it on the outside of the screen, just all over the bit where you're looking through and the droplets didn't hang about then, they just sort of went into overall water and you could see through it. You were thought to be quite fortunate if you had the car, otherwise you had to depend on buses, you see, and you didn't get so far away. And it gave you a lot of privacy, having the car. It was so nice to get away up in the hills, away from home and away from other people, just your own family around you, to get away from the busy town. In those days, the cars were small so you were quite tightly packed in it. But we were just a nice family party.....We lived in Motherwell. Twelve miles away we were right up into the Clyde valley.... We used to take the picnic up there — fruit, biscuits, flask of tea and sometimes we'd make a fire and boil a kettle, get a lot of little twigs and have a real camp fire, and all the kids used to enjoy that, playing about with the fire. (James Hardie in Humphries and Gordon, 1993, p.113-4)

The Great Depression

The depression is one of the subjects recommended for study as part of learning about lives of people at different levels of society. It is a commonly held but mistaken belief that the depression struck equally across the land. In 1930-31 nearly twenty percent of the insured population was unemployed, but this doesn't include women, who weren't counted in the official figures. The most vulnerable were unskilled workers, and then semi-skilled, with white collar workers the least severely hit. Unemployment struck hardest in the North and in Wales, where the great textile, coal, iron and steel and ship-building industries were located. There is a poignant irony in the fact that the very places and industries that had accounted for British industrial supremacy in the mid-nineteenth century, were those affected by the depression in the 1920s and 1930s.

That other great symbol of class conflict, the General Strike of 1926, is just outside the period, but teachers might decide to focus on the extraordinary and moving evidence of the Great Jarrow March, in October 1936. Hunger marches had become a symbol of resistance and protest over the previous decade. The Jarrow March was led by their Labour MP, 'Red Ellen' Wilkinson; 200 men chosen from the thousands who volunteered, walked three hundred miles from their home town to Westminster, supported along the way by well-wishers. Twelve thousand people had signed the petition which Red Ellen presented on behalf of the unemployed shipbuilders. The only tangible result at the time seemed to be that the marchers' unemployment allowance was docked for the time they were away and 'not available for work'. Despite the failure of its overt intention, the Jarrow March has achieved enormous publicity and, like the story of the Tolpuddle Martyrs a century before, the Great Hunger Crusade has become part of labour folk memory (commemorated by Alan Price in the *Jarrow Song* on Merlin Records, 1993, Alan Price: Live in Concert).

The longer term significance of the March and the existence of a considerable quantity of pictorial evidence, would allow children to consider aspects of historical cause and consequence in some depth. Why did the ship-building industry fail? Why did people decide to go on a Hunger March? What improvements did they hope for and what did they actually get? Children could develop role-plays and dramatic presentations about deciding whether or not to join the March — not knowing the outcome. Or they could imagine that they were doing a television documentary at the time about the March. They might take the roles of people on the March itself (using the pictorial evidence to choose roles): the Government officials who spurned them, individuals from the industry with background information about dwindling orders for British ships, those who were sceptical about the value of the protest, and those who enthusiastically supported it. One verse of Allan Price's song has the words:

My name is little Billy White
And I know what's wrong and I know what's right,
And my wife says 'Billy go to London town.
And if they won't give you half a bob,
And they won't give you a decent job,
Well Billy with my blessing burn them down!

Children could go further, imagining they were radio producers/directors making a documentary for the sixtieth anniversary of Jarrow. Sixty years on, people hold conflicting opinions about the March. Some see it as a misguided and pointless gesture, others as a noble demonstration of workers' solidarity.

In working class autobiographies from the time there are vivid descriptions of the effects of the depression on ordinary lives. The following excerpt comes from the first book of Kathleen Dayus' autobiography, called *Her People*.

(It is 1931. Kathleen's husband Charlie is seriously ill. She is trying to support him and four small children.)

> I managed to find a job with a Mr Brain who allowed me to bring my baby to work so I could feed her during working hours.... however this good fortune didn't last. Mr Brain closed down because he had so little work and I was out of a job. I had to look for work, it was either that or parish relief and rather than this I took in washing and mending, but the earnings from this were nothing like sufficient. In common with most women then I knew nothing about birth control and I became pregnant again at about this time. This meant I was less capable of the heavy work involved in washing and mangling but I had to struggle on. The illness which Charlie suffered from became much worse as well.... Poor Charlie did not live to see his daughter, he died three days later (after the birth of Kathleen's baby) on 26 April 1931. I was shattered. I had no real home, no job and no money. I was turned down when I applied for a widow's pension because Charlie didn't have enough insurance stamps on his card. How could he, when he'd been unemployed most of our married life? I had to turn to the parish [Poor Relief] and I'll never forget the humiliating and degrading way that the stern-faced inquisitors treated me. ....
> I was given food and coal vouchers eventually, but not before I had pawned everything except the clothes we stood up in... Life was unbearable with Mum, and I was at my wits' end. Finally, I had to let my children go into a Dr Barnardo's home. I was heart-broken, but what could I do? We were starving and helpless; there was only Mum and me and so I decided to let them go where they would at least be clothed and fed... I visited my children regularly, but it took years for me to fulfil my promise to myself and to them to have them home and they were growing up and away from me... (Kathleen Dayus, p.192-3)

[Kathleen Dayus was born in Birmingham in 1903. The early chapters of the book are based on memories of her poverty-stricken childhood. Although technically the Edwardian era had begun, little had changed since the Victorian period, and teachers might find her accessible style helpful primary evidence for domestic life in the Victorian Study Unit, 3a.]

One would not want to give children an impression of unadulterated gloom in the pre-war years. Some more fortunate upper working and lower middle class lives are recorded in vivid oral evidence and photographs in *Just like the country: memories of London families who settled in New Cottage Estates* 1919-1939 (Rubenstein, 1991) and *Fifty Years Ago: Memories of the 1930s* (Age Exchange Theatre Company, 1983). Advertisements for new cleaning materials to suit the beautiful new houses that were being put up, and photographs of gleaming bathrooms from the 30s are among the pictorial evidence that might help children understand about the nature of change.

Resources

(The majority of these books are annotated in Chapter 13, denoted by *[anno]*. Please check by title.)

Fiction

Second World War

Bawden, Nina, 1973, *Carrie's War*, London, Puffin

Gutman, C., 1989, *The Empty House*, London, Penguin Plus *[anno]*

Kerr, Judith, 1989, *When Hitler Stole Pink Rabbit,* London, Collins *[anno]*

Lively, Penelope, 1986, *Going Back,* London, Puffin

Magorian, Michelle, 1981, *Goodnight Mr Tom*, London, Puffin *[anno]*

Magorian, Michelle, 1983, *Back Home*, London, Penguin *[anno]*

Moon, Pat, 1993, *Double Image,* London, Orchard Books *[anno]*

Serraillier, Ian, 1956, *The Silver Sword*, London, Puffin

Tomlinson, Theresa, 1990, *The Secret Place,* London, Walker Books *[anno]*

Walsh, Jill Paton, 1969, *Fireweed*, London, Puffin

Pre- and post-war

Breslin, Theresa, 1993, *Kezzie*, London, Methuen *[anno]*

Ernest, Kate Elizabeth, 1993, *Hope leaves Jamaica*, London, Methuen *[anno]*

Moon, Pat, 1993, *Double Image*, London, Orchard Books *[anno]*

Kidd, Diana, 1989, *Onion Tears*, London, Viking Kites *[anno]*

Non-Fiction — *Photographic and oral history resources (available from local community bookshops, local libraries)*

Adi, Hakim, 1994, *African Migrations*, Hove, Wayland *[anno]*

Age Exchange Theatre Company, 1983, *Fifty years ago: Memories of the 1930s*, London, Age Exchange Theatre Trust

Age Exchange, 1993, *What did you do in the War Mum?* London, Age Exchange Theatre Trust *[anno]*

Alleyne, Mekada J., 1989, *African Roots in Britain*, London, Kemet Nubia Press *[anno]*

Arapoff, Cyril, *London in the Thirties*, London, Nishen Photography Series. (Also in this series: *Blitz and Shelters.*) *[anno]*

Braithwaite, B., Walsh, N. and Davies, G., 1987, *The Home Front: the best of good housekeeping 1939-1945*, London, Ebury Press

Bristol Broadsides, 1987, *The Bristol Picture Book, Part 2: twenty years of people's lives in photographs 1940-1960*, Bristol, Bristol Broadsides

Davies, Jennifer, 1993, *The wartime kitchen and garden. The Home Front 1939-45,* London, BBC Books

Dodgson, Elyse, 1983, *Motherland: West Indian Women to England in the 1950s*, London, Heinemann

ECOHP (ed) 1993, *Asian Voices: life stories from the Indian subcontinent,* London, Ethnic Communities Oral History Project *[anno]*

ECOHP, *Such a long story — Chinese voices in Britain*, London, Ethnic Communities Oral History Project

ECOHP, *Sailing on two boats, — second generation perspectives*, London, Ethnic Communities Oral History Project

File, Nigel and Power, Chris, 1981, *Black Settlers in Britain 1555-1958,* Oxford, Heinemann Educational *[anno]*

Gate House Project, 1985, *Day in, Day out: Memories of North Manchester from women in Monsell Hospital,* Manchester, Gate House Project *[anno]*

Hewitt, Maggie and Harris, Annie, *1992, Talking Time! A guide to oral history for schools*, London, Learning by Design, Tower Hamlets Education

Hilliman, C. and Hassan, L., 1987, *The Arrivants: a pictorial essay on blacks in Britain*, London, Race Today Collective *[anno]*

Kramer, A., 1988, *Women in Politics*, Hove, Wayland *[anno]*

Imperial War Museum, 1995, *'Together!' The contribution made in the 2nd World War by African, Asian and Caribbean men and women,* London, Imperial War Museum (Resource pack with video, audio cassette, posters, documents, black and white and colour photographs)

London Transport Museum, 1995, *'Sun a-shine, Rain a-fall': London Transport's West Indian workforce*, London, London Transport Museum *[anno]*

Miller, L. and Bloch, H., (eds) 1984, *'Black Saturday' the first day of the Blitz — East London memories of September 7th 1940*, London, Tower Hamlets Arts Project *[anno]*

Pettit, Jayne, 1994, *A Place to Hide: True stories of Holocaust rescues,* London, Piccolo

Rubinstein, A., 1991, *Just like the Country: memories of London families who settled in new cottage estates 1919-1939*, London, Age Exchange Theatre Trust *[anno]*

Schweitzer, P., (ed) 1990, *Goodnight Children Everywhere: memories of evacuation in World War II,* London, Age Exchange Theatre Trust

Schweitzer, P., (ed) 1984, *A Place to Stay: memories of pensioners from many lands*, London, Age Exchange

Schweitzer, P., (ed) 1992, *The Time of our Lives: memories of leisure in the 1920s and 1930s*, London, Age Exchange

Symons, Julian, 1972, *Between the Wars: Britain in Photographs,* London, Batsford *[anno]*

Schweitzer, P., (ed) 1993, *Reminiscence projects for children and older people,* London, Age Exchange

Taylor, S., 1992, *A journey through time,* London, London Transport

Van der Rol, Ruud and Verhoeven, Rian, 1993, *Anne Frank: Beyond the Diary — a photographic remembrance*, London, Viking *[anno]*

Visram, R., 1987, *Indians in Britain*, London, Batsford *[anno]*

Visram, R., 1995, *A history of the Asian community in Britain*, Hove, Wayland *[anno]*

Adult Resources

Adams, C. (ed) 1987, *Across Seven Seas and Fifteen Rivers: Life stories of pioneer Sylheti settlers in Britain*, London, THAP

Dayus, Kathleen, 1982, *Her People, Volume 1 of her autobiography*, London, Virago

Humphries, Steve and Gordon, Pamela, 1993, *A Labour of Love: the experience of parenthood in Britain 1900-1950*, London, Sidgwick and Jackson

Humphries, Steve and Gordon, Pamela, 1994, *Forbidden Britain — our secret past 1900-1960*, London BBC publications *[anno]*

Johnson, Buzz, 1985, *'I think of my Mother': Notes on the life and times of Claudia Jones*, London, Karia Press

Lennon, M., 1988, *Across the water: Irish Women's Lives in Britain*, London, Virago

Sherwood, M. 1985, *Many Struggles: West Indian workers and service personnel in Britain 1939-1945*, London, Karia Press

Spring Rice, M., 1981, *Working class wives (original 1939)*, London, Virago (primary evidence)

Supple, Carrie, 1993, *From Prejudice to Genocide: learning about the Holocaust*, Stoke-on-Trent, Trentham Books.

Notable people for this study unit included in Chapters 12 and 13 — Lives and Annotated Resources

Angelou, Maya *[anno]*

Baker, Josephine *[anno]*

Constantine, Lord Learie *[biog]*

Earhart, Anne *[biog, anno]*

Frank, Anne *[anno]*

Fitzgerald, Ella *[anno]*

Garvey, Marcus *[anno]*

Gies, Miep *[biog]*

Henry, Lenny *[anno]*

Johnson, Amy *[biog, anno]*

Jones, Claudia *[biog, anno]*

King, Martin Luther *[anno]*

Malcolm X *[anno]*

Mandela, Nelson *[anno]*

Moody, Dr Harold *[biog]*

Pitt, David Thomas, Lord Pitt of Hampstead *[biog]*

Ride, Sally *[anno]*

Wilkinson, 'Red Ellen' *[biog]*

Chapter 10

Study Unit 5: Local History

Reclaim your past!

The 1995 History Order gives teachers a choice for the local study unit. They can focus on one of three approaches:

- ☐ an aspect of the community studied over a long period of time — such as education, leisure, religion, population change, settlement and landscape, law and order, the treatment of the poor
- ☐ the way in which their local community was involved in a short term event (the italicised examples in the Order make it clear that this approach need not necessarily connect to the other study units)
- ☐ local illustration of developments taught through the other study units — for instance child labour, new towns in the twentieth century, life in a country house (presumably Tudor or Victorian).

The flexibility in potential content returns to teachers considerable control over the history curriculum. Now, with careful thought and research, schools can make sure to include issues of relevance and importance to their community and their educational philosophy. It is some compensation for the forced choice between Victorians and Britain since 1930. The local study can be the framework within which to tackle issues which come just outside the period of particular units, or were crowded out, or somehow seemed less central in the other statutory units for example women's suffrage, involvement in workers' or anti-slavery campaigns (as discussed in Chapters 8 and 9). Some challenging suggestions for a long thematic study have been added and some are explored in this chapter, making links with material already introduced elsewhere in the book. The local history unit, in other words, is one major avenue for schools to 'reclaim their pasts'.

The status of local history in the academic discipline

In the last few decades, there have been significant changes in the academic discipline, notably a move away from 'top down' political history, and local history has achieved far higher status. Studies in local history have necessitated revisions of universalist interpretations of the past. They have challenged stereotypes and metanarratives, offering insights into the contributions and participation of small communities in large events. Local history is not a ragbag of oddments of variable value and interest, however. It entails asking and trying to answer specific historical questions. 'Antiquarianism', or the indiscriminate collection of facts for their own sake, without any sense of questions to be answered, or relationships to wider issues, can be a hazard in local history studies. There is a sense in which local studies can overlap with anthropology in concern with the detail of customs and practices in small communities; it is important to focus and contextualise the local history within wider analysis and narrative.

From children's point of view, local studies can be fascinating. They can see the traces of the past in the very surroundings that they inhabit daily. By reducing the physical scale to the manageable area that children can walk around and probably know intimately, local history can become the most child-centred and child-friendly apprenticeship to the discipline. The eminent local historian William Hoskins reminds us that the first thing to do when embarking on local history, is to walk around with one's eyes wide open, noticing the detail of buildings, roads, parks, and open spaces, and asking questions about how they came to be like this, what has changed, and what the area might have been like before. Local history gives children the opportunity to become involved in small-scale research — asking real questions about places and people that are familiar — even if only by name — trying to find the evidence and then interpret it. This is at the heart of doing history, and could be one of its most valuable and memorable experiences that schooling offers.

Local history enables children to understand that though the history books remember the Duke of Wellington, at grass roots level 'Private William Wheeler, and thousands like him also won the battle of Waterloo' (Sharpe, in Burke, (ed) 1991). They can tap into the intentions and experience of ordinary people who lived, as they themselves do now, in these streets, these houses. Although, as I explore later in this chapter, there is certainly a place and the potential in local study to do work about notable people who lived in the area, children can also do 'history from below', with all that it implies in its rejection of elitism.

Ideally, the history co-ordinator in a school would take responsibility for researching and resourcing the potential for the local history unit in the vicinity, building up a bank of material which would contain enlargements of old maps, copies of photographs and pictorial evidence, newspaper articles and other useful documentary material such as excerpts from the censuses and extracts from parish registers. Oral history records — whether tapes or transcripts made with members of the community at different times — could be stored for other classes to draw on.

This chapter, like the others in this book, does not consider every possible way to interpret the choices for the unit. All kinds of opportunities exist for local study which don't relate particularly to my theme of inclusivity. Once more, I have chosen content which could develop an inclusive curriculum, organising the material broadly round the first two choices given in the unit. All that is offered are examples and ideas which, I hope, will stimulate teachers to research their own areas, as I have done mine.

A focus over a long period of time

i) Population change, settlement and landscape

A study of population change and settlement over a long period should always aim to move beyond collecting facts and descriptions to asking deeper questions about the reasons for changing patterns. The explanations might be very obvious — enclosure, drainage, or mechanisation of farming perhaps, accounting for moves away from traditional agricultural areas to where new work could be found in the towns — or even emigration. Modern industries have acted as magnets for those seeking a livelihood, just as the factories of the nineteenth century Industrial Revolution did for our ancestors. In our own times, closure of mines and factories have turned some towns into ghosts of their former selves; in other areas the establishment of new industries has led to new estates springing up, shopping and leisure centres, the infrastructure of schools, railways and new bypasses. Transport is always important, for some localities rely on easy commuting to a nearby area of work.

Population change is not just about movement into an area but also about people leaving. It's about industries growing up and then dying and the people moving away as the work vanishes. It's about new estates replacing slums, or being erected for newly arrived communities; the way neighbourhoods change in character over a generation — warehouses becoming gentrified and converted into expensive town houses and wine bars, new shops to serve new needs, different foods in the markets; new places of worship, clubs, community centres. These are the kinds of patterns that children can trace over a number of centuries, using parish registers, Post Office and street directories, census figures and old maps to help them establish the extent and nature of change.

For some areas, particularly in the inner city, the study of population change and settlement would be rich in possibilities for an historical project which reflected the children's own family life stories and addressed the main themes of this book. This interpretation of the local study theme would be literally about the nature and connections of the community currently living in the area. Chapter 9 explores the ways in which emigration and immigration are conceptualised by historians, and teachers planning a theme on population change and settlement

These houses were built by the Huguenot silk weavers who settled in Spitalfields in the middle of the C17th. The looms were on the first floor, and the large windows allowed in plenty of light. (Photo Hilary Claire)

through the local study unit might find p.170-173 helpful. Background information about the impact and importance of immigration and emigration in the nineteenth and twentieth centuries is in Chapters 8 and 9. The chart in Appendix 2, showing patterns of migration, would provide the framework for a time-line, which could concentrate on specific periods and people relating to the local community. Perhaps the area was a starting point for Puritan emigration to America in the seventeenth century. Connections with Canada, South Africa, Australia and New Zealand — which were all the destinations for major British settlement schemes — might be a theme that certain children could pursue through their own personal and family connections. The gold rushes in America, Australia and New Zealand (in the 1840s and 1860s respectively) account for considerable British connections with those countries.

British settlement in Africa largely dates from the end of the nineteenth century, reflecting the 'Scramble for Africa' in which the continent was 'carved up' between the European nations. Southern Africa is the exception. The Cape was first taken over from the Dutch and settled by the British during the Napoleonic Wars; a fairly substantial number of British settlers, including missionaries, went to the Eastern Cape in 1820. From the middle of the nineteenth century a second wave of British emigrants went to South Africa: the discovery of diamonds and then the goldrush on the Witwatersrand in the 1880s acted as a magnet for British fortune-seekers. Zimbabwe, Zambia, Malawi, Botswana and other Southern African countries were all settled by British colonists from the last decade of the nineteenth century. From the end of the nineteenth century white missionaries, traders, Chartered Company officials, soldiers, farmers and civil servants, people seeking their fortune and children sent by charities to find a better life, went out to Africa. There was a reciprocal journey of Africans to England, usually to acquire professional qualifications, which continues in our own time, along with Africans fleeing political troubles.

The same is true of connections with the Asian sub-continent. From the middle of the nineteenth century when India became part of the Empire, considerable numbers of British people went out to serve in the civil service and the army. Indians also came to England. Some achieved fame in public life, others remained for a while then returned.

'Wolf Pack no 15' (Worsnop, 1994) has a map showing British 'possessions' at the turn of the century. It could be used to explain why people from remote countries have come to Britain because of colonial and Commonwealth connections.

Local sites or museums provide excellent evidence for the very early periods of history, whether they be Celtic, Roman, Saxon or Viking. Local history libraries will be able to help with information and resources about particular patterns of settlement in later periods. Changes in the nature of agriculture and work opportunities are often at the heart of changing population. An area might have

The Eel Pie Shop in Kingsland High Street, Hackney.
(Photo Hilary Claire)

The drapers' shop in Kingsland Road, Hackney, hardly changed in fifty years (Photo Hilary Claire)

been the focus for Italian, Irish or French immigration, and evidence of specific trades or crafts can be perceived in the design and function of buildings, even if they are no longer used for their original purpose.

Sometimes the changing history of a place of worship, or the local market, factories or shops in the high street might show the impact of population change. The local history library will usually hold photographs showing the urban landscape of a different era, which can be compared with the contemporary scene. Victorian shop fronts on my local High Street in Hackney have been transformed into Turkish and Greek travel agents, a Pan-African Centre selling a range of African artefacts and foods, a Chinese herbal medicine centre, an African-Caribbean bakery. Among them there is still the Edwardian Eel and Pie Shop with its art nouveau mirrors and tiles, the modernised Sainsburys which dates from the 1870s, the old butcher shops, a drapers that sells threads, tapes and zips in a setting that has not changed since the 1920s. Post Office Directories in the local history library are the best source for information about previous use of commercial or industrial buildings.

Places of worship are often interesting markers not only of growing populations but also of changing ethnicity. In the mid to late nineteenth century speculative builders in my area put up row upon row of semi-detached houses for the burgeoning middle class. An Anglican Church was built to serve the suburban parishioners. In the 1960s and 1970s the Church stood empty, marking not so much a decline in population as a decline in local church-going Anglicans. In the 1980s it became the home of an Evangelical African sect; in the mid-1990s, dangerously in need of repair, it has been boarded up to await rebuilding. The local mosque is new — testimony to the arrival of large numbers of Turkish immigrants, and a reminder of more recent Muslim arrivants — Kurds and Bosnians — though whether they share the mosque I do not know. Down the road from the mosque, a big factory has been converted into a centre for the Kurdish community — till recently many refugees were sleeping in its vast central area. As Hoskins (1984) has observed, unless we understand the social and economic significance of issues in our own times, we will neither notice nor ask the right questions about the past.

ii) Work on notable people who lived in the area

The theme of population change and settlement is a sensible vehicle for work on notable women, black and ethnic minority people who have lived or worked in the area at some time. Alternatively, such study could be part of the second option in the Unit: 'involvement in a short term event'. Someone buried in the local cemetery may be worth researching (see Greenwood 1990). Blue plaques may mark those who have been canonised by the historical establishment. The local history library often has a pamphlet about local heroes and heroines — I discovered, for example, that both Elizabeth Fry and Florence Nightingale had been connected to local hospitals in Hackney — but one needs a beady eye, and a browse in the community bookshop to find out about others.

The names of buildings, streets and parks often signify the connection of a place with notable people. Dalston, for example, has a whole neighbourhood of Tudor names — from a newish block called Tudor House, to a much older road — King Henry's Walk — leading into Boleyn Road, and Mildmay Grove. Apparently Henry VIII had a hunting lodge near here. Nearby in the High Streets, are Claudia Jones House — an African-Caribbean Women's Organisation — and the CLR James Library, named for the eminent black socialist historian and novelist.

Sometimes names are indicative of prevailing attitudes or national or international events of the time beyond the local boundaries, for example the enclaves of Victorian roads named after famous battles of the Crimean War, or victories in the Boer War (defeats are seldom commemorated!). The roads or buildings named after Mandela do not indicate that he was personally there, but rather that the local council wished to honour him. Was Despard Road in North London named after the suffragist, Irish nationalist and pacifist Charlotte Despard or Colonel Edmund Despard, a Jacobin conspirator who went to the scaffold for conspiracy in 1803?

On Stoke Newington Green is the Unitarian Chapel, built in 1746, which served the local dissenting community. Mary Wollstonecraft probably attended in 1784-6, when she lived on the Green and ran a school there (there is no blue plaque marking her house and it is possible that it has been demolished).

The school that the pupils attend may be named after someone worth studying. There are brief biographical pen portraits of a number of notable black people and women from the past (including Claudia Jones) in Chapter 12, indicating where they came from, worked or lived during significant periods of their lives. At the end of this chapter, other reference works are listed but teachers will need to research their own localities, drawing on the resources of their local community bookshops and history library for information.

Featuring the work of such people (or others like them who lived in your area) in a local study could be a fruitful way to broaden the history curriculum and make children more aware of the lives of people who deserve to be remembered. There could be someone currently living in the area who has achieved eminence, or whose life is interesting and illustrative of a broader theme. Neither national fame nor being dead need be the criterion for study! The local newspaper is always a good source about interesting local people — be it an artist, writer or community activist. For example, as part of their local history project, children in a Lewisham School interviewed the black activist Sybil Phoenix, who lived nearby and has been honoured for her community work.

iii) Poverty and illness: class, philanthropy and self help

Work on this theme would probably mean starting with the actual physical environment near the school and looking for the history attached to the existing buildings and open spaces. Blackheath, for example, is the site of a huge graveyard dating from the Black Death. Old maps show clearly where the workhouses, poorhouses and charitable establishments stood, even though they have now been demolished. These buildings were put up as part of the national response to poverty and illness and old age. A local building like this, or what used to be on a site, could be the starting point for work on what life was like in a system where the state did not take responsibility for any but the very poorest, and then made sure that the help was so humiliating and punitive that people would make every effort to avoid, rather than call on it. (See the excerpt from Kathleen Dayus's autobiography, p.177) The Tudor Poor Law, which continued to operate until 1834, was considerably less harsh than the so-called Victorian 'New Poor Law'. Under the Old Poor Law destitute or unemployed people were supported by the parish and could continue to live at home. They even received a form of subsidy related to the current price of bread, which would bring their wages up to the amount needed to support their families.

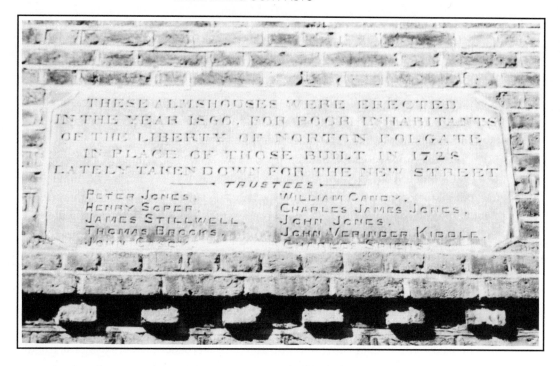

Plaque on almshouses erected in 1860, Puma Court, Spitalfields
(Photo Hilary Claire)

The New Poor Law operated an ideology which assumed that the poor were basically lazy and feckless; people who fell on hard times were to blame for their own misery, and the appropriate response was punishment. The Boards of Guardians for the Poor Law were issued 'Instructional Circulars' which had been drawn up by the same Dr Edwin Chadwick responsible later for sanitary improvements in the towns, whose basis was psychological deterrence. In the words of an Assistant Commissioner of the time, 'Our intention is to make the workhouses as like prisons as possible'. Another wrote 'Our object .. is to establish therein a discipline so severe and repulsive as to make them a terror to the poor and prevent them from entering.' The poor in workhouses were subject to a minimal diet, a harsh regime of inhumane routines, religious exercises, silence during meals, prompt obedience, total separation of the sexes, separation of families (even where of the same sex), labour and total confinement. In a clear statement of underlying intention, Dr Chadwick specified that

> ... neither widows with families, nor the aged and the infirm, nor the sick... should be spared these workhouse humiliations for fear of sustaining improvidence and imposture and of sapping the motives to industry, frugality, prudence, filial duties, independent exertions of the labourers during their years of ability and activity. (Thompson, 1980, p.295-6)

The Victorian Metropolitan Hospital, Hackney, derelict for several years, and now converted to a Business Enterprise Centre.
(Photo Hilary Claire)

Many areas have huge redbrick Victorian hospitals; some have been shut down, or converted into enterprise centres for the 1990s. These vast hospital buildings, erected at the end of the nineteenth century, were normally funded through charities. There was no National Health Service until 1944. Medicine was not free and working class people could not always afford the medical services that were available. Some areas have Victorian dispensaries where women who were excluded from conventional medicine sometimes set up practice. Women's hospitals were actually staffed by male doctors, using the services of nurses trained through Florence Nightingale's austere methods. Only in the latter part of the nineteenth century could ill women be treated by a woman doctor, following the struggle for recognition of pioneers such as Elizabeth Blackwell and Elizabeth Garrett Anderson who challenged male domination of the profession. (See Chapter 8, p.158 and information on Anderson in Chapter 12.)

As part of their developing understanding of chronology, children might consider change and continuity in medicine and health, in relation to our own times. How different was it to be old and ill in the seventeenth and eighteenth century, in the days of the Old Poor Laws, or after the New Poor Laws were introduced in 1834, compared with now? What were Victorian values really about regarding poverty and the so-called 'undeserving poor', and is the claim that we are reverting to such attitudes justified? What about the first half of the twentieth century, which was a period when new social security measures were first being introduced, or the late 1940s, when the National Health Service was set up as part of the Welfare State? There is a great deal of evidence from the late nineteenth and early twentieth century, about 'managing', childcare and illness, and the experience of maternity.

Children could read excerpts from contemporary books for their insights on local poverty and the resilience and courage of women (see resources at the end of this chapter for books edited by Margaret Llewelyn Davies and Maud Pember Reeves). Pember Reeves' book is a mine of information about women's daily routines, their children, the ways they made do on small amounts. Even if children do not actually live in Lambeth, where the survey was made, this is a fascinating comparative resource about working lives in the pre-First World War period. For more recent times, it is usually not difficult to find material that comes from local people, often recorded for local history reminiscence groups. Closer still to our own times, the best source of all is people who can come and talk to the children about what they remember. Here comparisons with accounts by people who grew up abroad would give a broader focus. Local history surely includes the experience of all those currently living in the area, even if some spent their earlier years elsewhere.

iv) Education: gender and class

There may be a great or minor public or grammar school in the area dating back more than a century that could provide the subject for analytic study of the class and gender-based nature of provision for children, which continues in our own time. Some of the boys' public schools date back to the Tudor period, when there was pressure to educate the sons of the growing professional and merchant class, but no equivalent provision for working class children or girls. Charitable schools, too, are often very old, reflecting who took responsibility for children fallen on hard times. Girls' education is a possible theme in areas where there is (or was) a girls' public or grammar school, even if it has now been amalgamated into the state system. Children could find out about the resolute Victorian women who worked for (middle class) girls' education so that they could escape the stultifying constrictions of the domestic 'separate sphere'. The headteacher and their staff in such schools were often involved in the suffrage movement, as some local studies make clear (e.g. Dove 1988) and this could be followed up in the school's own records, drawing on the gender and class issues in education in Chapter 8.

Whether their own school building dates from before the 1870 Forster Act, or is an original Board School, or more modern, children could start with their own school and move back in time to study comparative provision for children in an earlier period. The development of working class schooling in the nineteenth century before 1870 is often charted in local buildings. Before the Forster Act secured Elementary Education for all, the National Schools run by the Church of England, and their great rivals, the 'British and Foreign Schools' established by dissenting Christians, were responsible between them for the education of the majority of those children who went to school at all. In some areas there are also Sunday School buildings and Ragged Schools, usually with the date over the front entrances, no longer used for their original purpose. Barnardos archives keep the records of Ragged Schools (contact the Ragged School Museum Trust in Bow) and the parish church is the first place to look for the Sunday School records, although they might have been transferred to County Archive offices. In London, the Greater London Records Office keeps the archives for most schools, or can tell you where they are kept now. The local history library will also tell you where the records are kept.

v) Law and order

This theme appeared as part of Local Study for the first time in the 1995 Order and, so far, I have not come across any commentary on the intentions of the Dearing Committee who added this topic to the rewritten unit. Law and order is a controversial historical topic, and its treatment in the academic literature will reflect the values and ideology of the historian. You have only to think about the ways in which, say, the Right to Silence, the Criminal Justice Bill, views on capital punishment or arming the police are debated in our own time to understand the inevitable existence of very different agendas — sometimes implicit, sometimes spelled out. Some historians concentrate 'top down' on the actual laws and how order was maintained. Others chart changes in definitions of crime and criminality, looking at patterns of law-breaking, or at the underbelly of criminality, from the experience of the criminal.

The theme of law and order could quite possibly be treated as a narrative of the ways in which the established social order is imposed and maintained and the occasional challenge suppressed. Order is taken to be 'a good thing', not to be problematised. In this conservative view, the law is understood as embodying the will of the ruling class (whoever they may be at any time) without asking about whose interests are served, and how far the legal system is considered ethical and legitimate by those who are subject to it. Such a history would take the Romans' part in their imposition of order over the Britons; Mary Tudor's and then Elizabeth's actions in the suppression of rebel religious groups would be understood as part of monarchic necessity. The Civil War would be reduced to a narrative of alliances and battles, rather than a deeply complex movement in which various interest groups challenged the legitimacy of the crown and the oligarchy, and then each other. In such a reading of history, children might learn about their area's participation in the Civil War on one side or another, or conditions in a local prison, or the use of the militia and its replacement by the police force in the middle of the nineteenth century. They could quite easily avoid troubling questions about why some people don't keep the law, why the law and methods of enforcing conformity have changed, whether the law itself has been oppressive, and how one might now evaluate some of the punitive procedures of the past.

On the other hand, a study of law and order could reflect contemporary perspectives in academic history. Formerly, historians tended to study law and order through the acts of Parliament and official legal records. Recently, rather than focus solely on the evidence of those who made and administered the laws, historians have used the records to interpret the attitudes of ordinary people to crime and the social order, and their attempts to change or resist their situation. Changing legislation and how it is enforced, reflects the ways in which people do or don't conform to an establishment view of proper behaviour.

So for example, the records for witchcraft and 'scolding' trials (see Chapter 7) can be used to consider women's power and agency in the community. The records of parents taken to court for their children's truancy, after education became compulsory in the early 1880s, tell a story not just about non-compliance and disinterest in education, but about poverty and the shame of families who couldn't afford to send their children to school in boots, or manage without the contribution to the family budget of the children's wages.

Clashes with the police and army during demonstrations and strikes are interpreted not just in terms of law-breaking but of people's resistance to what they saw as exploitation or oppression. For many centuries, the collection of petitions, demonstrations and marches (which occasionally degenerated into riots) were the customary way to make one's political preferences known to the government, in the years before ordinary men and women had the vote and thus a voice in public policy making.

A study of law and order is unavoidably about the politics of a period, since it entails looking not just at the ways in which 'ordinary' law was imposed but at the various events that have precipitated unusual resort to force. On the whole, this has been in response to demonstrations and demands, often backed up by force, which have challenged the ruling establishment: for example, the Peasants' Revolt of 1381, led by Wat Tyler, which originated in a village in Essex; the many demonstrations from the end of the eighteenth century into the nineteenth against rising bread prices and taxes of one sort or another; Luddite revolts against the introduction of new machinery; the Chartist demonstrations of the 1840s; and the Trade Union marches and strikes towards the end of the nineteenth century, with their twentieth century heritage. Strikes, including school strikes, were very much a feature of the late nineteenth and early twentieth century. Some schools have discovered this hidden history in their local archives or school log-books. The law- breaking which was the hallmark of the militant suffragette movement in the early twentieth century thus had a long history in struggles for social change.

In Elizabethan times, certain people who wrote blasphemously against the Queen had their right hand cut off; in early Victorian times, young children were kept on prison hulks or deported to Australia for minor thefts. Capital punishment was gruesomely turned into a public spectacle. A case study perhaps reported in an early local newspaper, could initiate fascinating ethical discussions with children. One village school in the Midlands found a record of a young girl brought to court for 'stealing water' from a hand-pump in the 1840s and set up their own trial based on the newspaper report. Through thinking how our conception of misdemeanours has changed, and how law-breakers have been dealt with in history, we would be asking children to reflect seriously on the nature of the social order, the reasons why people might test the boundaries of conformity. (See also short-term involvement below, for further ideas about law and order in local history.)

Involvement in a short term event

The best way to find out about the involvement in any movement or event is through the local historian at the library. Most local history libraries keep files of cuttings and photographs; the archivists are well informed about local people as well as the history of the buildings. Local community bookshops are also often a mine of information and resources, and usually have books of photographs of the area, the history of a particular community's settlement, and publications from the local history society, which often include booklets produced by local people

A section of the large mural in Copenhagen Road, London N1,
commemorating the March in support of the 'Tolpuddle Martyrs'.
The main inscription reads:
On Copenhagen Fields, just north of here in 1834, over 100,000 Londoners
met to march for pardon of the 6 Dorset farm labourers, known as Tolpuddle
Martyrs, transported to Australia for joining a trade union. 12 Trade Unionists
carried a huge petition mounted on a roller at the head of the 6 mile long
procession to Parliament at Westminster. The government was forced to give
pardons and eventually all of the deported labourers returned.
(Photo Hilary Claire)

about their lives. For example I recently came across a book produced by a Local
History Group in Dorset: a woman, in her 80s in 1972 when the book was
published, told about her life with foster parents at the turn of the century, going
into service and her eventual marriage in the 1920s.

Sometimes a space or a commemorative mural or plaque will mark where some
great event happened, or testify to strong local commitment to a movement. For
instance the mural in Copenhagen Road, London N1, commemorates the huge
demonstration in support of the 'Tolpuddle Martyrs', the six Dorset agricultural
workers who were tried and deported to Australia in 1834, for forming a Trades
Union. Banners on the mural proclaim 'Women workers say support the Charter'
and demand 'Votes for Women and Equal Pay and Equal Work'. Though some

Chartists did support female suffrage, this campaign actually took second place to the demand for workers' rights and male suffrage.

The peace mural depicting the multicultural community in Hackney, with its CND signs and musical instruments, is emblematic of issues and attitudes and this community's participation in what was, after all, the international history of the early 1980s. Before the Soviet Block collapsed, when Britain was still an important base for American warheads, and Hackney was on the 'nuclear route', local people were involved in anti-nuclear protests. It should go without saying that recognising such movements as part of history implies nothing about personal sympathies, rather the ability to acknowledge the relationship of personal and local commitments to national and international events.

A municipal building or a church such as Holy Trinity on Clapham Common, might have been the focus for an important movement. Holy Trinity was the local church for the 'Saints' as they were known — the High Church Evangelical Tories who, led by William Wilberforce, played an important role in getting abolition of slavery through the Houses of Parliament. Another such building is the Free Trade Hall in Manchester, built on St Peter's Fields, the site of the notorious Peterloo Massacre. Here, on August 16th 1819, a crowd of 60,000 including women and children had gathered to hear the orator Henry Hunt speak about electoral reform. The local magistrates panicked and ordered the mounted troops to charge the crowd. Eleven people were hacked to death and 600 were wounded. The Manchester Free Trade Hall is where Annie Kenny and Christabel Pankhurst — representing the newly formed Women's Social and Political Union (the WSPU) — famously challenged Sir Edward Grey in 1905 about votes for women, during his electioneering for the Liberal Party. They were ejected and so began the militant action of the campaign which soon became better known as the 'Suffragettes'.

The non-militant Suffragists, a far larger and longer standing organisation, if less concerned with publicity and image, had a tremendous following throughout England, particularly in the textile areas of the North. Burnley, Manchester, Chester, Nelson-and-Colne and Bolton are all associated with suffragist women (see Liddington and Norris, 1978).

Rosemary Taylor has documented the places where Sylvia Pankhurst worked with East End women, first as part of the WSPU and, after she broke with her militant mother and sister, in the East London Federation of Suffragettes (which she founded in 1914, giving us a memorable acronym — the ELFS). Soon after the war started in August 1914, the ELFS opened a cost price restaurant in Old Ford Road, a nursery which looked after the local children, a boot factory and a toy factory nearby where women could get work. In 1915 they took over a pub in Old Ford Road, the Gunmaker's Arms, and turned it into a mother and baby clinic and creche, with a Montessori school upstairs. They regularly held meetings and parties for local children and women at the Bow Baths in the Roman Road.

The Peace Mural at Dalston Junction, Hackney
(Photo Hilary Claire)

(The ELFS changed its name in 1916 and became the Workers' Suffrage Federation, fighting for universal suffrage.)

It is not just those forbidding nineteenth century prisons, Holloway in London and Strangeways in Manchester, which locked up the suffragettes arrested for breaking the law in the militant period between 1905 and 1914. It is worth checking the local records to see if suffragettes were active in the neighbourhood of your school. Feminist local historians such as Iris Dove have started to uncover the involvement of local women in the suffrage movement, and their monographs are often in the local history library or bookshop.

Kennington Common in London SE 11 is connected to another campaign of major importance in Britain's history, the Chartist movement demanding a public voice for British working men, and major reforms of the democratic system. Fear and paranoia about imminent revolution was very high in 1848, when news of the Chartist demonstration in London became public. Queen Victoria fled from London to the Isle of Wight. The authorities called together a large counter-revolutionary police force drawing on local tradespeople, shopkeepers and so on to supplement the militia. The last great Chartist march gathered in 1848 on the Common, intending to take a huge petition demanding the 'Charter' into Parliament, but they were outmanoeuvred, their leaders in disarray over their conflicting ideas about how to handle the opposition, and they never got over Westminster Bridge. William Cuffay, the black tailor from Chatham, born a slave on board a ship coming from St Kitts to England, was involved in leading the Chartist movement. Like other leaders, he was deported after the failed demonstration, and died in Tasmania. Chartism was by no means confined to London and there is substantial evidence for Chartist activity in the North of England and most major towns.

The Docks in London, Liverpool and Bristol stand witness to the importance of sea power to Britain in former centuries, and her involvement not just with international trade in goods but also, far more notoriously and tragically, the trade in human beings. From these three ports the majority of ships came and went on the triangular trade, starting small in the seventeenth century and expanding throughout the eighteenth. They took goods produced in British factories and mills to Africa, where they were bartered for slaves. This human cargo was carried to England's own colonies in the Caribbean islands and Southern States of America and the plantations and mines of their international rivals — whom they supplied with slave labour to work the plantations and mines of South America and other Caribbean islands. From the end of the sixteenth century, British ships made the voyages to India, first round the Cape and, after Suez was opened in 1869, through the Canal, and were inextricably connected with the economic and military subjugation of the Indian subcontinent.

Liverpool and Bristol docks were the site of anti-black riots just after the first world war. Stranded and looking for work, black sailors were the victims of violent attacks from white workers who believed the jobs were theirs by right.

The Bryant and May factory in Bow, London E3, still stands. Here, in 1888 the famous match girls' strike took place. Led by Annie Besant, the women workers went on strike, and won, against the use of the dangerously unhealthy phosphorus, which caused 'phossie jaw'. One of the best ways to discover participation in such major local events, certainly from the final quarter of the nineteenth century, is through postcards sold at the local public library. Some local libraries have street by street historical directories that tell not just who lived in a certain street but whether events of importance happened there.

Cato Street in Westminster, and Cable Street in East London are both sites of famous 'battles'. (For Cato Street see the entry in Chapter 12 for William Davidson.) Rather like the Jarrow March or the Tolpuddle Story, Cable Street has achieved symbolic significance in history. In 1936, Moseley's fascist Black Shirts, a legal group, planned a march through the heart of the East End, a highly provocative move since this was the home of a considerable number of Jews. Some were the descendants of people who had settled there in the late nineteenth century, fleeing the pogroms in Eastern Europe; others were refugees from the growing Nazi threat in Europe, after Hitler came to power in 1933. Jews and local radicals combined to stop the march and, united under banners reading 'They shall not pass', effectively barricaded Cable Street. They also forced a government which was ambivalent about taking a strong stand against fascism, to ban all uniformed marches in future. Nearer our own time, streets in Notting Hill Gate, New Cross and Brixton in London, St Pauls in Bristol, the centre of Liverpool, and Handsworth in Birmingham are all part of a history of black demonstration and resistance to racism (see 'law and order' above).

On a different note, 1994 was the 150th anniversary of the foundation of the Co-operative movement in Rochdale. The town commemorated this anniversary with exhibitions, street drama and publications still available after the year ended. If there is a local co-op, then this could be the starting point for some work on this nineteenth century working class movement that was about far more than shopping. In the early part of this century, the Co-op movement created a forum for women where they learned how to manage their budget and their homes, but also became involved in political debate about suffrage and peace, as the women who contributed to Margaret Llewelyn Davies' book, *Life As We Have Known It*, testify.

Resources
Children's Fiction
Scobie, Pamela 1991, *School Strike*, Oxford, Oxford University Press

Classroom Resources
Hilliman, C. and Hassan, L., 1987, *The Arrivants: a pictorial essay on blacks in Britain*, London, Race Today Collective *[anno]*

Bristol Broadsides, 1987, *The Bristol Picture Book, Part 2: twenty years of people's lives in photographs 1940-1960*, Bristol, Bristol Broadsides

Gate House Project, 1985, *Day in, Day out: Memories of North Manchester from women in Monsell Hospital*, Manchester, Gate House Project *[anno]*

London Transport Museum, 1995, *'Sun a-shine, Rain a-fall' London Transport's West Indian workforce*, London, London Transport Museum *[anno]*

Visram, R., 1987, *Indians in Britain*, London, Batsford *[anno]*

Visram, R., 1995, *The History of the Asian Community in Britain*, Hove, Wayland *[anno]*

Worsnop, R., 1994, *The British Empire (Expansion)* Wolf Pack 15, Huntingdon, Cambs, Elm Publications *[anno]*

Adult Resources and References
Burke, P. (ed), 1991, *New Perspectives on Historical Writing*, London, Polity Press

Clarke, J., 1984, *In our Grandmother's Footsteps: A Virago Guide to London*, London, Virago, (Notable women connected with London: brief biographies and place of connection but disappointingly short on black women)

Collicott, S., 1986, *Connections: Haringey Local-National-World Links*, Haringey Community Information Service in association with the multi-cultural support group

Dove, Iris, 1988, *Yours in the Cause: suffragettes in Lewisham, Greenwich and Woolwich*, Lewisham and Greenwich Library Services

File, N. and Power, C., 1981, *Black Settlers in Britain 1555-1958*, Oxford, Heinemann Educational Books

Greenwood, Douglas, 1990 (2nd ed) *Who's buried where in England*, London, Constable (rather male in focus)

Hoskins, W., 1984, *Local History in England*, Harlow, Essex, Longman

Legget, J., 1988, *Local Heroines: a women's history gazetteer to England, Scotland and Wales*, London, Pandora (Area by area details of women connected with different localities; includes brief biographies)

Liddington, Jill and Norris, Jill, 1978, *One Hand Tied Behind Us: the rise of the women's suffrage movement*, London, Virago

Llewelyn Davies, Margaret (ed), 1978, *Maternity: letters from working women*, (original 1915), London, Virago.

Llewelyn Davies, Margaret (ed), 1977, *Life as we have known it by co-operative working women* (original 1931), London, Virago.

Manchester Women's History Group, 1995, *Resources for Women's History in Greater Manchester*, Manchester, National Museum of Labour History

Mayhew, Henry, (1985) *London Labour and the London Poor* (original 1851-2, 2nd enlarged edition 1862) London, Penguin Classics

Merriman, N., 1993, *The Peopling of London: fifteen thousand years of settlement from overseas*, London, Museum of London Press

Reeves, Maud Pember, 1979, *Round About a Pound a Week* (original 1913) London, Virago, (an investigation into the lives of women in Lambeth)

Sturtevant, Katherine, 1990, *Our Sisters' London: Feminist Walking Tours,* Chicago, Chicago Review Press

Taylor, Rosemary, 1993, *In Letters of Gold: The Story of Sylvia Pankhurst and the East London Federation of the Suffragettes in Bow*, London, Stepney Books

Thompson, E.P., 1980, *The Making of the English Working Class*, London, Penguin

Visram, R., 1986, *Ayahs, Lascars and Princes,* London, Pluto Press (History of Indian people in Britain, particularly in nineteenth century)

Chapter 11

Study Unit 6: a past non-European society
General issues and an exemplar: Benin

This chapter is mainly about teaching the Benin option in Study Unit 6, but considers some general ideas relevant to all the non-European study units. Ancient Egypt has been rather better resourced than others in Study Unit 6, so I shall make just one point with respect to African civilisations which has relevance to the Ancient Egypt option. It is this: till quite recently, white writers have attributed Great Zimbabwe to Arab builders, apparently unable to accept that black engineers could have designed and achieved this magnificent stone enclosure. Similarly, as writers such as Diop and van Sertima have pointed out, some European textbooks portray Egyptian people as white or pale brown, emphasise Greek and Middle Eastern influences and play down the black cultural aspects, which were also important.

Recognising the possibility of children's negative stereotypes about non-European civilisations and particularly Africa

The following paragraphs focus particularly on Africa as the object of negative stereotypes, but it is worth considering that the racism that underpins such stereotypes has a tendency to shift and get directed at different targets. Currently it appears to be people of Asian origin who are the main victims of negative attitudes and personal attacks. It is difficult to feel confident that negativity about people considered as an 'out-group' will vanish entirely from our shores.

Some teachers who have introduced work on Africa or other developing countries into their curricula have been dismayed to discover the negative images and stereotypes that children hold — and not only white children. Given the powerful socialisation of children into the dominant white culture, with several centuries of deprecating and disparaging non-European civilisations, this is hardly surprising.

Attitudes about black people may be changing among the younger generation in Britain, due possibly to the influence of official and unofficial positive action in America, the very positive coverage given to recent changes in South Africa, increasing familiarity and the strong influence of black youth culture. Fewer comics, television shows and children's books are overtly racist, but many children (and adults) still harbour residues of ignorance and prejudice about the developing world. These historically based images are further distorted by current media presentations which focus exclusively on war, poverty, disease and famine, or additionally in the case of Africa, on wild animals, game parks and safari. Many children are unaware that Africa consists of many countries, each with its different languages, history, geography and culture. They do not get the opportunity to see African cities and villages functioning normally, people going to work in cars and buses, living in houses with televisions, cookers and fridges (see Grunsell and Wade, 1995). Many young children believe that all Africans live in villages, as a recent Development Education Centre teachers' project discovered (DEC, 1994). In consequence, many children will come to a study of, say, Benin, with a jumble of ideas about jungles, wild animals, naked savages and poverty — ideas which can only subvert teachers' attempts to treat the history of a black civilisation with dignity and respect.

DEC (1994) includes the guidelines from the Council on Inter-Racial Books for Children, which is worth consulting for criteria for evaluating children's resources. Some resources for primary schools tackle the problems of negative stereotyping head-on and realistically advocate work on images of the contemporary country as an essential precursor to the historical work. This is particularly relevant as History Study Unit 6 is often presented through a cross-curricular history/geography project, covering the geography requirement to teach about a locality in a foreign country (not the EC). The Development Education Centres and agencies, (e.g. Oxfam Education, Christian Aid and Cafod) have produced excellent resources using photographs which help children explore and broaden their own knowledge. Photographs of people and places abroad often draw attention to and compare similar representations of children's own local community, to highlight how media representations can distort or be used for specific ends (see Chapters 13 and 14 for resources and organisations).

Teachers wanting to know their pupils' starting points might find it illuminating to ask them to draw or write about what they would expect to see and find if forced to make a crash landing while travelling over some part of Africa (or the Middle East, India, or Central America). Working from their existing images means teachers have a much clearer set of goals about attitudes they may need to counteract, information they need to teach, and mistaken views they need to dispel.

Conflicting values between a non-European civilisation and contemporary mainstream British culture

As we have seen, dealing with moral issues and value conflicts cannot be avoided in history. Indeed, such discussions are essential if history is to be taught honestly and well. I have noted the necessity of dealing with different attitudes and values about for example, child labour, gender roles, or crime at different periods in British society. Children are more likely to be able to handle different values in non-European societies in a rational manner if equivalent conflicts and moral problems relating to the British units are also acknowledged and dealt with openly.

Historical work on a non-European civilisation must seek to study the culture in terms of the people who developed and lived it. Historians of non-European societies are sometimes compared with anthropologists, subjecting a society to the researchers' gaze while striving to remain dispassionate and non-judgmental. Work on say, the Maya or the Aztecs must somehow take on great cultural differences, try and understand them in their own terms, and avoid making judgements against a yardstick of European value systems. There is no point in sweeping the dilemma under the carpet, since the children are bound to raise the issues themselves or, worse, to retain chauvinist views, which go unchallenged. It would be no more appropriate simply to ignore the difficult issues than, for example, to refuse to debate the historical context and value system in which Victorian child labour prevailed.

Bruner discusses the issue of absolute values and relative preferences and suggests that, rather than assume that 'anything goes', one should ask 'how does this view affect (one's) view of the world or (one's) commitments to it?'. 'Open mindedness' he says, 'is the keystone of what we call a democratic culture — (namely) the willingness to construe knowledge and values from multiple perspectives without loss of commitment to one's own values' (Bruner, 1990, p.30). It is hardly surprising that non-European societies — just like Western ones — have been less than perfect with respect to human rights. For example, some practised slavery, and gender relations generally disadvantage women, just as they do in the West. It is important that teachers have examined their own prejudices and attitudes but also that they are well informed. As in Western society, there are conservatives who defend the status quo and progressives who struggle for change. For most controversial issues — slavery, gender relations, treatment of enemies or sacrifice — a broad comparative approach is most helpful, since children who are already becoming aware of the nature of current and historical inequalities in their own society, are less likely to harbour the impression that discrimination or cruelty is, or was, somehow uniquely characteristic of non-European cultures.

Gender

Teachers need to discuss the role of women in non-Western societies honestly and comparatively with other civilisations, remembering that there are feminists in developing countries struggling against patriarchy and oppression, as well as women who collude — as there are elsewhere. It is impossible to generalise. Historically, Egyptian women had different experiences to Greek women, and were less subordinated to a patriarchal system — and yet the female pharaoh Hatshepsut is portrayed with a beard and in masculine dress in contemporary images. Does this suggest that she had 'manly qualities', or that her authority depended on being seen as masculine? Unfortunately, we do not know. Nor do we know much about ordinary women in the Edo Empire (Benin) but several noble women had special status. If the children have worked on gender in the Victorian and Tudor periods, they should have had a fair grounding in the notion of 'separate spheres', the ways in which women were treated differently to men, and should be alert to the difference gender made to everyone's life.

Polygamy is the norm in a number of non-Judaeo/Christian societies, including Benin. Polygamy was problematic for the missionaries who were among the early explorers and settlers in Africa and elsewhere, and still clashes with the mind-set of those deeply committed to the system of monogamous relationships. Implicit prejudgments based on romanticising monogamy as universally fault-free will make it difficult to consider polygamy from the point of view of the women involved. My own acquaintance with some African women in Southern Africa who live in polygamous relationships, suggests that while *patriarchy* can be problematic (particularly if it is very conservative), polygamy itself holds no more difficulties for them than monogamy, and has advantages in terms of shared work, childcare and friendship. A recent video about Benin made for primary children by IBT, deals matter-of-factly with polygamy: a middle class family made up of a university teacher, his three wives and their children living in a communal setting, are shown all getting along with each other and with their own lives.

Human sacrifice

Human sacrifice, practised by both Maya and Aztecs (but not by the Edo of Benin) can challenge teachers' and children's fundamental moral values. Confronting and trying to come to terms with value conflicts, teaching or learning about another cultural system and according it dignity and respect, demands great maturity. On the other hand, it is not right to demand that children or teachers put aside their ethical views when they study history. Few of us, presumably, would want to explain away slavery or condone the Holocaust. I would want to argue that it is irresponsible to teach about genocide as if we had no view on the moral issues. But it is worth keeping a sense of chronology. The Mayan civilisation peaked between 250 and 1200 AD, and the Aztecs slightly later, in other words contemporary with the Middle Ages in Europe. This period was not noted for tolerance or putting great store on the sanctity of human (or animal) life. Perhaps one way to deal with the issue of human sacrifice is to remind children that the records of modern Western civilisations, let alone those contemporary with the Maya and Aztec, are not squeaky clean with respect to human life and that comparing them in these terms does not get one very far. This does not prevent one having a moral view about human sacrifice, but avoids pointing a judgmental finger at another civilisation and ignoring the sins of one's own.

Change and continuity

Partly because the chosen option of Study Unit 6 is frequently taught through a cross-curricular project involving geography and perhaps art and design and technology, there is a danger of teachers ignoring the historical concepts of change and continuity and freezing the non-European society in a timeless frame. The civilisation is treated as if it were static and unchanging over the centuries. This is ahistorical and, incidentally, contributes to the stereotypes which ignore the impact of modern life in developing countries. While it is true that the pace of change was slow in some cases where communities had established satisfactory ways of doing things and were largely immune to the influences of the outside world, no civilisation remained the same at all times. History's basic concepts are change and continuity, and while children will need to understand the long continuities in customs and political and economic arrangements, they will also need to get a sense of how, why and when changes occurred. Ancient Egyptian civilisation is commonly considered to have lasted 3,000 years and is divided into different periods signified by distinctive features and people. It can no more be treated as unchanging over time than can the period of British Invasion and Settlement covered in Study Unit 1. In the case of Benin, using chronology, change and continuity as substantial planning concepts will mean concentrating not just on the 'high period' of the Empire but considering Benin's decline from the eighteenth century, and certainly including work on the sack of Benin, and its incorporation into the British colonial system at the end of the nineteenth century.

LEARNING ABOUT BENIN
How shall we find out about the Empire of Benin?

The main evidence about the Empire of Benin is from artefacts (particularly the bronzes which decorated the royal buildings, sculptures, carvings, domestic objects), oral history and some archaeology in the form of remains of huge earthworks which were built to fortify Benin City. The National Curriculum Council produced an excellent booklet (1993) on the non-European study units in Key Stage 2. The first chapters outlined the methods and difficulties of archaeology. The document also noted the difficulty of finding evidence of women's work. Sensibly, it recommended that children discuss the effects of lack of evidence, and not be left with the impression that women had no important role. Children might consider how it would be if all evidence about one group of people in their own society somehow did not survive (babies say, or school-age children). Future historians would quickly establish that the absence of evidence just creates a great question mark about them, since all societies had babies and children.

Appreciating that all historical knowledge is more or less approximate and tentative is a valuable lesson. Not only do new discoveries often overturn old certainties, but the imperfect and incomplete nature of our knowledge about the Benin Empire can help children realise that historians can only build on what is available and that some questions may never be answered. Finding out about Benin means detective work, 'interrogating' the evidence, trying to make sensible hypotheses about the period. Children need to work critically and with open minds, using their imagination and empathy but always acknowledging that there are some things we'll never know, and that all our speculations should be tentative, until a better explanation or interpretation comes along.

Study of the Benin Empire creates an opportunity to get into the real excitement and techniques of archaeological research. Archaeological remains, drawings done by Europeans in the seventeenth century — based on hearsay and not personal visits — and aerial photos show the layout of the old Benin city, and the earthworks which acted as defence and fortification. To help them appreciate the problems of limited evidence about Benin, children might consider how much of our knowledge about, say the first few centuries AD in Britain, depends on archaeological and artefactual evidence. Quite specific characteristics, like what things were made of and the acidity or moisture level of the soil, have determined how well they were preserved or survived. Children might consider why most old artefacts we have from Benin are made from metals, clay or very hard woods, and that this partly explains the under-representation of some groups in society. Clothes, basketware, woven hangings typical of contemporary West African society would all have disintegrated long ago in the tropical climate. In addition to artefactual evidence some drawings and accounts from contemporary travellers or people who heard about Benin exist.

British and European museums hold a considerable quantity of sculptures, bronze plaques and artefacts made in wood, ivory and metal. Some were gifts from the early encounters, dating from the sixteenth century, between Portuguese explorers and the Edo, but most come from the conquest and plunder of Benin by British colonial officers in 1897. Most of the artefacts we have were probably made by men and often depict men. Most were made for and belonged to the elite ruling class, and though they tell us quite a lot about their customs and authority, we often cannot do more than hypothesise about the ordinary people. The NCC document recommends that children think about the ethics of taking the valuable and often sacred objects to museums in another country. In some cases this has saved irreplaceable remains from vandals, but some artefacts have ended up in

European museums as a consequence of conquest and looting. Should we return Benin's art?

Luckily, this part of Africa has a very strong oral tradition; history has been preserved and handed down by trained story-tellers going back many generations. Like medieval chronicles, this is not of itself 'history' in the way we have been discussing in this book, but rather evidence which still has to be interpreted. In addition to oral evidence, many traditions have continued over the centuries. These help us know something about people and times long past, since we can extrapolate from current practice to earlier periods.

Respecting history in a cross-curricular project on Benin

Few of the existing resources (with the exception of Andrew Forson's pack and the time-line produced by PCET) develop the history aspects of the cross-curricular topic as fully as they might, or give a coherent and detailed chronological context to the work, so there is a sense of fragmentation and discontinuity. To help teachers overcome this there follows an outline chronological narrative of the Benin Empire. If children are to move beyond a static and ahistorical approach to this study unit, they will need some knowledge of chronology and sequence, of *when* and *in what order* things happened, so that they can think about cause and consequence, or the nature of change and continuity.

Working from the brief history provided here, children could construct a time-line of the major events of the Benin Empire over several centuries. On the other side of the time-line they could show how its history fitted with world events, for example the Norman invasion of England; Portuguese explorations down the coast of West Africa and round the Cape; changing Tudor monarchs; the Spanish discovery of the New World; the developing slave trade which undermined the Oba's power (though Benin was not directly involved in slavery); the establishment of the Royal African Company in 1660, licensed to trade in slaves; The British East India Company's first 'factory' in Bombay in 1668, which increased sea traffic round the coast of West Africa.

In the Victorian period, the development of bicycles with pneumatic rubber wheels (from 1888), and then cars, made Benin's native rubber extremely attractive to Western traders. The increasing popularity of soap and margarine in England also affected Benin, since palm oil, which Benin produced, was the major ingredient. Mary Kingsley, the eccentric Victorian traveller, traded in rubber and oil a little further down the coast. Benin's other main export, ivory, was used for the handles of cutlery for the prosperous Victorian middle classes and for piano keys and ornaments. Such evidence connects with museum work on Victorian daily life. Finally, the last years of Victoria's reign saw the fall of Benin, a victim of Britain's commercially-based political conquest of Africa.

A short history of Benin Empire

The old Empire of Benin was not the territory now called Benin, but lay in what is now modern Nigeria. Benin City, the home of the chief rulers, the Obas, was not on the coast but up river, to the west of the great Niger delta and east of Lagos. This secluded position meant that it was not directly involved in the slave trade, though it was certainly influenced by it. Initially, Benin's rulers had a 'closed-door' policy towards Europeans, and kept them at arms' length for a century after they had landed on the coast and established 'factories' and commercial forts.

The Empire of Benin appears to have changed little over several centuries. As far as we are able to discern, change was connected with changes in rulers, and the impact of foreign visitors. The arrival of Europeans on the coast in the fifteenth century and the transatlantic slave trade affected Benin in the long run, and led to its ultimate decline. Finally it lost its power through direct invasion and conquest by British troops at the end of the nineteenth century. However, there is still an Oba of Benin and some continuities in tradition.

Prehistory

Archaeology has revealed that Africa is the birthplace of humankind. In the Stone Age, about 10,000 years ago, when the first humans were developing tools, the Sahara was not a barrier between West Africa and the East and North. Much of the Sahara was rich and fertile and here agriculture and herd raising developed. The great climatic change seems to have come round about 2,000 BC and led to migrations which were largely over by about 500 BC.

Iron Age West Africa

Two thousand years ago, the descendants of Stone Age people in West Africa had invented methods of farming and metal working. Early evidence of ironworking in what is now Nigeria, dates from round 300 BC. The ability to use iron to make tools and weapons opened up new forms of agriculture, hunting and military power for the West African people. Gradually, more organised forms of society developed, with settlements based round crafts, agriculture and trade, and simple government. This might be headed by chiefs or, as in the case of the Igbo of Nigeria, organised more communally.

The growth of many varied civilised states in West Africa

Throughout West Africa significant forms of government developed, along with sophisticated and beautiful art and crafts in wood, metal, cloth and clay. Benin Empire was one of a number of organised, wealthy and complex civilisations co-existing in this part of Africa. Just as European societies were not insulated from one another, so Benin did not evolve in isolation from its neighbours. Some ideas and developments were learned from neighbours like the Yoruba, and equally, other states learned skills from Benin.

Early trade with North and West Africa and countries of the Middle East

The African states were at the southern end of the great trading caravan routes across the Sahara, maintained by the Berbers. Gold and ivory were the main trading goods desired by the peoples of the North and East, and in return they supplied West Africans with salt, copper and silks. Trade led to the growth of cities — the administrative and religious centres and also the centres for craftsworkers. Trade generated empire building in West Africa. Indeed, Benin Empire started as a trading settlement on the Niger Delta. The importance of trade with the North and the necessity for strong government to maintain this trade, are the key to understanding its history. Children could be reminded of the importance of trade for the development of Britain in the Roman period.

Early history of Benin from about 900AD — sources and evidence

Our knowledge of the early history of Benin is fragmentary. Most of what we know now comes from the interpretation of archaeological and artefactual evidence, and from the oral histories which have been passed down through the centuries since the first dynasties of Obas ruled on the banks of the Niger from about 900 AD.

From the end of the fifteenth century onwards, Benin was a power in this part of Africa. There is some documentary evidence from visitors to Benin from this period, and authentic records from the Empire itself. However, there was no written history till Chief Egharevba wrote his *Short History* in 1934. It was based largely on oral evidence collected from authoritative informants who had grown up in the nineteenth century, steeped in the oral traditions. Egharevba's book chronicles the political history of Benin through its Obas, and is largely devoted to the power struggles and military fortunes of the Empire. In time-honoured West African fashion, much historical information comes through parables and legends about the ruling class, and there is little in the history about ordinary people who lived by farming yams and other vegetables on small farms cleared from the tropical forest.

The dynasties of Obas in Benin from about 900 AD

Egharevba's history begins like a legend 'Many many years ago, the Binis came all the way from Egypt to found a more secure shelter in this part of the world.' The dynasty of the first rulers was founded in roughly the tenth century. The history of the early years is that of the wise deeds and innovations of the Kings, who established their power through tranquil and prosperous rulership, developed crafts, founded villages, often headed by sons who became hereditary chiefs. The rulers were themselves the sons of kings, who took office one after the other according to their age. They were trained by advisors and protectors to assume their important roles.

There are stories too, from this early period, of maladministration and intrigue. Sometimes civil war was deflected by the migration of a group under their leader, and according to Egharevba some settlements were the result of emigration from Benin to avoid bloodshed. Much of this early history of Obas and their wives, mothers, sons, daughters and rivals is carried through legend. For instance, a monster which has been devouring the people is defeated by the brave hero Evian, and his courage is celebrated in yearly performances which have continued to the present day. Other traditions, like a ceremonial crossing of the river Niger by the Oba on his coronation day, celebrate real historical events.

The introduction of brass casting

Though some historians believe that brass work dates from the tenth century, the introduction of brass casting to Benin is attributed to Oba Oguaola, who ruled Benin in about 1280 AD. Apparently he wanted to produce works of art similar to those made in Ife — where he had been fighting a war. The practice of recording events in brass dates from this period. We know that Benin must have been involved in foreign trade at this period, because there is no copper (an essential ingredient of brass) in Benin itself.

The system of government

The political system and customs of Benin were well established by the fourteenth century. Some of the oral history explains changes and developments introduced by different Obas or resulting from internal clashes. In this period, trade — the production and exchange of goods — was an important focus for growth of the Bini empire. Gold in particular was taken by Arab traders across the Sahara and the Mediterranean into the Middle East and Europe. Arab accounts from the period (e.g. Ibn Battuta) indicate the extent of contact with West Africa.

Considerable areas of territory round Benin city had been conquered and were ruled by the Bini (also called the Edo). The hereditary Obas were supported by administrators centred on the court in Benin. The Obas ruled their Empire somewhat like the rulers and monarchs in the same period in England, i.e. they were autocratic and had special powers, but were still dependent on chiefs and officials who administered the territory. One way in which Bini and European monarchies differed is in the respect and status accorded to the Queen Mother.

Benin Empire at its height in the fifteenth and sixteenth centuries

Benin was at the height of its powers from the middle of the fifteenth to about the end of the sixteenth century (i.e. contemporary with Tudor rule in England) under Obas renowned for sensible policies and wise rule. At its height, Benin Empire exerted influence over Lagos in the West, Sierra Leone, and south to the Congo River.

Oba Ewuare the Great (approx. 1440-1473)

Oba Ewuare, the 'powerful, courageous and wise', was responsible for considerable expansion of Benin, developed Benin city, built roads and a great fortified inner wall and ditch and reorganised the State under a central government. In 1472, during his rule, Europeans and the Bini first met, when the Portuguese captain Ruy de Siqueira brought a sailing ship up the Bight of Benin, and subsequently set up trade on the coast. Ewuare wanted to keep control of trade and territory, and wouldn't allow the foreigners into the interior. However this first meeting initiated important trade directly between West Africans and Europeans, without the intermediation of Arabs, which continued for 400 years. Amongst other things, the Portuguese traded brass ingots made in Holland for Benin's brass casting. Very few Europeans were allowed to visit Benin city at this time. Ewuare prophesied that one day the Oba would be deported and the chiefs would rule in his place. This doom-laden prophecy partly accounted for the suspicion towards the European visitors in 1896, whose massacre led to the imposition of British rule (see pages 215-6).

Oba Esigie (1504-1550) and the arrival of Europeans in Benin

Ewuare was succeeded by various sons. Finally in 1504, a younger son, Oba Esigie, came to power and ruled for nearly 50 years, continuing his father's expansionist policy and statesmanlike rule. He challenged the power of the nobility by making it possible for commoners to achieve power in government (in contrast to the former criterion of noble birth). Oba Esigie was a man of learning. During his rule the Portuguese missionary John Affonso d'Aveiro visited Benin city and persuaded Esigie that Christianity would benefit the country. Esigie sent his own ambassador to the King of Portugal, requesting missionaries to teach and convert the Bini, and large Catholic mission stations were established in Benin. Esigie himself learned to speak and read Portuguese from the resident missionaries, who were close to the royal court. He was also interested in astronomy. In contrast to earlier periods, foreign visitors were encouraged. During Esigie's time, guns were first used in Benin.

In 1553, during Mary Tudor's reign the first Englishman, a man called Windham, came to Gwato, the port of Benin, trading English metal pots and other goods for a cargo of peppercorns. Two other Englishmen visited in 1588 and 1590. In 1602 a Dutchman visited Benin city, and from his account we have one of the earliest descriptions of Benin city (published in O. Dapper's *Description of Africa*, 1668).

The impact of changes elsewhere in the world and greater contact with Europeans

For many centuries West Africa was largely immune to changes elsewhere and there were no important external challenges to the political and social systems developing there. However, from the late 1400s Benin's fortunes were tied to the important changes in North Africa and the Islamic Empire and also to the ambitions and maritime growth of the seaboard Europeans. During the Middle Ages rumours and mythical stories about West Africa, along with the beginnings of more factual information, spread into Europe via Arab traders and mapmakers. In 1067 Abdullah Al Bekri, a Muslim who lived in Granada in Spain, visited Ghana overland, and wrote about the pageantry surrounding the powerful king, and the wealth of Ghana, particularly the gold. Another Arab explorer, Muhammad Ibn Battuta journeyed overland through Asia and Africa and visited Mali in 1352. Like his predecessor Al Bekri, he was impressed and he noted that the 'negroes are of all peoples those who most abhor injustice' (Killingray, 1973, p14). Ibn Battuta also commented on the honesty of the people, who would protect a traveller's goods, and that one could travel in complete safety. But not all Arabs responded to Africans with equal respect, and there is evidence that Arabs were taking Africans into slavery from the Middle Ages.

From the early 1430s, Portuguese sailors were exploring the West coast of Africa. 1441 is the fateful year in which the first African slaves were taken to Europe, by Portuguese. In 1455 a Venetian explorer ventured up the Senegal River and, in 1470, Portuguese navigators were back on the West Coast, this time reaching the Gold Coast. By 1484 Diego Cam had discovered the mouth of the Congo and before the century ended Vasco da Gama had gone round the Cape of Good Hope.

Meanwhile, the westward expansion of the Ottoman Empire after the fall of Constantinople in 1485 undermined the security and continuation of the overland trade routes from North Africa into West Africa, on which West Africa's prosperity depended. On the other hand, the expanding commercial, military and sea power of Portugal, Spain, the Netherlands, England and France — their ability to sail round the coast of Africa to India, and the new connections with the West Indies — put West Africa on the European map. The West African states were strong enough to resist initial aggressive European raids, and peaceful partnership in coastal trade developed. But even if the impact was not immediate, these new developments were to alter the patterns of West African history forever.

The impact of the triangular slave trade

Like its neighbours, Benin had remained largely immune from outside interference for several centuries. However, European slave trading, which began small in the middle of the fifteenth century, developed alongside the opening up of the New World thereafter. From the time when the Spanish realised that the indigenous people in their newly conquered American lands would not make good workers on their plantations and mines, the fate of millions of Africans was irrevocably caught up in an increasingly brutal European history. From the second quarter of the seventeenth century when Jamaica, Cuba and Bermuda established plantations of sugar cane, which was highly labour intensive, the triangular trade and thus the slave trade, gathered momentum, dominating the coastal markets. West Africa started to lose its most valuable source of wealth — its own young and energetic people — in exchange for the manufactured goods of Europe — guns, cloth, trinkets. Not all the states were equally affected, Benin less so initially than some of the coastal states. But there is no doubt that this was the beginning of destabilisation in the area.

The decline of Benin Empire

The slave trade was well under way by the third quarter of the seventeenth century. Benin Empire went into slow decline from the end of the century. Although reports from Benin City tell of continuing peace and prosperity in weaving and metal working, in the outlying regions, the rot was starting. As the coastal regions on the Guinea coast became involved in the slave trade, and increasing quantities of firearms became available to the Oba's subjects, it became more difficult to keep control of rebels and rivals, who now had the means to defy the Oba's authority. The Obas and their priests became increasingly dictatorial. Sculptures in later periods reflect an increasingly warlike ethos.

Benin is taken by force and becomes a British colonial possession

There is not space here to go into detail about the history of the eighteenth and nineteenth centuries. The British established a small colony in Sierra Leone in 1780, partly to settle ex-slaves from America who had supported the English side in the American War of Independence. European commercial interests in West Africa increased, even though the British slave trade itself was formally ended in 1807. Explorers started to visit the area as part of the great Victorian push to extend scientific knowledge and the commercial and political power of the British Empire.

The history of the Obas of Benin, though still in power, is less impressive than at their height in earlier centuries. In the 1870s both the French and the British were active commercially in West Africa, interested in its rubber, cocoa and palm oil. The invention of quinine had made voyages of exploration in West Africa and living there a less fatal project for Europeans. Commercial rivalry moved into a different gear in the years of the 'Scramble for Africa', during which power struggles for control of Africa were played out between Germany, Belgium, France and England, at gunpoint against local rulers who did not fall in with the treaties brought by the Europeans. During the 1890s the West African coast and hinterland, where previously French and British commercial companies had maintained their respective countries' spheres of interest, were caught up in what became increasingly an armed power struggle.

In 1897 Benin was taken over forcibly by British troops, with considerable vandalism and destruction. Egharevba tells the full story of this disaster. A British deputation under the Acting Consul General — Mr Phillips — was waiting to see the Oba Obaramven about the terms of a treaty to allow Europeans to trade freely with his people. The envoy to the Oba requested permission to come up river but was sent back with a message requiring the British party to delay its arrival till an important festival was over. The British ignored this request and proceeded up river. Before they reached Benin City the seven unarmed Englishmen were ambushed and massacred by one of the Chiefs sent to escort them, who could not stomach the insult to his King. The Oba himself was concerned and angry at this action and immediately tried to retrieve the situation. However the British sent a large force of retribution which successfully attacked and destroyed the palace. After a trial to determine guilt for the massacre of Phillips' party, the Oba was sent in exile to Calabar. Most of the valuable brasses and sculptures were stripped and stolen, removed to England and elsewhere in Europe and most are still there. Though the British maintained the Oba as ceremonial ruler, they imported their own systems of colonial government and established the Anglican church to rival Catholic Christianity — the legacy of the Portuguese connection.

Benin is now part of federal Nigeria, and during this century has shared in that country's vicissitudes and varying fortunes.

Some teaching approaches

This chapter has raised the question of contextualising a study of Benin within a wider framework which aims to counter stereotypes and raise awareness of black African pre-colonial culture and history.

The following pages summarise some of the concepts about Benin which could be developed with children and used to plan the historical aspects of a cross-curricular topic. There is more detail about these broad issues in the outline history above, and in some resource packs produced for primary use (see page 221).

a) The historical concepts through which the children will learn and do history

Chronology
☐ work with time-lines showing developments in Benin, indicating changing Obas and activities associated with them, and marking up contemporary important events and people in other parts of the world.

Change and continuity
☐ use the time-lines to note continuities over long periods in customs, trade patterns, political organisation

☐ use the time line to note where changes occurred and what they were connected with, particularly the changes effected by the first European explorers, the slave trade, the Scramble for Africa and the establishment of trade settlements by Victorians, and the sack of Benin.

Cause and consequence

☐ work from the changes and continuities noted to hypothesise about what caused change, or to explain continuities

☐ use changes and continuities in a similar way to think about consequences for the Edo (Bini) themselves, and how changes in other communities and parts of the world affected the Benin Empire.

Human motivation

☐ why did different Obas act in the ways they did?

☐ why did the Europeans come to West Africa?

☐ why did Phillips try to enter Benin City in 1896 and why did the Oba refuse him?

☐ why did the British invade? ... and so on.

Interpretations and use of evidence

☐ Work from brasses, artefacts, musical instruments, documents and pictures from visitors: what do they tell us about the skills, wealth, culture, political systems of Benin society?

☐ Work from legends, stories, oral evidence handed down and symbolised in artefacts to think about religious and cultural aspects of society.

☐ Work from evidence eg from modern television, showing traditions which have continued to the present to reflect on what the past might have been like.

☐ The original evidence itself, from Europeans and Edo, offers different perspectives on the Empire. Attempts by children to interpret some of the evidence, which is obscure and even now open to debate, will give them insights into the problems of reconstruction and the way interpretations of the past can differ.

b) Concepts about the Benin Empire which need to be developed through the project

Politics and power

☐ Benin was one of the most powerful empires in West Africa from the tenth century or so; its height in the fourteenth and fifteenth centuries coincides with the beginnings of Tudor rule.

- [ ] The political system and customs of Benin were well established by the fourteenth century; rulership of hereditary Obas (kings) was supported by administrators etc centred on the court in Benin. Obas were somewhat like monarchs in the same period in England — ie autocratic but still dependent on chiefs and officials who administered their territory.

- [ ] Considerable areas of territory around Benin City were ruled by the Bini, who gained them through conquest and settling the Oba's relatives.

- [ ] The earthworks around Benin City suggest that fortification was needed against enemies.

Trade

- [ ] Trade — production and exchange of goods was the important focus for the growth of the Bini Empire.

- [ ] Long before the sea routes to Europe were opened up by Portuguese navigators, West Africa was in contact with the Mediterranean through its trading links.

- [ ] Trade was carried on between West Africa and North Africa by Arabs who moved in caravans across the Sahara and back from the shores of the Mediterranean and also brought goods from North Africa into West Africa.

- [ ] Gold was the most important export from West Africa to Europe and Arab countries. Knowledge about African gold and searching for its source was an important motive for European exploration of this coast.

Bini culture

- [ ] Like other West Africans, the Bini practised brass casting using copper and zinc, from about the tenth century on, but didn't have enough of these metals themselves and obtained them through trading, initially with Arabs and later from Portuguese who traded brass ingots and 'manillas' (bracelets) made in Holland.

- [ ] The brasses depict important legends, significant symbolic creatures denoting the power and status of the Obas and also historical events, including battles and conquests. They also reflect historical episodes and are helpful in understanding Bini response to outsiders.

- [ ] Music and songs were an important part of the cultural and religious traditions. Calabash shakers, drums, flutes and horns made from metal, bells, thumb pianos and stringed instruments similar to guitars were used.

- [ ] On ceremonial occasions the Oba wore (and still wears) a head-dress and necklaces of coral beads. These can be seen in the brasses.

☐ The Bini had guilds which organised the cloth, leather, ivory, woodworking and brass industries. They made clay pots and other cooking utensils and wove mats and baskets.

☐ Many utensils, ornaments, domestic goods and sculptures were elaborately carved from local hard woods.

☐ Ordinary people lived by farming yams and other vegetables on small farms cleared from tropical forest.

Meetings with the Europeans

☐ The first meeting of Europeans and Bini (and other West Africans) at the end of the fifteenth century set up trade on the coast. Though the Oba initially would not allow Europeans to enter the interior, important trade began which continued for 400 years. Very few Europeans were allowed to visit Benin city, but we have records of early visitors and know that the Oba sent an ambassador to Portugal. Oba Esigie learned Portuguese.

The decline of Benin

☐ Benin Empire went into gradual decline from the end of sixteenth century. Trade in guns, and rival groups' participation in the slave trade meant they could defy the Oba's authority. Sculptures in later periods reflect an increasingly warlike ethos.

☐ Benin was taken over forcibly by the British in 1897, with considerable vandalism and destruction. Most of the valuable brasses, sculptures etc. were stolen and removed to England and elsewhere.

Starting points

1. *What do children know about contemporary Africa* — where is it, images of Africa.
   Supplementary question — what are their images and ideas of Africa in earlier periods, compared to now?

2. *Work on old maps* — The old maps reveal geographical misconceptions, but can also be used to explore mythologies, stereotypes and fears. European people hardly knew about this part of Africa and had all kinds of fanciful ideas, as old maps show, depicting the interior of Africa inhabited by monsters and deformed creatures.

   Question: Do children think this also applied the other way around?
   Did African people know about, fear or misrepresent Europeans?
   Find Benin on old and current maps and trace the old Saharan trade routes.

3. *How long ago was the Benin Empire?* — Introduce time-line. Use postcards, pictures of Europe at the time showing something of buildings, clothes, art, ships etc.

   What was going on in Benin?

4. *How can we find out?* — Discussion of how historians work using artefacts, documentary evidence, archaeology, oral history (make connections with other history units — need for primary evidence).

   What are the primary sources for learning about Benin?

   - ☐ brasses and other artefacts

   - ☐ earthworks (in Guiness book of records)

   - ☐ remains of Benin city shows how old it is

   - ☐ traditional stories

   - ☐ accounts and pictures from Arab and European visitors.

Interrogating evidence to find out about the people and the period

- ☐ Can we date the sources?

- ☐ Who was responsible for making them?

- ☐ What could they have been for and what does this tell us about people who made and used them?

- ☐ Meaning of symbols — leopard, bird, snake — into oral history and traditional stories;

- ☐ Lost wax process itself — technological sophistication, where materials mined, craftsworkers;

- ☐ Value of artefacts;

- ☐ What they can tell us about Benin court life?

- ☐ What they can't tell us — ordinary people, women — will we ever know?

The layout and structure of Benin city and the Oba's palace

- ☐ compare current and old pictures;

- ☐ explore information on plaques in British Museum and Museum of Mankind in London — look for similarities and differences in the plaques;

- ☐ critique the Dutch painting — how much can we believe, since the artist never went there?

Europeans in Brasses

- ☐ make clear the chronology and change that this involved;

- ☐ who were they and what were they doing?

☐ ...leads into visits of Europeans and ambassadors' accounts;

☐ Drama/role-play techniques for interrogating them and looking at their perspectives on these encounters and those of the Bini.

Using oral history and traditional stories

☐ the role of the Queen Mother;

☐ the story of Emotan;

☐ stories of conquest, bringing in the symbolism of animals and birds on brasses and artefacts.

The sack of Benin

Use drama techniques to explore motives, feelings and reactions of different participants:

☐ role play trials: of the Oba; of Phillips; of the British Colonial Secretary who sent in the troops to destroy the Oba's power.

☐ stills, hot-seating.

Finally — a presentation from different groups about what they have learned — have their images and views changed?

Resources

Development Education Centre, 1994, *Long ago and far away: activities for using stories for history and geography at Key Stage 1*, Birmingham, Development Ed. Centre

Isaacs, D. and Isaacs, I., 1994, *Benin: An African Kingdom, The Story Book: traditional stories*, London, International Broadcasting Trust

Betlem, Sandy, 1993, *Benin: some resources and ideas for teachers,* Suffolk Humanities Advisory Team (from Norwich Education and Action for Development)

Eureka! *Benin: An African Kingdom,* 1994, Channel 4 Schools, ETC, PO Box 100, Warwick, CV 34 6TZ

Forson, A., 1992, *Benin History Project Source Pack*, Wellingborough District Racial Equality Council, Wellingborough, Northants, NN 8 1HT (by far the best of the Benin packs available)

Midwinter, C., 1994, *Benin: An African Kingdom*, (Topic Pack) World Wildlife Fund for Nature

NCC, 1993, *History at Key Stage 2: an introduction to the non- European study units*, York, NCC (now available from SCAA)

Osoba, Funmi, 1993, *Benin Folklore: a collection of classic folktales and legends*, London, Hadada Press

PCET, 1994, *Poster and Timeline: The Kingdom of Benin.* Teachers' notes by Cathy Midwinter, PCET Wallcharts, 27 Kirchen Road, London W 13, OUD

Adult Resources and References

Bruner, J., 1990, *Acts of Meaning,* London, Harvard University Press

Davidson, Basil, 1977, *A History of West Africa 1000-1800*, Harlow, Longman

Egharevba, J., 1968, *A short history of Benin*, Ibadan, Nigeria, Ibadan University Press

Grunsell, A, and Wade, R, 1995, Where do we go from here? in *Multicultural Teaching,* Vol. 13, no. 3 Summer

Killingray, David, 1973, *A plague of Europeans: Westerners in Africa since the fifteenth century*, Harmondsworth, Penguin Education

Museums with artefacts from Benin

British Museum, Great Russell Street, London WC1B 3PS

Horniman Museum, 100 London Road, London SE23 3PQ

Museum of Mankind, Burlington Gardens, London W1X 1LG

Chapter 12

Lives of distinction connected with Britain
Resources for KS 1 'Famous People' and KS 2
— Study units 3a and 3b

This chapter contains brief biographical notes about black women and men and some white women whose contribution to British history may not be widely known, and is generally excluded from conventional mainstream histories. As the chapter on the Victorian period discusses, the first wave women's movement provides a rich seam to counteract a typically male-dominated curriculum. Mainstream publishers are increasingly making available excellent resources designed for school pupils about these women (see for example catalogues from Wayland, Franklin Watts and A. & C. Black). *The Macmillan Dictionary of Women's Biography* (2nd ed 1989) edited by Jenny Uglow, is comprehensive and includes a number of black and ethnic minority women.

However, it is less easy to find school texts and resources about notable black people in Britain, particularly for the nineteenth century. These life stories could be used by KS 2 teachers as part of Study Unit 3a, as well as Key Stage 1 teachers looking for resources on black people connected with Britain, to include in this part of the Programme of Study. Some who might be included (like the famous African-American abolitionist Frederick Douglass) were visitors; others lived in Britain for most of their lives (like ex-slaves Olaudah Equiano and William Cuffay), or for an extended period, (like the black feminist, Sarah Parker Remond, and the fugitive slaves Ellen and William Craft). A useful source for contemporary lives is the obituary sections in newspapers, the 'qualities' as well as the Black press. The *Times* obituaries are collected and published in book form, which is normally held in local reference libraries.

Teachers who want to do more research can follow the references to further reading, or consult a good dictionary or biography in their local library. Children's resources about some of the people in this chapter are available from smaller community as well as mainstream publishers. So readers should check names in Chapter 13, which lists and annotates further published resources.

Aldridge, Ira (1807-1867) A free black American, he was born in New York and educated at the African Free School. He worked his way on a ship to Liverpool when he was seventeen, determined to enter the theatre. He first played at the Old Vic in London in 1825, but took many years to become accepted and established. He became a British citizen in 1863 at the age of 56. He lived in Upper Norwood, South London. He acted at the Theatre Royal in Liverpool, in Manchester, Bristol, Bath, Dublin, and in London at Covent Garden, the Lyceum and Haymarket. He was famous for performances as King Lear, Macbeth, Shylock and Othello (see File and Power, 1981 [includes picture], Fryer, 1984).

Anderson, Elizabeth Garrett (1836-1917) achieved a number of 'firsts' in her lifetime and was one of the band of nineteenth century feminists who struggled on several fronts to improve women's situation. The Hospital at Euston and (former) Elizabeth Garrett Anderson School in Islington, London both commemorate and are named for her. Anderson was not in fact the first qualified female doctor in England; this was Elizabeth Blackwell, an Englishwoman who qualified in America, and inspired and helped Elizabeth Garrett. Anderson's first 'dispensary', actually a hospital for women and children, opened in Seymour Place, Marylebone in 1866, the year after she qualified as an apothecary, at that time the only route open to women who wanted to enter medicine. This later became the New Hospital for Women and Children (see photograph p.157). There are a number of women's hospitals round the country which date from the following decade and are testimony to the struggle fought by women in the nineteenth century to break down the prejudice of a male-dominated profession (but check — many Hospitals for women were run exlusively by men!). She became a lecturer and then Dean and President of the London School of Medicine for Women. Between 1873-1892 she was the first and only woman on the British Medical Association. As well as her involvement in opening up the medical profession to women, Anderson was part of the women's suffrage movement (suffragists) and was on the London School Board. She was also the first woman mayor in England, in 1880 (see Forster, 1984).

Archer, John (born Liverpool 1863, died London 1931) The son of a West Indian, he became Britain's first black mayor, in 1913. He was elected thirty to twenty nine by the Progressive Party of Battersea and said in his election speech: 'My election tonight marks a new era. You have made history. For the first time in the history of the English nation a man of colour has been elected mayor of an English borough. That will go forth to all the coloured nations of the world.' He lived and died in Battersea Park Road where he had his own photography business (see File and Power, 1981).

Besant, Annie (1847-1933) was a socialist and free-thinker who in the late nineteenth century was publicly vilified for challenging the prevailing views about women's subservient role to their husbands, and the conventions against birth control. In 1888 she organised the famous — and successful — Match Girls' Strike against their conditions of work. From 1887-90 she was on the London School Board, representing Tower Hamlets. From 1898 she became increasingly involved in Theosophy and Eastern religious movements. She lived for most of the rest of her life in India, supported Indian independence and died there. (Also see *[anno]*.)

Bodichon, Barbara (1827-91) Florence Nightingale's cousin, she was a leading figure in the middle class women's movement in the mid-nineteenth century. She was involved in every important woman's issue of her time, from property rights for married women, to education and suffrage. The headquarters for her group was at 19 Langham Place, London W1. She was able to exert an important influence through the magazine she owned and edited, called *The English Woman's Journal*, which published all the major feminists of the day (Spender, 1983, Lacey, 1987, Kramer, 1988).

Chuma, James, Susi and Jacob Wainright (mid nineteenth century) The African men responsible for bringing Livingstone's body back from Central Africa to be buried in England. In 1873 David Livingstone died of fever in a remote area in Central Africa 1,500 miles from the coast. He had spent twenty five years wandering round Central Africa with prayerbook and maps, sounding a clarion call for a crusade against the brutal slavery, which he uncovered for Western eyes. Africa, he claimed, would be redeemed by the 'three C's' — commerce, Christianity and Civilisation. As Thomas Pakenham has brilliantly chronicled (Pakenham, 1991) these were soon followed by the fourth C, conquest at gunpoint. Two loyal and canny Africans who had been with Livingstone during his journeys, Chuma and Susi, preserved his corpse. Then they led their little party one and half thousand miles back to the coast at Bagamoyo, carrying the body on a specially made stretcher. The journey took them nearly nine months through hostile territory along the trails mainly made by slave traders. They disguised the body as a bundle of cloth on one occasion, and pretended to bury it on another, in order to get it safely to its destination. Livingstone's body finally arrived in London for burial at Westminster Abbey in April 1874, nearly a year after his death. Jacob Wainright, who had accompanied the body home from the coast to England, had the place of honour as a pall bearer (see Pakenham, 1991 for a photograph). Chuma and Susi were brought to England the following month by the London Missionary Society to see for themselves where the journey had ended. (See photo on p.137.) As Pakenham writes 'The story illustrated not only Livingstone's extraordinary moral power. It showed that Africans too could display initiative and leadership. Black Africa had stretched out a hand to Britain....' (Pakenham, 1991, p 7).

Coleridge Taylor, Samuel (1875-1912) The composer of many operas and operettas performed in England, perhaps best known for the music *Hiawatha's Wedding Feast* . He was born in Holborn, London and lived most of his life in Croydon. His father was from Sierra Leone and became a doctor. His mother was English. Coleridge Taylor was involved in the Pan Africanist movement and concerned with the poverty and difficulties of the black community in London (see File and Power, 1981).

Constantine, Lord Learie (1901-1971) first came to Britain as a member of the West Indies cricket team in 1923 from Port of Spain Trinidad, and returned in 1928, when he made his name by scoring an incredible 1,000 runs and taking over 100 wickets. The following year he returned with his wife to live in England and settled in Nelson, Lancashire, but continued to play for the West Indies in Test matches. He was employed by the Ministry of Labour during the war as labour officer for West Indians working in Manchester. He achieved fame in 1944 for challenging the racism of a large London hotel, when he was asked to leave because he was black. He took the case to court and won. He became a barrister after the war and returned to Trinidad where he became a member of Parliament and member of the Cabinet. He was High Commissioner in England for Trinidad and Tobago from 1962 and continued to work for race relations and against discrimination. He was made a life peer in 1969 (see File and Power, 1981).

Craft, Ellen (1826-1891) and William (1825-?1891) Fugitive slaves from North Carolina who came to Britain in 1851 and lived here till 1870. Ellen and William's flight to freedom just before Christmas in 1848 is one of the exciting dramas of all time. Ellen was just 22 and had been married to her twenty-four-year-old carpenter husband for two years, when they decided they could not bear to have a child born in slavery, who might be sold away from them. Ellen herself had been taken from her mother when she was eleven. Her new owner was in fact her half-sister, the legitimate daughter of her master and mistress, for Ellen was the child of a white slave owner, Major James Smith and one of his young slaves Maria. Neither William nor Ellen could read or write, for under the cruel laws of the Southern States it was an offence for slaves to become literate, or for others to teach them.

The plan they made required Ellen to disguise herself as a young white man — William Johnston — (she was very light skinned). They had saved up some money and Ellen would travel first class in the train going north, with William, who was dark-skinned, pretending to be her faithful slave, in the 'Jim Crow' carriage reserved for blacks. To carry off her impersonation, Ellen pretended to have a variety of maladies — she wore huge dark glasses and an enormous overcoat to hide her woman's face and figure, a bandage round her face as if she had dreadful toothache, and since she couldn't write, her right hand in a sling to provide an excuse. The four day journey from Georgia to Philadelphia was a nightmare of tension and near misses. It was not just that Ellen had to pretend to be a white man. There was the dreadful moment when William was turned off the train because 'Mr Johnston' did not have the certificate proving ownership, required for a slave to leave Baltimore. Ellen and William were literally saved by the bell announcing that the train was leaving. The station master, outfaced by Ellen's stare through her dark glasses, decided to let them go on.

They reached Philadelphia and freedom on Christmas morning and went on to Boston where they were drawn into the anti-slavery circuit of public speechmaking and celebrity. Some people thought they were impostors so they had to decide whether to prove the truth of their story by revealing their real names and owners. That would also give them the opportunity to let their families know they were safe — but what if their owners came after them? It was a desperate dilemma, for in 1850 a new Fugitive Act was passed which allowed owners to chase up their escaped slaves into the northern states even though slavery itself was illegal there. Soon the slave hunters were on their tracks. William realised that the suspicious character from the South who wanted to be shown the sights of Boston was actually a slave hunter and barricaded himself inside his own shop. The slave hunters tried to get a warrant for the Crafts' arrest, and with the help of sympathetic abolitionists the Crafts went into hiding.

Realising that they were no longer safe in America, the Crafts embarked on a second voyage of escape, this time by boat to Liverpool in England. They did not dare to leave from Boston itself, where spies might report them, so they joined the Underground Railroad to get over the border into Canada. They had a terrible journey in the dead of winter to Nova Scotia, where they would board the ship. The stage coach that they were on overturned and they had to walk the last seven miles, exhausted and bruised from the accident, through the mud, in driving rain. Finally, in December 1850 they arrived in Liverpool carrying letters of introduction to English abolitionists. Once again they were caught up in the abolition campaign and spent the next few months on the road, from Edinburgh in the north to Wales in the West and Bristol in the South. With Ellen sitting near him on the platform, William told their extraordinary story and spelled out for their British audience the hardships and torments of a slave's life. In June 1851 they visited the Great Exhibition in Crystal Palace, London. But they were no ordinary visitors, for the abolition campaign had planned a public demonstration with the Crafts in central roles. For maximum publicity, they had chosen a Saturday when it was known that members of Parliament and Queen Victoria herself would be there. Each black campaigner strolled round with a white companion, as a statement of the equality between white and black.

At the end of the summer, the Crafts were invited to live in the tiny village of Ockham in Surrey. Harriet Martineau and Lord Byron's widow had raised money to send them to school and here Ellen and William finally learned to read and write, at a progressive school founded by Lady Byron's daughter. In the afternoons, both turned teacher, William teaching the boys carpentry, and Ellen taking the girls' sewing class. After two years they decided to try and 'go it alone' and moved to London, where William hoped to open a lodging house. Ellen meanwhile was busy with the children whose birth she had been so anxious to postpone until she and William really were safe from slavery.

They settled in Hammersmith in London and published the story of their flight to freedom. Sarah Remond came to stay with them in 1859-60 while on tour with the abolition campaign, and Ellen went with her to meetings and lectures. The Crafts stayed in London for another 10 years. William worked in Dahomey for a while, leaving Ellen alone for nearly three years while he was abroad. There was a high point for Ellen in 1865, a year after the Civil War ended, when her abolitionist friends tracked down her mother Maria and brought her to visit Ellen in England. Ellen had grown in confidence by now and was no longer the shy twenty-four-year-old who sat quietly listening to her husband telling their story. With William away so much, she entered London society on her own, working on various organisations and attending smart dinner parties.

Finally however, in 1869, the Crafts decided that it was a good time to return to their home in America. They had a chequered career over the next twenty years. They bought a plantation in South Carolina, where Ellen opened a little school for ex-slaves, the children coming by day, and adults in the evening, only to have it burned down by the Ku Klux Klan. They moved to Woodville in Georgia, the state where both had been born into slavery, and whence they had fled nearly a quarter of a century before. Again Ellen set up a school for ex-slaves and she also took on community work with the women who had grown up in slavery. William opened and managed the first black-owned plantation in the county. But as the political climate deteriorated for black people in the South, they fell victim to libel from whites determined to destroy them and their good name. They were forced to give up the school but struggled on with the plantation, just making ends meet. In 1890, now both in their early sixties, they moved to Charleston in South Carolina to live with their daughter, also called Ellen. Ellen Craft died in 1891 and was buried under a pine tree at Woodville in Georgia (See Sterling, 1988).

Cuffay, William (1788-1870) the grandchild of an African slave, born to a slave family on board ship from St Kitts to England; his family were freed in England and settled in Kent. William was increasingly involved in politics and joined the Chartist movement. He was elected a delegate at the National Chartist Convention and in 1848, when the Chartist movement failed and was mopped up by the authorities, he was tried and transported to Tasmania for his political activism. (For a contemporary portrait, see File and Power, 1981; Fryer, 1984.)

Cuguano, Ottobah (?1757-?early C19th) was also a freed slave, living in London at the end of the C18th. Cuguano was born on the coast of what is now Ghana, kidnapped when he was about 13 and taken to Grenada. He was brought to England and set free by his owners in 1772. Like Equiano (see below) he wrote in protest against the scheme to round up black beggars in London and get them to move to Sierra Leone. His book *Thoughts and Sentiments on the Evils of Slavery* (1787), possibly written with the help of his friend Equiano, was a very strong argument against slavery; many of his ideas were used by white abolitionists in their campaign. He argued that all English people should take responsibility for the evil institution of slavery and make a stand by immediately abolishing the trade and emancipating the slaves. He advocated that the British navy should patrol the coast of West Africa and intercept slave ships — which is exactly what happened some 20 years later. He maintained that free labour was more productive than slave labour — in advance of Adam Smith who put forward the same argument. Cuguano sent copies of his book to members of the Royal family, but they were solidly against abolition, and probably never even read it. We do not know much about him after the publication of the book, but he is believed to have opened a school in London for Christian black people who wished to be educated.

Davidson, William (1786-1820) member of the Cato Street Conspiracy. William Davidson was born in Kingston, Jamaica, the illegitimate son of the island's (white) attorney general and a black woman. When he was fourteen he was sent by his father to complete his education in Edinburgh and started to train as a lawyer but ran away to sea. He became apprenticed to a cabinet maker and learned his craft. Moving to London, he set up as a cabinet maker and became a preacher at a Wesleyan Sunday school. He eventually married a widow with four sons and they settled near Lord's Cricket Ground in Marylebone. He had two sons and seems to have been popular with his neighbours and loved by his wife, stepsons and his own children. Davidson read and was influenced by Tom Paine's book, *The Rights of Man*.

After Peterloo (1819), when eleven unarmed demonstrators were killed by the militia in St Peters Square in Manchester, Davidson became involved in radical politics. Many working people at the time were deeply discontented by the repressive government and were discussing the necessity of rising up against it. Davidson was part of a small group plotting at a dinner party to blow up the Cabinet. There was a police spy in the group, George Edwards, who had actually introduced 'Black Davidson' into the group. The plot was Edwards' idea — the attack on the Cabinet would be the signal for a general uprising. Davidson was entrusted with raising money to buy weapons, which the group stored in a loft in Cato Street, just off the Edgware Road. However, they were betrayed by Edwards (shades of Guy Fawkes), set upon by the police (one of whom was killed in the affray but not by Davidson) and arrested. Strikes and small risings around the country fizzled out. Davidson and four of his co-conspirators were put on trial for high treason, condemned to death and died on the scaffold on May 1st, 1820. (For more information see Fryer, 1984.)

Davies, Emily (1830-1921) was largely responsible for opening up higher education to women from the mid-nineteenth century, in schools and then universities, particularly London University and Cambridge. In the late 1860s when the education of middle class boys was under review by a Royal Commission, she persuaded the commissioners to take an interest in the dire situation of girls' schools. This eventually resulted in several new girls' schools, and 'sister schools' to the existing boys' schools being established. In 1868, more or less single-handed, she collected the funds and set up a university college for young women in Hitchin. This was affiliated to Cambridge University; in 1873 the small college moved into Cambridge, and was renamed Girton.

Emily Davies was also a central figure in the women's (non-militant) suffrage movement, from its earliest days. In her late 70s she was still participating in demonstrations. She was born in Southampton and lived in Gateshead, Newcastle from the age of ten, till she was 30, when her father died and she moved with her mother to Cunningham Place, St John's Wood, in London. Her last years were spent in Hampstead (see Forster, 1984).

Despard, Charlotte (1844-1939) was a wealthy middle class Irish Catholic who became a radical and a socialist. At the end of the nineteenth century she worked with poor people in Nine Elms, Battersea and set up a child welfare centre in Currie Street. She took a particular interest in mothers and children in the Lambeth workhouses. She also established 'Despard Clubs' for poor children in her own house in Wandsworth, South London. She provided pots and pans, tables and benches for school dinners herself, when the School Board would not vote money for this purpose. She became involved in the militant suffragette movement when it was first formed, but broke away quite early to form the Women's Freedom League, objecting to Christabel and Emmeline Pankhursts' autocratic style and military discipline in the WSPU. Influenced by Gandhi's ideas of non-violent resistance, the WFL took a pacifist stand in the Great War. When women over 30 were granted the vote after the war, Despard stood for Parliament for Battersea, but was unsuccessful. Late in life she went to live in Ireland, sharing a house with Maud Gonne. She was a firm supporter of Irish freedom and Sinn Fein. After the war, she continued to be part of the international peace movement and in the thirties, along with Sylvia Pankhurst, Ellen Wilkinson, Vera Brittain and others, was in the British section of the Women's World Committee against War and Fascism. In 1935, at the age of 91 she spoke in an Anti-Nazi rally in Hyde Park. As well as opposing fascism, this Women's anti-fascist group produced a women's charter asserting the right of married women to work and to obtain birth control at local clinics. Despard was considered eccentric in her old age and died bankrupt, having given most of her money to progressive causes (See Mulvihill, 1989).

Earhart, Amelia (1898-1937) was an American woman who was determined to become an aviator at a time when such vocations were very difficult for women to enter. In 1928 she became the first woman aviator to fly across the Atlantic, and in 1932 she flew the Atlantic solo. She established a number of flying records before disappearing in 1937 on a round-the-world flight. Her husband received a letter after her death which said that 'women must try to do things as men have tried. When they fail, their failure must be but a challenge to others.' The folk singer Joni Mitchell has paid tribute to Amelia's courage and adventurous spirit in a song called 'Amelia', on the album *Hejira* (Elektra 1976) (see Tames, 1989, *Amelia Earhart [anno]*).

Edwards, Samuel Celestine (1858-1894) was born to a poor Dominican family and stowed away on a French ship to come to Europe. He settled in England in the 1870s, and became a strong supporter and advocate of human rights and brotherhood and a public speaker on temperance and religion. From the 1880s he lived in Hackney in London, working as a casual building labourer. He travelled all over England giving speeches denouncing racism here and in America, and the increasingly militaristic, British imperialist interventions in Africa in the 1890s. He was part of the new and growing Pan Africanist movement, many of whose supporters lived in Britain at the time. He enrolled as a medical student at the London Hospital, but the punishing programme of public speaking took its toll. He sailed to Dominica to try and recover his health, but died there (Fryer, 1984)

Equiano, Olaudah (1745-1797) was captured on the coast of the Bight of Benin as a child of ten and taken to Barbados as a slave. He finally purchased his freedom and settled in England. He wrote his autobiography in 1789, which received immediate acclaim, and he was invited to lecture around the country as part of the anti-slavery campaign. His book continued to be widely used for its authentic and moving detail, as part of the campaign which led to the abolition of the slave trade (though not slavery itself) some eight years after his death. Equiano's story has been published in an abridged form and is not beyond the understanding of junior children. It was used with top juniors as part of a project in a London school recently by one of my students (see Edwards, 1967, File and Power, 1981 [including portrait]; Fryer, 1984).

Gies, Miep (1909-) was sent in 1920 from her native Austria via a foreign aid programme for children affected by the First World War, to live with foster parents in Holland. From 1933 she worked for Otto Frank, Anne Frank's father, who had fled with his family from Germany when the Nazis came to power. In 1942, as the situation for Jews became more dangerous, Otto took Miep into his confidence about his plans for the whole family to go into hiding. Despite the edict that ordered death by hanging for Jews and anyone who helped them escape or hide, Miep and her husband Henk agreed to help the Frank family. For two years Miep and Henk were their chief contact with the outside world, and the main source of food and other supplies (including books) to the seven and later eight people hidden in the annexe at the back of Otto's business premises at 263 Prinsengracht.

More than 20,000 Dutch people helped to hide Jews and other fugitives from the Nazis during the war. Like everyone who made this stand, Miep and Henk ran considerable risks every day in their attempt to save the lives of the Jewish families in the annexe — the Franks, the van Daans, and Dr Albert Dussel. They used illegal ration cards to buy food, smuggled rubbish and ashes out of the building, and brought in extra clothing through the freezing winter of 1942, always under the watchful eyes of the 'Green Police' and Dutch collaborators. Signs were everywhere, ordering death to people in the Dutch Resistance, and anyone caught hiding Jews. In the spring of 1943 the Gieses took a refugee into their own home, compounding the danger to themselves.

On August 4th, 1944 the Jews in the annexe were betrayed and arrested, and taken away to concentration camps; it was Miep who saved Anne's diary. When Otto, the only survivor, returned after the war, he lived with Miep and Henk for seven years, before moving to Switzerland. (See Gies, 1987, Pettit, 1993; contact Anne Frank Educational Trust.)

Hobhouse, Emily (1860-1926) exposed conditions in the concentration camps in the Boer War. The daughter of a Liberal Anglican archdeacon, she became involved in an organisation of Liberal and Fabian women concerned with working women's wages and conditions. She joined the South African Conciliation Committee, formed to condemn and try and end the involvement of the British in the Boer War. When the news of the scorched-earth policy, farm burning and incarceration of Boer women and children in British-run concentration camps reached England, she formed the South African Women and Children Distress Fund and decided to sail personally to South Africa to deliver the funds she had collected.

She travelled to Bloemfontein and visited some of the camps. When she returned to England, she published her reports from the camps; these raised questions in the House and initiated condemnation of what were now called atrocities. Her message was that women — non-combatants — bear the brunt of war. The imperialist and patriotic Liberal suffragist, Dame Millicent Fawcett (Elizabeth Garrett Anderson's younger sister), was sent out by the British government to South Africa. Her Report, published just as peace was declared, was less critical. Emily Hobhouse continued to support the Peace Movement, and was involved in a project to help women and children affected by war (such as children like Arefo Gies, starving and ill in Austria, see above), and in protesting against violence in the Great War. (See Liddington, 1989; Pakenham, 1979, for photographs of the concentration camps.)

Johnson, Amy (1903-1941) defied the conventions and was determined to become an aviator, like her American contemporary, Amelia Earhart. She was the first woman to fly from London to Australia, which she achieved in 17 days, and to fly the Atlantic east to west. She joined the Women's Auxiliary Air Force at the start of the war, and disappeared over the Thames estuary (See *[anno]*).

Jones, Claudia (1914-1964) a Trinidadian socialist, fled from McCarthyite persecution in the United States in 1955, and made her home first in Notting Hill and later in Hampstead. She founded the Carnival, was founder-editor of the *West Indian Gazette*, active against racism in Britain, and part of the anti-bomb movement in the early 1960s till her premature death in 1964, shortly before her fiftieth birthday. She is buried in Highgate Cemetery, next to Karl Marx (see Chapter 13 for books about her).

Kingsley, Mary (1862-1900) was the niece of Charles Kingsley, famous for his novels and social tracts (including *The Water Babies*, a moralistic tale for children). Mary's father, George was a doctor who spent his life roaming the world collecting curios and from him Mary learned natural history and acquired a fascination for distant places and strange adventures. Orphaned at the age of thirty, she had a little money and no ties. So against all conventions and advice, she took off for the coast of West Africa, to be an explorer and collect specimens of rare fish.

Her explorations were remarkable not for new discoveries, but because this rather sheltered middle class woman, without any knowledge of the language, people or places she was going to, seems to have been oblivious to the prevailing conventions about femininity, extremely independent even by today's standards, and apparently quite fearless. Quite unsuitably for the heat, swamp and jungle of the Congo and Cameroon, she always dressed in button boots, heavy Victorian long dress with petticoats, and a neat little hat. She went everywhere without any European companions through dangerous and inhospitable terrain, hiring African guides to take her where she had decided to go, and learning enough of the local language to get by. She traded in oil and rubber and brought back specimens for the British Museum. She had many adventures, such as sleeping in a tent along with the wizened head of her host's enemy. She waded rivers, encountered crocodiles, caught snakes, got soaked to the skin in jungle storms, ate whatever was going, determinedly climbed a mountain when even her guides had lost heart, and learned to sail. Nothing seemed to phase her.

Though she is sometimes condescending, she was an outspoken critic of moralistic judgmental Europeans who, she claimed, understood little about the African society they condemned and wished to convert. Though she clearly thought trade in West Africa was 'a good thing' and that Africans would benefit from European technical knowhow, she questioned the destruction of African mores and imposition of European ways. She argued that Africans were not childlike, but full of common sense and mental acuity.

She achieved considerable fame back in England, where she gave talks at the Royal Geographical Society, following the publication of her *Travels in West Africa* in 1897. In 1900 she had decided to 'make herself useful' in the Boer War and sailed for Cape Town. Although she was critical of the British in Africa, she did believe in the Imperialist ideal and was not pro-Boer (unlike Emily Hobhouse, see above). Presenting herself to the Principal Medical Officer for the Army, she was asked to nurse sick Boer prisoners detained at Simonstown. She died of typhoid and dysentery a few months later, and was buried at sea (see Birkett, 1991, Kingsley, 1993, Chandler, 1994, for children's biographical notes).

Moody, Dr Harold (?-1947) the founder of the League of Coloured Peoples was a Jamaican doctor who specialised in opthalmics. He came to London to study medicine in 1880 and qualified, but colour prejudice prevented him working in his specialism in Britain, and he became a family doctor in Peckham, South London. He was a devout Christian, and member, then president of the London Missionary Society. He lived in Queen's Road, Peckham. His house was a centre for black people in Britain and black visitors (see File and Power, 1981).

Naoroji, Dr Dadabhai (1825-1916) was born in Bombay and came to England in 1855 as part of an Indian commercial firm involved in importing cotton. He set up his own business in 1859. He quickly became involved in academic life in England and, at the age of 29 became the first Indian professor of mathematics and natural philosophy (at University College London). An Indian nationalist, he soon started to agitate against discriminatory recruitment to the newly formed Indian Civil Service. He believed in India for the Indians, and formed the London Indian Society with the intention of promoting mutual understanding. He first stood for Parliament in 1886. The Prime Minister, Lord Salisbury declared publicly that 'however great the progress of mankind as been, and however far we have advanced in overcoming prejudices, I doubt if we have yet got to that point of view where a British constituency would elect a black man'. The insult propelled Naoroji to instant celebrity. Though he failed to get elected on that occasion, he became the first Indian member of the House of Commons in 1892, standing as Liberal MP for Finsbury Central in London.

Naoroji supported women's suffrage and Irish Home Rule, major national issues of the time. He was instrumental in the formation of the Indian National Congress, and devoted considerable energy to campaigns to inform British people about the situation in India, and in particular the links between political domination and economic exploitation. Gandhi, who was in England from 1888-1892, was among his friends. (For other notable Indians in Britain at the time, and more about Naoroji, see Fryer, 1984, Visram, 1987, 1995.)

Pankhurst, Sylvia (1882-1960) Emmeline's second daughter and Christabel's sister, was initially an active member of the militant suffragette movement, the WSPU (Women's Social and Political Union). She trained as an artist and designed many of the striking posters, banners and badges that helped to publicise and give the WSPU its image of disciplined, organised cohesion. In 1912 she went to live in Bow in East London and became involved with the socialist movement. Like other former suffragettes, she became increasingly disenchanted with her mother and sister's autocratic and militaristic strategies in the WSPU. In 1913 she split from them to found a pacifist, socialist suffrage movement, the

ELFS (the East London Federation of Suffragettes); Christabel responded by expelling the ELFS from the WSPU. The ELFS published its own journal called the *Woman's Dreadnought* (later the *Workers' Dreadnought*). As Editor of the *Workers' Dreadnought*, Sylvia Pankhurst was the first to publish and give a regular column to a black journalist in a 'white' newspaper (see Benjamin, 1995).

While Christabel and Emmeline became enthusiastic patriots during the war, Sylvia devoted herself to the cause of peace, and to the welfare of East End women. She pointed out that in wartime, women always suffered but in less heroic ways than the soldiers at the front. Financed by well-off supporters, she set up a toy factory to provide work for women, a cost-price restaurant, a nursery and creche for their children. She petitioned for equal pay for women, for maternity and infant clinics, and free public nurseries. After the war she set up an orphanage in Woodford. She moved away from pacifism in the face of growing fascist threats and together with Ellen Wilkinson, Vera Brittain and Charlotte Despard, joined the inter-war women's organisation against War and Fascism. For the last quarter of her life she became increasingly involved with the anti-fascist movement, particularly in Africa. She knew Jomo Kenyatta and George Padmore and was a friend of Emperor Haile Selassie. She spent the last years of her life in Ethiopia where she died (see Taylor, 1993, (plenty of photographs); Pankhurst, 1977, Marcus, 1987).

Pitt, Dr. David Thomas, Baron Pitt of Hampstead (1913-1994) was born and educated in Grenada. He won a scholarship which allowed him to come and study medicine at Edinburgh University, where he became involved in student politics. He went back to the Caribbean in 1938 and spent the war in Trinidad, at the San Fernando Hospital. He became a town councillor, and a founder member and then president of the West Indian National Party, which campaigned for Trinidad's independence. In the 1950s he and his wife returned to England, where he established a surgery in Gower Street London, thus becoming one of the very few black doctors to serve the growing Caribbean community.

Faced with racism and rising hostility against black people, he decided to join national politics. His initial attempts to become a member of Parliament failed, some believe because of the colour of his skin, but he was elected to the LCC as member for Hackney. He remained on the Council when it became the GLC and was its Chair in 1974-5. He fought for the rights of oppressed communities, black and poor. In the 1960s he was Chair of the Campaign against Racial Discrimination, and in 1977 Chair of the Community Relations Commission. From 1979 he was Chair of the charity Shelter. He gained eminence in the medical world, and became president of the prestigious British Medical Association in 1985. He was awarded the title Lord Pitt in 1975 and went up to the House of Lords, but maintained his medical practice. One of his last public acts was to protest in the House of Lords against the immigration authorities' refusal in 1993 to allow Jamaican visitors who had arrived at Heathrow to spend Christmas with their relatives and friends (*Guardian* obituary, 19.12.94).

Prince, Mary (1788-?) was the first black British woman to escape from slavery and publish a record of her life story. Her autobiography gives a vivid account of the torments of slavery in the Caribbean, but also describes how slaves brought to Britain, continued to be maltreated. Prince's story was used as part of the British anti-slavery campaign, but is also important because it indicates that black women were not the passive, docile creatures often portrayed in white accounts. Born a slave in Bermuda, she came to London in 1828 with her owners, having asked to accompany them because she knew that she might obtain her freedom in England. She ran away because they maltreated her (forcing her to do 'mountains of laundry' when she was ill and suffering from rheumatism).

Prince was more or less destitute in London and desperately tried to survive as a charwoman. She was initially taken in by a poor working class couple called Mash. Then she sought help from the Anti-Slavery Society, whose secretary Thomas Pringle took her in as their household servant. Mary Prince's case went to the British courts and came to the attention of Parliament through her private petition. In this way her unfortunate story became part of the movement to introduce a bill for the emancipation of all slaves brought to England. Mary Prince also contributed directly to the anti-slavery movement through her very successful autobiography: *The History of Mary Prince by Herself,* published in London in 1831, in which she declared that she intended 'to let English people know the truth about slavery'. She had dictated it to a white woman, Susannah Strickland, who edited it and got it published. (Moira Ferguson's introductory chapter in the Pandora edition (1987) gives a useful background to interpreting the History. Also see Midgley, 1992.)

Remond, Sarah Parker (1826-1894) lived in England between 1859 and 1866. She was a free black woman from New York, from a middle class family who encouraged their daughters as well as son to get an education. Her brother Charles was a prominent abolitionist who went on speaking tours against slavery in America and England. Sarah was a feminist: she lodged with and worked closely with members of the First Women's Movement in England, who were agitating for a number of feminist causes (for example, Barbara Bodichon, Bessie Parkes and Emily Davies). British women as well as men had been centrally involved in the British campaign to end slavery in the 1820s and 1830s and once this was achieved, many turned to the campaign to abolish slavery in the United States of America. The first International Anti-Slavery Convention was held in London in 1840. Sarah's brother Charles Remond had also been at the 1840 London convention and had supported the women's right to be part of the proceedings, a protest which failed at the time. The American Abolition campaign continued actively in Britain through the next twenty years, with many American speakers — black and white — giving public lectures against slavery.

Sarah Remond had already been a public speaker in America when she came to Britain in 1859. She came partly to further her education and partly to support the anti-slavery cause in this country. In Britain she was to be the first woman — black or white — to lecture publicly on the abolition platform. (Ellen Craft, who had come eight years earlier, had appeared on the platform when her husband spoke, but not taken the stage to speak). This was at a time when Victorian morality made it very difficult for women to take any part in public work, except through philanthropic 'good works', for example visiting the poor or producing uplifting pamphlets to educate working class children. Sarah was invited to join the London Emancipation Committee but, like other women, was outraged by the sexism of men on the Committee who believed it was not ladylike for women to speak in public. She left and soon became active in the Ladies' London Emancipation Society, which was organised by feminists to circumvent the narrow-minded approach of the other Committee. Other members of the 'Ladies Society' were well known women such as Harriet Martineau the political writer and journalist, Harriet Taylor, Emily Davies and Frances Power Cobbe, all of whom were involved in a variety of feminist movements in the second half of the nineteenth century.

In the early 1860s, after the American Civil War had seemed to solve the problems of American slavery, Remond found that support for black people's rights fell away. She was aware that the end of the Civil War had cured neither racism nor the problems of survival for American blacks and she was also disturbed to note the growing racism in England itself, which had been so welcoming of her, her brother and other black people from the States, like Frederick Douglass and the Crafts. She wrote an angry letter to the *Times* to protest against the insulting way in which the Morant Bay uprising in Jamaica (1865) had been reported, and the credibility given to Governor Eyre's brutal suppression of black people, in the British press (See entry in Chapter 13 on Paul Bogle.) A growing sense of isolation led Sarah to leave Britain in 1866. She decided not to return home to America but to go to Italy, one of the few places in the world where medical training was open to women, to fulfil her dream of becoming a doctor. She married an Italian and lived the rest of her life in Italy, where she died in 1894 (see Midgley, 1992).

Saklatvala, Shapurji was only the third Indian to reach the Houses of Parliament when he was elected as Labour member for Battersea North in South London in 1922 (see Visram, 1987, 1995).

Sancho, Ignatius (1729 -1780) was born in mid-Atlantic on a slave ship and brought to England when he was two. He was butler to the Duke of Montagu. He became a free man, and wrote poetry, plays and Letters published after his death, and became very popular. He was a member of the smart literary set in London, and for a time ran a fashionable grocery shop in Westminster. He also lived and worked in Greenwich (see File and Power, 1981, Fryer 1984).

Seacole, Mary (1805-1881) was born in Jamaica and is famous for her nursing work in the Crimean war. Settling in England after the war, she made her home in Covent Garden. She is buried in St Mary's Cemetery, Harrow Road, Kensal Rise, London (see Chapter 13 for numerous resources).

Swanwick, Helena (nee Sickert) 1864 -1939, Suffragist and Pacifist, was one of the first woman students at Girton College Cambridge in 1882, where she studied 'moral sciences' — psychology, philosophy, economics and politics. Married to a university lecturer, and living in Manchester, she knew the Pankhursts. In 1905, she was living locally when Christabel and Annie Kenny challenged Sir Edward Grey and Winston Churchill about Votes for Women, at a Liberal Party election rally in the Manchester Free Trade Hall. She said she could not work with them, and instead joined Mrs Fawcett's suffragist National Union of Women's Suffrage Societies and worked with them throughout the next ten years. During the war she became increasingly disenchanted with Mrs Fawcett's jingoism and moved into the developing international women's peace movement, largely organised by socialist women. After the war she was a leading light in the pacifist Women's International League of Peace and Freedom and an organiser of the Woman's Peace Crusade in 1929. She continued to uphold her anti-war stance right to the end of her life, unlike some younger feminists for whom fascism seemed to demand a non-pacifist response (see Liddington 1989).

Wilkinson, 'Red Ellen' (1891-1947) was one of the people who led the famous Jarrow Hunger March in 1936. At the time she was a Labour MP for Jarrow, having become the first woman Labour MP (for Middlesborough) in 1924. As a young woman she had been a working class suffragist, was active in the Peace movement from 1919, part of a women's delegation to Ireland in 1920 which supported Irish self-determination, a main speaker in Hyde Park for the Peace Pilgrimage (June 1926) and a member of the British delegation at the Women's World Committee against War and Fascism set up in 1934 as the risk of war became more apparent. Before her death in 1947, she was Minister for Education.

Bibliography

Some of the sources quoted in this chapter are annotated in Chapter 13, designated by the symbol *[anno]*.

Benjamin, Ionie, 1995, *The Black Press in Britain*, Stoke-on-Trent, Trentham Books

Birkett, D., 1991, *Women and travel*, Hove, Wayland *[anno]*

Chandler, C., 1994, *Victorians*, Hove Wayland [anno]

Edwards, P. (ed), 1967, *Equiano's Travels — his autobiography: the interesting narrative of the life of Olaudah Equiano or Gustavus Vassa the African*, (original 1789), Oxford, Heinemann Education

File, N. and Power, C., 1981, *Black Settlers in Britain 1555-1958*, Oxford, Heinemann Education *[anno]*

Forster, M., 1984, *Significant Sisters: the grassroots of active feminism 1839-1939*, London, Penguin

Fryer, P., 1984, *Staying Power*, London, Pluto Press

Gies, M. (with Alison L Gould), 1987, *Anne Frank Remembered: the story of the woman who helped to hide the Frank family*, London, Touchstone, Simon and Schuster

Kingsley, M., 1993, Travels in West Africa (original 1897), London, Everyman

Kramer, A, 1988, *Women in politics*, Hove, Wayland *[anno]*

Lacey, C. (ed), 1987, *Barbara Leigh Smith Bodichon and the Langham Place Group*, London, Routledge and Kegan Paul

Liddington, J., 1989, *The long road to Greenham: feminism and anti militarism in Britain since 1820*, London, Virago

Marcus, J. (ed), 1987, *Suffrage and the Pankhursts*, London, Routledge and Kegan Paul

Midgley, C., 1992, *Women against slavery: the British campaigns, 1780-1870*, London, Routledge

Mulvihill, M., 1989, *Charlotte Despard: a biography*, London, Pandora

Pakenham, T., 1979, *The Boer War*, London, Weidenfeld and Nicolson

Pakenham, T., 1991, *The Scramble for Africa*, London, Weidenfeld and Nicolson

Pankhurst, S., 1977, *The Suffragette Movement* (original 1931), London, Virago

Pettit, J., 1993. *A Place to Hide: True Stories of Holocaust Rescues*, London, Piccolo

Prince, Mary, 1987, *A history of Mary Prince by herself* (original 1831) edited by Moira Ferguson, London, Pandora

Spender, D. (ed) 1983, *Feminist theorists: three centuries of womens intellectual traditions*, London, Womens Press

Sterling, D., 1988, *Black Foremothers: three lives*, New York, Feminist Press

Tames, Richard, 1989, *Amelia Earhart*, London Franklin Watts [anno]

Taylor, R., 1993, *In letters of gold: the story of Sylvia Pankhurst and the East London Federation of the Suffragettes in Bow*, London, Stepney Books

Visram, R., 1987, *Indians in Britain*, London, Batsford, [anno]

Visram, R., 1995, *The history of the Asian community in Britain*, Hove, Wayland, [anno]

Chapter 13

Annotated Resources

This is an annotated list of:

☐ **Books about famous people**
   listed alphabetically by the name of the person, or by the title of the book if
   a compilation (eg Seacole, Mary or *Famous Women in the Struggle*).

☐ **Children's fiction**
   listed alphabetically by title, ignoring 'The' or A' if these are the first words
   (eg look for *A Twist of Fate* as 'Twist of Fate').

☐ **Non-fiction, primary evidence or adult resources**
   listed alphabetically by title (eg *What did you do in the War Mum?*).

Each entry is annotated as follows:

Name or title
Author, *date, title*, publisher
Reading level — infants, juniors, or adults   period covered by publication
*('Good' readers indicates that competent pupil
readers could read this on their own, but that the
book could be read aloud in class.)*
Notes about content of the publication
Suggested relevance to KS 1 or KS 2 history curriculum

African Migrations

Hakim Adi, 1994, *African Migrations*, Hove, Wayland

Juniors   mid C20th

Useful resource with photographs for Britain since 1930, information on forced migrations. Some information about notable individuals.
KS 2: SU 3b — Britain since 1930

African Roots in Britain

Mekada J. Alleyne, 1989, *African Roots in Britain*, London, Kemet Nubia History Series

Juniors, adapt for infants   Whole period from Romans

Short biographical details of a number of notable Africans from Emperor Severinus through to nineteenth century.
KS 1: Famous people; KS 2: SU 1, 2, 3a, 3b, 5

Angelou, Maya

Frank Forde, Lesnay Hall, and Virginia McLean, 1989, *Not Just Singin' and Dancin'*, London, The Peckham Bookplace

Juniors, adapt for infants   Mid — end C20th

Maya Angelou's life story reveals courage, commitment and artistic integrity. Angelou is a regular visitor to Britain, where she talks and performs. See also other books in this series
KS 1: Famous people — artists; KS 2: SU 3b — Britain since 1930

Arrivants: a pictorial essay on blacks in Britain

C. Hilliman and L. Hassan, 1987, *The Arrivants: a pictorial essay on blacks in Britain*, London, Race Today Collective

Primary evidence   1950s-present

Photographs of people who came from the Asian subcontinent, East Africa and the Caribbean, taken in the 50s, 60s and 70s. Themes: work, classrooms, resistance and demonstrations, carnival, sport, shops, family history and domestic life.
KS 2: SU 3b — Britain since 1930

Asian Community in Britain

Rozina Visram, 1995, *The history of the Asian community in Britain*, Hove, Wayland

Juniors and adult resource   C17th — present

Useful accessible resource covering ordinary and outstanding Asian lives — including women — from 1630 to the present. Plenty of carefully researched illustrations and other primary evidence.
KS 1: Famous people; KS 2: SU 3a and b

Asian Voices

ECOHP, 1993, *Asian Voices: life stories from the Indian subcontinent*, London, Ethnic Communities Oral History Project

Juniors and adult resource   Mid-C20th

Autobiographies from Indian, Pakistani, Bangladeshi and East African people who migrated to Britain. Useful source of primary evidence.
KS 2: SU 3b: Britain since 1930

Back Home

Michelle Magorian, 1983, *Back Home*, London, Penguin

Fiction: good readers, junior   Late 1940s

The sequel to *Goodnight Mr Tom*; just post-war
KS 2: SU 3b — Britain since 1930

Baker, Josephine

Alan Schroeder, 1989, *Ragtime Tumpie*, London, Little Brown & Co

Juniors, top infants   1920s — mid-C20th

Josephine Baker, a black girl from New Orleans, was determined to be a singer and dancer and eventually found fame in Paris. She worked in the French Resistance and later gathered a large 'family' of orphan children of all races, nicknamed the 'Rainbow Tribe'. A project on Josephine Baker would need supplementary material on the Paris years, French Resistance and 'Rainbow Tribe' which are not included in this book.
KS 1: Famous people — artists

Banneker, Benjamin

Jeri Ferris, 1988, *What are you figuring now?*, Minnesota, Minneapolis, Carolrhoda Books, Inc.

Juniors, teacher's resource for infants   Mid — late C18th

Free black American, self-taught astronomer and mathematician, who built one of the earliest clocks, and developed an almanac. He was invited by George Washington to help survey the land for the new capital city of the United States in 1792 (see also next entry).
KS 1: Famous People — inventors

Banneker, Benjamin

Andrea Pinkney, 1994, *Dear Benjamin Banneker*, Gulliver Books, Harcourt Brace Jovanovitch

Infants, lower juniors   1731-? end C18th

Banneker, a free black man, was a self-taught mathematician and astronomer, who struggled to get his almanac recognized; he corresponded with and was sponsored by Thomas Jefferson, one of the authors of the Declaration of Independence. In 1791 he was employed by George Washington to survey the boundaries for the new capital of Washington.
Biographical detail in author's notes.
KS 1: Famous people — inventors and scientists

Bennett, 'Miss Lou'

Frank Forde, Lesnay Hall and Virginia McLean, 1989, *Not Just Singin' and Dancin'*, London, The Peckham Bookplace

Juniors, adapt for infants   Early — mid C20th

Popularised Jamaican culture, music and art in Britain and America as well as working in her native Jamaica. See also other books in this series.
KS 1: Famous people — artists; KS 2: SU 3b — Britain since 1930 — women at work; leisure

Besant, Annie

Olivia Bennett, 1989, *Annie Besant,* 'In her own time' series, London, Hamish Hamilton

Juniors — source for teachers; needs adaptation for pupils   Late C19th

A prominent radical at the end of the C19th, Besant was involved in publicising birth control. She supported the Match Girls Strike in 1888. She also worked actively for female suffrage.
KS 2: SU 3a — Victorian Britain — public health, domestic life, work — trade unionism

Bethune, Mary McLeod

Ray Uter, Virginia McLean, Lesnah Hall and Frank Forde, 1987, *Four Women: Black Makers of History,* ALBSU, London, The Peckham Bookplace

Infants, juniors   Late C19th, early C20th

Black American woman, worked for educational opportunities for black people
KS 1: Famous people — pioneers

Bi Sheng

S.Z. Zhong, 1984, *Ancient China's Scientists*, The Commercial Press Ltd, Hong Kong

Juniors, adapt for infants, teacher's resource   Roughly 1040 AD

Invented moveable type made of baked clay, which revolutionised process of printing, compared to earlier carved wood blocks process. From C13th this was introduced to other parts of world.
KS 1: Famous people — inventors, scientists

Bishop, Isabella Bird (1831-1904)

Anne Gatti, 1988, *Isabella Bird Bishop,* 'In her own time' series, London, Hamish Hamilton

Juniors and adult resource   C19th

Bishop was a Victorian middle class woman who travelled alone in many different parts of the world, with little regard for comfort or convention. She was a competent and talented photographer, recording the places and people she met, and wrote travel diaries which achieved fame in her own lifetime. Plenty of illustrations.
KS 1: Famous people — explorers and pioneers; KS 2: SU 3a — Victorians

Black American scientists and inventors

Eugene Winslow, 1975, *Black Americans in the founding of our nation*, Chicago, Afro-American Publishing Co Inc.

Resource for primary teachers, text for able juniors   C18th — C20th

A salute to black scientists and inventors, in C18th, C19th and C20th. African-Americans involved in USA history — mainly after 1770 but some from earlier.

KS 1: Famous people — inventors and pioneers

Black heroes and heroines

Wade Hudson and Valerie Wilson Wesley, 1988, *Afro Bets Book of Black Heroes from A — Z, An Introduction to Important Black Achievers*, Orange, New Jersey, Just Us Books

Juniors, adapt for infants   C18th — C20th

49 men and women who have excelled in different spheres — one page per person.

KS 1: Famous people; notable local and national past events, including in other countries

'Black Saturday'

L. Miller and H. Bloch, (eds) 1984, *'Black Saturday', the first day of the Blitz — East London memories of September 7th 1940*, London, THAP

Juniors, primary evidence   WW2

Graphic accounts, good pictures and reading level simple enough for children

KS 2: SU 3b — Britain since 1930

Black scientists and inventors

Empak Enterprises, Inc, 1985, *A Salute to Black Scientists and Inventors*, Chicago, Empak Publishing Co

Teachers' resource   Mid C18th — mid C20th

Eighteen men who have contributed to scientific and medical advances over two centuries.

KS 1: Famous people — inventors, pioneers

Black Settlers in Britain 1555-1958

Nigel File and Chris Power, 1981, *Black Settlers in Britain, 1555-1958*, Oxford, Heinemann Educational Books

Top juniors, adult resource   Tudors — mid C20th

Excellent primary sources, including drawings, cartoons, documents on the presence of black people in Britain. Short biographies of such as Equiano, Cuguano, Cuffay, Dr Harold Moody. Indispensable resource for teachers.

KS 1: Famous people — pioneers; KS 2: SU 2, 3a, 3b, 5

Black Women in Britain
Jacqueline Harriott, 1992, *Black Women in Britain*, 'Women Making History' Series, London, Batsford

Resource for teachers, upper juniors   Mid-C20th

Resource for black women's involvement in the war; lives of black women in post-war Britain.
KS 2: SU 3b — Britain since 1930 — impact of WW2, changes in roles of men and women

Bly, Nellie
Sue Davidson, 1992, *Getting the Real Story*, 'Women who Dared' Series, Seattle, Washington, The Seal Press

Top juniors, source for KS 1 teachers   End C19th, early C20th

Courageous journalist involved in social investigation; beat Jules Verne's 'Round the World in 80 days' record. Useful background resource to support *'Nothing is Impossible'* — children's version on Nellie Bly.
KS 1: Famous people — Pioneers

Bly, Nellie
Judy Carlson, 1989, *'Nothing is Impossible' said Nellie Bly*, Milwawkee, Raintree Publishers

Infants, juniors   Late C19th

In 1888, aged 20, Nellie Bly was breaking all the conventions and working as a journalist for a New York newspaper. In 1889 she took up the challenge to beat the 80 day Round the World Record — and did it! In this book the story ends there, but her life as a mature reporter is also worth exploring with older children.
KS 1: Famous people — pioneers

Bogle, Paul and Gordon, George William (? -1865)
Mary Dixon, 1990, *The Morant Bay Rebellion: the story of George William Gordon and Paul Bogle*, Birmingham, Handprint, Jamal Heritage Readers

Juniors   Mid-C19th

The story of the Morant Bay Rebellion, 1865, in which Bogle and Gordon, both Baptist preachers lost their lives. The Morant Bay Rebellion created a stir in Britain and considerable disquiet. Sarah Parker Remond (see *[biog]*) wrote to the *Times* about Eyre. Questions were asked in the House, Governor Eyre removed from office and improvements made in the colonial government of Jamaica.
KS 1: Notable local and national past events, including in other countries;
KS 2: SU 3a — Victorian Britain

Boudicaa
Jayne Woodhouse, 1991, *Boudicaa*, History Stories Set A, London, Ginn

Infants, young juniors   AD 65

Very simplified version for infants of Boudicaa's leadership of the Iceni against the Romans.
KS 1: Famous people; KS 2: SU 1 — Romans

Boudicaa

Ian Andrews, 1987, *Boudicaa against Rome*, Cambridge, Cambridge University Press

Juniors, adapt for infants   AD 65

The story of the famous leader of the Iceni who challenged the might of the Romans and was only defeated after destroying several of their newly established British towns.
KS 1: Famous people — rulers; KS 2: SU 1 — Romans

British Empire (Beginnings)

Sue Mullard, 1994, *The British Empire (Beginnings)* Wolf Pack W14, Huntingdon, Cambs., Elm Publications

Junior resource pack — primary evidence   C15th, C16th and C17th

Excellent resource to support work on wider connections in Tudor period; reproductions of maps from the period; information on food and beverages brought from New World eg, coffee, sugar; information on wool trade, slave trade, Drake, Raleigh.
KS 2: SU 2 — Tudor Times

British Empire (Expansion)

Richard Worsnop, 1994, *The British Empire (Expansion)* Wolf Pack W15, Huntington, Cambs., Elm Publications

Juniors, resource pack, primary evidence.   C18th, C19th, C20th

Excellent resource supporting SU 3a, with information about extension of empire into India, South and East Africa, Autralasia in C19th. Useful map showing extent of Empire at end of C19th.
KS 2: SU 3a — Victorian Britain

Cai Lun

S.Z. Zhong, 1984, *Ancient China's Scientists*, The Commercial Press Ltd. Hong Kong

Juniors, adapt for infants, teacher's resource   First Century AD

Invented paper and reported invention to Emperor of China in AD 105
KS 1: Famous people — inventors

Carson, Rachel (1907-1964)

Leila Foster, 1990, *The story of Rachel Carson and the environmental movement,* Chicago, Children's Press

Juniors, adapt for infants   C20th

Carson was a scientist and marine biologist who worked on the dangers of pesticides to the environment. Her book *Silent Spring* gained her international recognition and marked a change in official policy in the USA towards the environment, which spread round the world.
KS 1: Famous people — pioneers; KS 2: support for geographical work on environment

Cavell, Edith (1865-1915)

Nigel Richardson, 1985, *Edith Cavell*, Profiles Series, London, Hamish Hamilton

Juniors, resource for teachers   Late C19th — early C20th

After a happy, rural, middle class childhood, Cavell began nursing in the London Hospital, East End at the turn of the century. She established a Red Cross clinic in Brussels during WW1 and stayed on after the German invasion, helping British soldiers escape back to England. Executed by the Germans as an informer in 1915.

KS 1: Famous people — pioneers, people of courage; KS 2: SU 3a — Victorian Britain, public health and medicine

Coleridge Taylor, Samuel

Frank Forde, Lesnay Hall and Virginia McLean, 1989, *Not Just Singin' and Dancin'*, London, The Peckham Bookplace

Juniors, adapt for infants   Late C19th — early C20th

Father a doctor from Sierra Leone, mother English. Studied classical music. Friends with Longfellow, Put *Hiawatha's Wedding Feast* to music. His operas and musicals were seldom off the English stage in the early C20th. See also other books in this series

KS 1: Famous people — artists; KS 2: SU 3a — Victorian Britain, music

Dagger in the Sky

Alan Gibbons, 1992, *Dagger in the Sky*, London, Dent

Fiction: junior good readers   early C19th

Not strictly Victorian, since it deals with events in the second decade of the nineteenth century before Victoria came to the throne, but well worth reading for an introduction to life in a working class community in the early Victorian era. Set in the textile country of the North of England among cloth weavers, it tells about the famous Luddite uprisings in which people smashed machinery to register their protests against unemployment caused by the new technology.

KS 2: SU 3a — Victorians

Day in, Day out: Memories of North Manchester

Gate House Project, 1985, *Day in, Day out: Memories of North Manchester* from women in Monsell Hospital

Primary evidence   1930s to present

Pictures of school, work, wash houses, shops. Oral history with original interviews published. Very accessible — children could act out these accounts, or base drama on them.

KS 2: SU 3b — Britain since 1930; SU 5 — Local Study

Double Image

Pat Moon, 1993, *Double Image*, London, Orchard Books

Fiction: good junior readers   1960s

A boy discovers some faded photographs and a suitcase full of books and papers and the story of the boy whose things they were — a child in the 60s — gradually unfolds.

KS 2: SU 3b — Britain since 1930

Douglass, Frederick

Sharman Apt Russell, 1988, *Frederick Douglass*, 'Black Americans of Achievement' Series, Chelsea House Publishers, obtainable from New Beacon Books

Resource for teachers, secondary   Mid-C19th

Important figure in American abolition; adviser to Lincoln on Black issues. Lectured in Britain and Ireland on slavery in the 1840s and achieved an important following. Edited anti-slavery *North Star*. Supported women's suffrage. See other books in this series. More information than in next entry.

KS 1: Famous people — pioneers; KS 2: SU 3a — Victorian Britain

Douglass, Frederick (1818-1895)

Linda Walvoord Girard, 1994, *Frederick Douglass: The slave who learned to read*, Illinois, Albert Whitman & Co.

Infants, adapt for juniors   C19th

Douglass' early life as a slave, learning to read and write, escape on underground railway, brief biographical details about subsequent life as abolitionist, career after Civil War as Recorder of Deeds in Columbia, and US minister to Haiti. (See entry above for more detailed biography.)

KS 1: Famous people; notable local and national past events
KS 2: SU 3a — Victorian Britain

Dumas, Alexandre

Frank Forde, Lesnay Hall and Virginia McLean, 1989, *Not Just Singin' and Dancin'*, London, The Peckham Bookplace

Infants, juniors   Mid-C19th

Grandmother from Haiti, grew up in France. Author of *The Three Musketeers*. Statue in his memory in Paris. See also other books in this series.

KS 1: Famous people — artists

Earhart, Amelia (1897-1937)

Richard Tames, 1989, *Amelia Earhart*, London, Franklin Watts

Juniors, resource for teachers   C20th

Earhart was the first woman to make a transatlantic solo flight, in 1932. She disappeared during a flight in 1937. The book is illustrated with photos and includes material on other aviators.

KS 1: Famous people — pioneers; KS 2: SU 3b — Britain since 1930

Empty House

C. Gutman, 1989, *The Empty House*, London, Penguin Plus

Fiction: good junior readers   1940s

Harrowing — for older juniors — a young Jewish boy's parents are abducted by the Gestapo from their home in Paris and he spends the war in the occupied city, on the run.
KS 2: SU 3b — Britain since 1930

Famous Campaigners for Change

Nina Morgan, 1993, *Famous Campaigners for Change*, Hove, Wayland

Juniors   C19th and C20th

Five to six pages each, with biographical material and excellent colour and black and white photographs of ten campaigners: Frederick Douglass, Florence Nightingale, Mahatma Gandhi, Maria Montessori, Mother Teresa, Nelson Mandela, Martin Luther King, the Dalai Lama, Chico Mendes and Aung San Suu Kyi.
KS 1: Famous people — courage, pioneers
KS 2: SU 3a and b

Fanny and the Monsters

Penelope Lively, 1983, *Fanny and the Monsters*, London, Mammoth, Heinemann

Fiction: easy read, young juniors   mid-C19th

Funny and full of contemporary detail about life in a large middle class Victorian family. Eight year old Fanny is unconventional, won't conform to the expected behaviour for nice little Victorian girls, and is determined to be a palaeontologist.
KS 2: SU 3a — Victorians

Fitzgerald, Ella (1918-)

Bud Kliment, 1988, *Ella Fitzgerald*, 'Black Americans of Achievement' Series, New York, Chelsea House Publishers

Juniors, teachers' resource   C20th

Going from strength to strength since her first success as a teenager in the 30s, Fitzgerald has been called the 'First Lady of Jazz'. She has entertained presidents and American troops in WW2 and won numerous awards. This book catalogues the great period of the Harlem Renaissance and includes material on a large number of jazz musicians with whom Fitzgerald has been associated.
KS 1: Famous people — music
KS 2: SU 3b — Britain since 1930: leisure — jazz

Forbidden Britain

Steve Humphries and Pamela Gordon, 1994, *Forbidden Britain — our secret past, 1900-1960*, London, BBC publications

Adult resource and juniors   Early and middle C20th

Excellent resource with photographs on social, economic and political history; includes Hunger Marches, unemployment and depression years, homelessness in 30s and as result of bombing in war, 'labour camps' for unemployed, Cable Street 1936, Notting Hill Gate 1958.

KS 2: SU 3b — Britain since 1930 and some material for SU 3a — late Victorians

Frank, Anne

Ruud van der Rol and Rian Verhoeven, 1993, *Anne Frank: Beyond the Diary*, London, Viking

Teachers' resource, top juniors   1930s and 40s

'Photobiography' of Anne Frank's life with details and excerpts from the Diary, plenty of other writtten and photographic evidence — school before they went into hiding, the annexe where they hid, Amsterdam etc. Produced by Anne Frank Foundation. Good resource to support work on why Britain entered the war, and presence of refugees in Britain.

KS 1: Famous people; notable local and national past events, including in other countries, KS 2: SU 3b — Britain since 1930

Frank, Anne

D. Adler, 1993, *A picture book of Anne Frank*, London, MacMillan Children's Books

Juniors and infants   mid C20th

Excellent version of Anne Frank's story for infants and juniors. Continues to end of Anne's life, so be prepared for some harrowing detail. Uses drawings based on photographs.

KS 1: Famous people; KS 2: SU 3b — Britain since 1930

Frank, Anne

Anne Frank, 1995, *The Diary of Anne Frank*, London, Penguin

Junior readers, adult resource   WW2

New edition with foreward by Hugo Gryn.

KS 1: Famous people; KS2: SU 3b — Britain since 1930

Fry, Elizabeth (1780-1845)

Angela Bull, 1987, *Elizabeth Fry,* London, Hamish Hamilton

Juniors   Early C19th

The story of the Quaker philanthropist who worked to improve conditions for women and child prisoners in Newgate and on the convict ships bound for Australia. The early part of the book deals with Fry's conventional happy middle class upbringing and supports work on Victorian families.

KS 2: SU 3a — Victorian Britain — public health, religion, home life

Gandhi, Mahatma (1869-1948)

M. Nicholson, 1989, *Mahatma Gandhi: the man who freed India and led the world in non-violent change*, Wisbech, Cambs., LDA

Juniors, teachers' resource   Late C19th to mid C20th

This book includes material on the Victorian period when Gandhi was training to be a lawyer in London, and his work in South Africa. Support from Lancashire textile workers is mentioned in connection with the boycott of English cotton. Good photos.

KS 1: Famous people — rulers, pioneers; KS 2: SU 3a — Victorian Britain

Gandhi, Mahatma (1869-1948)

Sarojini Sinha, 1985, *A Pinch of Salt Rocks an Empire*, New Delhi, Children's Book Trust, available from Soma Books

Teachers' resource   Mid-C20th (1930s)

Fascinating story of the Salt March, an important event in the long Indian struggle to compel the British to grant independence.

KS 1: Famous people — rulers; notable local and national past events, including in other countries.

Gandhi, Mahatma (1869-1948)

B. Clarke, 1988, *Gandhi*, Children of History, Bath, Avon, Cherry Tree Books

Juniors, adapt for infants   End-C19th to mid-C20th

Easy to read biography with drawings.

KS 1: Famous people — rulers, pioneers

Garvey, Marcus (1887-1940)

Lottie Betts-Priddy, 1988, *The Life and Times of Marcus Garvey 1887-1940*, London, ACER Books

Juniors   Early and mid-C20th

Black nationalist, controversial politician and founder of Universal Negro Improvement Association (UNIA). Born 17 August 1887 in Jamaica, died 10 June 1940 in London. Founded six black newspapers in USA and England, and a shipping line.

KS 1: Famous people; KS 2: SU 3b — Britain since 1930 — immigration and emigration

Garvey, Marcus (1887-1940)

Eric Huntley, 1993, *Marcus Garvey*, London, Bogle l'Ouverture

Juniors   Late C19th — mid-C20th

Life of Garvey who spent last thirty years of his life in England and lived and died in Chiswick, W4.

KS 2: SU 3b — immigration and emigration; SU 5 — Local History

Goodnight Mr Tom

Michelle Magorian, 1981, *Goodnight Mr Tom*, London, Puffin

Fiction: good junior readers   1940s

Evacuated from London, eight year old Willie Beech is billetted with old Mr Tom Oakley far from his East End home, and finds in him an unlikely friend who rescues him from awful abuse. A classic children's novel about WW2.
KS 2: SU 3b — Britain since 1930

Grace — a novel

Jill Paton Walsh, 1991, *Grace — a novel*, London, Viking

Fiction based on a true story: for able top juniors   early C19th

Grace Darling lived on the coast of Northumbria in the first half of the nineteenth century. On September 7th 1838 she made history by rowing with her father through a fierce storm to rescue the survivors of a shipwrecked paddle steamer. This is a fictionalised version of Grace Darling's momentous act of courage but stays close to the truth in recounting the way publicity, accusations and bitterness from the locals haunted Grace's short life afterwards. (She died of consumption in 1842.)
KS 2: SU 3a — Victorians

Great Women in the Struggle

Toyomi Igus et al 1991, *Afro Bets Book of Black Heroes*, Vol 2, Orange, New Jersey, Just Us Books

Juniors, adapt for infants, teachers' resource   C16th — C20th

Eighty-four black women of courage,who have made outstanding contributions in a variety of fields, from Queen Nzingha of Angola (1582-1663) to Mae Jemison (1956-), the first black female astronaut. One page for each woman with drawings, or photos. See also *Afro Bets Book of Black Heroes*, Vol 1.
KS 1: Famous people — pioneers, inventors; notable local and national past events, including in other countries

Henry, Lenny

Frank Forde, Lesnay Hall and Virginia McLean, 1989, *Not Just Singin' and Dancin'*, London, The Peckham Bookplace

Infants, juniors   contemporary

See also other books in this series
KS 1: Famous people — artists; KS 2: SU 3b — Britain since 1930, leisure, television

Herschel, Caroline (1750-1848)

Carole Stott, 1988, *Into the Unknown*, 'Women History Makers' Series, London, MacDonald

Juniors   Late C18th, early C19th

Together with her brother, Caroline Herschel was one of the foremost astronomers of her day.
KS 2: SU 3a — Victorian Britain

254

Hope Leaves Jamaica

Kate Elizabeth Ernest, 1993, *Hope Leaves Jamaica*, London, Methuen

Fiction/autobiography, junior readers   1960s

Described as 'an autobiographic telling' set in the 1960s, seven year old Hope and her younger sister and brother stay on in Jamaica with their grandparents when their parents leave to find work in England. They finally join them four years later.
KS 2: SU 3b — Britain since 1930

Indian Migrations

Rachel Warner, 1994, *Indian Migrations*, Hove, Wayland

Junior resource   C19th and C20th

Good resource for SU 3a — Victorians — army in India, Indian cloth manufacturers, Indians coming to Britain. Photos from the period.
KS 2: SU 3a — Victorians

Indians in Britain

Rozina Visram, 1987, *Indians in Britain*, London, Batsford

Junior resource   C17th — C20th

Includes maps, pictures, photographs and primary evidence about Indian people in Britain from C17th to C20th, including ordinary and notable people. Photo of Victoria with Indian servants and dignitaries, as well as Strangers' Home, Ayah's Home in Hackney etc.
KS 2: SU 3a — Victorians, and 3b — Britain since 1930

Jay, Allen

Marlene Targ Brill, 1993, *Allen Jay and the Underground Railroad*, Minneapolis, Minnesota, Carolrhoda

Infants and young juniors   1840s

True story of a Quaker family who were part of the Underground Railroad and especially how 11 year old Allen helped a slave on the first and most dangerous leg of the journey to freedom in Canada.
KS 1: Famous people — courage

Johnson, Amy (1903-1943)

Carole Stott, 1988, *Into the Unknown*, 'Women History Makers' Series, London, MacDonald

Juniors   Early — mid-C20th

Amy Johnson was the first person to fly from Britain to Australia in 1930. She was lost over the Thames estuary and her body was never found.
KS 1: Famous people — pioneers; KS 2: SU 3b — Britain since 1930

Jones, Claudia

Ray Uter, Virginia McLean, Lesnah Hall and Frank Forde, 1987, *Four Women: Black Makers of History*, ALBSU, London, The Peckham Bookplace

Infants, juniors   Mid-C20th

Deported to Britain after serving sentence for 'un-American activities' in USA. Helped organize first Notting Hill Carnivals and secure Carnival as an annual event. Active worker for black civil rights and Trade Unionism in England. Founded and edited *West Indian Gazette*.

KS 1: Famous people — pioneers; notable local and national past events, including in other countries; KS 2: SU 3b — Britain since 1930 — changes in roles of men and women, leisure, immigration and emigration; SU 5 — Local History

Jones, Claudia (and others)

Jacqueline Harriott, 1992, *Black Women in Britain*, 'Women Making History Series', London, Batsford

Teachers' resource for lower juniors and infants, pupils' text for   Mid-C20th upper juniors, secondary

Claudia Jones was a black Trade Unionist from Trinidad who had settled in Harlem, New York. Arrested under McCarthy for 'un-American activities' she was deported and came to Britain. She was involved in anti-racist work in the 50s and 60s in London, and was a founder member of the Notting Hill Carnival. Helpful resource for black women's lives in Britain since the 30s.

KS 1: Famous people; KS 2: SU 3b — Britain since 1930 — immigration and emigration

Just like the country

A. Rubinstein, 1991, *Just like the country*, London, Age Exchange

Primary evidence   1920s-30s

Memories of London families who settled in new cottage estates 1919-1939. Photos, oral history, adverts for cleaning equipment etc.

KS 2: SU 3b — Britain since 1930

Keller, Helen (1880-1968)

Carolyn Sloan, 1984, *Helen Keller*, Profiles Series, London, Hamish Hamilton

Juniors, resource for teachers   Mid-C19th to mid-C20th

The inspiring story of Helen Keller's struggle to overcome blindness and deafness with the support of her first teacher Annie Sullivan and her friend Polly Thompson. Helen Keller is known for her work for the blind, but she was also a supporter of female suffrage and a radical in politics.

KS 1: Famous people — pioneers

Kezzie
Theresa Breslin, 1993, *Kezzie*, London, Methuen

Fiction, good junior readers   1930s

Life in depression Scotland in the 30s, when tens of thousands of children were sent overseas by welfare institutions, often without even informing their family, in the misguided belief that they were being saved from poverty and squalor and offered a better life. Kezzie sets out to find her little sister who has vanished, and has to extend her search to Canada.
KS 2: SU 3b — Britain since 1930

King, Martin Luther
Rosemary Bray, 1995, *Martin Luther King*, New York, Greenwillow

Infants, juniors   mid-C20th

A beautiful picture book with bright paintings rather than photos or drawings. Text quite long and print small, but language accessible to infants.
KS1: Famous people — courage, pioneers

King, Martin Luther (1929-1968)
N. Richardson, 1983, *Martin Luther King*, Profiles, London, Hamish Hamilton

Juniors, teachers' resource   Mid-C20th

From the bus boycotts of 1956 to King's assassination in 1968, with a short historical chapter on racial discrimination in the USA. King's assassination had as great an impact as Kennedy's, on some communities in Britain.
KS 1: Famous people — pioneers, courage; notable local and national past events, including in other countries
KS 2: SU 3b — Britain since 1930

King, Martin Luther (1929-1968)
Valerie Schloredt and Pam Brown, 1988, *Martin Luther King: America's great non-violent leader who was murdered in the struggle for black rights*, Watford, Exley

Top juniors, teachers' resource   Mid-C20th (1960s)

Useful book on King's life, work and influence. King's birthday, Jan 15, 1929, death, April 3, 1968.
KS 1: Famous people — courage, pioneers; notable local and national past events, including in other countries; KS 2: SU 3b — Britain since 1930 (for influence of Black Civil Rights Movement)

King, Martin Luther (1929-1968)
Joanne Mattern, 1992, *Young Martin Luther King,* Troll Associates

Infants   Mid-C20th

Clear easy to read text, contextualises King's ideals in his childhood experiences. Uses drawings based on photographs.
KS 1: Famous men and women — pioneers, people of courage

Load of Unicorn

Cynthia Harnett, 1959, *A Load of Unicorn*, London, Puffin

Fiction for good junior readers   Early Tudor, C15th

Should the scriveners — the men who copied books by hand — be thrown out of work by the new printing presses? A mystery story set in London in 1482, at the time of William Caxton, the first English printer. The Tudors took over the throne in 1485, so technically the book is just outside the period, but the period detail is so good that it would be silly to quibble.
KS 2: SU 2 — Life in Tudor Times

Local Heroines

Jane Legget, 1988, *Local Heroines: A women's history gazetteer to England, Scotland and Wales*, London, Pandora

Adult and junior resource

Deals with women who have lived in Britain area by area. Includes brief biographies. Really useful!
KS 2: SU 5 — Local History

London in the Thirties

Cyril Arapoff, *London in the Thirties*, London, Nishen Photography Series

Primary evidence for KS 2   1930s

Pictures of women and children hop-picking, children playing in courtyards etc. (Also in this series: *Blitz and Shelters*.)
KS 2: 3b — Britain since 1930

Lu Ban

S.Z. Zhong, 1984, *Ancient China's Scientists*, Hong Kong, The Commerical Press Ltd.

Juniors, adapt for infants, teachers' resource   Roughly 300 BC

A carpenter and craftsman who invented the saw, plane, drill, spade, plumb line and set square. Also invented a stone mill for grinding rice and wheat. Attributed with invention of lock and key and China's earliest 3-D stone map.
KS 1: Famous people — inventors

Malcolm X (1925-1965)

Abdul Alkalimat, 1990, *Malcolm X for Beginners*, New York, Writers and Readers Publishers

Teachers' resource   Mid-C20th (1960s)

Birthday May 18, 1925 in Nebraska. Assassination February 21, 1965.
KS 1: Famous people — pioneers; notable local and national past events, including in other countries; KS 2: SU 3b — Britain since 1930 — for influence on local communities

Mandela, Nelson
Sue Adler, 1993, *Mandela: a time to be free*, London, Mantra

Juniors, adapt for infants   contemporary

Mandela's life from childhood in the hills of the Transkei, through to his release in 1991. Uses mixture of cartoons, direct quotations, news articles.
KS 1: Famous people — pioneers; notable local and national past events, including in other countries

Mandela, Nelson
Richard Tames, 1991, *Nelson Mandela*, Lifetimes Series, London, Franklin Watts

Top juniors, teachers' resource   contemporary

Good background material for teachers. Lots of photographs.
KS 1: Famous people — courage, pioneers; notable international past events; KS 2: SU 5 — Local History

Marley, Bob
Frank Forde, Lesnay Hall and Virginia McLean, 1989, *Not Just Singin' and Dancin'*, London, The Peckham Bookplace

Infants, juniors   Mid-C20th

One of the most important figures in reggae/roots music. Guest of Honour at Zimbabwe Independence celebrations, 1980. Died 11 May 1981.
KS 1: Famous people — artists

Nanny of the Maroons
Ray Uter, Virginia McLean, Lesnah Hall, and Frank Forde, 1987, *Four Women: Black Makers of History*, ALBSU, London, The Peckham Bookplace

Infants, juniors   C18th

Ashanti queen and leader of the Maroons in the Blue Mountains of Jamaica, who resisted British slavery in the late eighteenth century.
KS 1: Famous people — pioneers, rulers; notable local and national past events, including in other countries

Nanny of the Maroons
Lucille Mathurin Mair, 1975, *The Rebel Woman in the British West Indies during Slavery*, African-Caribbean Publications, Jamaica (available from New Beacon Books)

Adult, resource for teachers   C18th

Ashanti freewoman and guerrilla leader of the Maroon community of Nanny Town in the Blue Mountains of Jamaica, who resisted the attempts of English slave owners to recapture the free community. Informative on black female resistance throughout whole period of slavery till 1838.
KS 1: Famous people — rulers; notable local and national past events, including in other countries

Nanny of the Maroons, (?1680-?1750)

Karl Philpotts, 1990, *Nanny of the Maroons*, Birmingham, Handprint, Jamal Publications

Juniors   C18th

Brought as a slave from West Africa with her brothers, Nanny escaped and set up a free rebel area in the Blue Mountains which she controlled and defended against British attack for many years. She finally bargained for a land grant from the British where New Nanny Town was set up. Nanny is one of Jamaica's national heroes.
KS 1: Famous people — rulers; notable past events in other countries

Naoroji, Dadabhai

Zerbanoo Gifford, 1992, *Dadabhai Naoroji*, 'Makers of History' Series, London, Mantra

Juniors   late C19th

Came to England from India in 1855, first Indian member of Parliament in 1892, Liberal MP for Finsbury Central. Friend of Gandhi, worked for Indian independance, member of Indian National Congress.
KS 1: Famous people — pioneers; KS 2: SU 3a — Victorian Britain;
SU 5 — Local History

Nightingale, Florence

Angela Bull, 1987, *Florence Nightingale*, Profiles Series, London, Hamish Hamilton

Juniors, adapt for infants   Mid to late C19th

Accessible version for juniors. Illustrated with drawings.
KS 1: Famous people — pioneers; KS 2: SU 3a — Victorian Britain

Nightingale, Florence

Eric Huntley, 1993, *Two Lives: Florence Nightingale and Mary Seacole*, London, Bogle l'Ouverture Press

Juniors, adapt for infants   Mid to late C19th

Good source bringing these two lives together — comparable in some respects, very different in others.
KS 1: Famous people — pioneers; KS 2: SU 3a — Victorian Britain — public health, armed forces

Nightingale, Florence (1820-1910)

Pam Brown, 1988, *Florence Nightingale*, 'People who have helped the world' series, Watford, Exley

Juniors, teachers' resource   Mid to late C19th

This biography of Nightingale has useful detail on her early struggle against a conventional middle class upbringing (Victorian families) as well as material on her work in the Crimea, reform of the army medical service, and subsequent nursing career in England. Excellent illustrations.
KS 1: Famous people — pioneers; KS 2: SU 3a — Victorian Britain — public health, domestic life, the army

Notable Black Abolitionists

Empak Enterprises, Inc, 1991, *Historic Black Abolitionists*, Chicago, Empak Publishing Co

Juniors, teachers' resource   C19th

Thirteen men and women involved in anti-slavery campaign, largely in the earlier part of the century, before the Civil War.
KS 1: Famous people — pioneers; notable local and national past events, including in other countries

Notable Black Americans

Empak Enterprises, Inc, 1991, *Historic Black Firsts*, Chicago, Empak Publishing Co.

Juniors, teachers' resource   C19th and C20th

Twelve Americans, women and men, each the first black person in their field to achieve fame.
KS 1: Famous people — pioneers

Now Let Me Fly: the story of a slave family

Dolores Johnson, 1993, *Now Let me Fly: the story of a slave family*, New York, MacMillan

Juniors and top of Key Stage 1 — 'Faction'   C19th

An exquisite, realistic, historically accurate book tracing a child's capture in Africa to her old age in slavery in Georgia. Two of her children flee to freedom, two remain enslaved. Despite the almost unbearably sad resignation of Mina and her children's story, a book of quiet courage and dignity. In the spirit of modern historiography, it explores the textures and nuances of slaves' lives.
KS 1 and 2

Onion Tears

Diana Kidd, 1989, *Onion Tears,* London, Viking Kites

Fiction: easy read for young juniors   early 1980s

Easy enough for young juniors, this is the story of a young Vietnamese refugee. Though set in Australia, her memories of Vietnam and her problems with unsympathetic schoolmates would parallel the experience of Vietnamese children who came to England.
KS 2 : SU 3b — Britain since 1930

Our Sisters' London: Feminist Walking Tours

Katherine Sturtevant, 1990, *Our Sisters' London: Feminist Walking Tours*, Chicago Review Press

Adult resource   from Boudicaa to C20th

Absolutely fascinating book about the many notable women who have lived and worked at some time in London. Very readable and gives lots of information about the women featured. (See also *In Our Grandmothers' Footsteps* by J. Clarke, *Local Heroines* by J. Legget and *Feminist History A Sponsored Walk*, by Anna Davin.)
KS 2: SU 5 — Local History

Pankhurst, Emily

Linda Hoy, 1985, *Emily Pankhurst,* Profiles Series, London, Hamish Hamilton

Juniors, needs adaption for infants; teachers' resource Early C20th (pre-1914)

The charismatic leader (with her daughter Christabel) of the militant WSPU which brought the issue of women's suffrage to the attention of the British public through sabotage against property, and courage in face of imprisonment and forcible feeding. Though technically in the Edwardian era, many teachers are incuding the pre-war period in their Victorian studies.

KS 1: Famous people — pioneers; notable local and national past events, including in other countries; KS 2: SU 3a — Victorian Britain

Parkes, Rosa

Multicultural Education Service, 1986, *Black Heroes and Heroines,* Metropolitan Borough of Wolverhampton

Infants, juniors Mid-C20th

In 1954 Rosa Parkes refused to go to the back of the bus, to the section reserved for blacks. She is considered to be the 'mother of the Black Civil Rights movement'. Story suitable for reading/telling to infants.

KS 1: Famous people — courage, pioneers; notable local and national past events, including in other countries

Parkes, Rosa

Kai Friese, 1990, *Rosa Parks, The Movement Organizes, History of the Civil Rights Movement,* Silver Burdett Press, New York, Simon and Schuster, available from New Beacon Books

Top juniors, secondary, teachers' resource Mid-C20th (1950s-60s)

Describes growing up in the shadow of the Ku Klux Klan in 1920s, Jim Crow laws, her part in the 50s bus boycotts and Civil Rights movement, fight against segregation in education.

KS 1: Famous people — pioneers, courage; notable local and national past events, including in other countries

Pawan, Joseph Lennox (1887-1957)

Multicultural Education Service, 1986, *Black Heroes and Heroines,* Metropolitan Borough of Wolverhampton

Infants and juniors C20th

A West Indian, Pawan discovered vaccine against rabies. Chairman of World Health Organization from 1954.

KS 1: Famous people — inventors and pioneers

Playing Beatie Bow

Ruth Park, 1982, *Playing Beatie Bow,* London, Penguin

Fiction, good junior readers contemporary and late Victorian

Set in contemporary Australia, this is a haunting 'time travel' book in which a young girl is plunged back into a Victorian past.

KS 2: SU 3a — Victorians

Question of Courage

Marjorie Darke, 1989, *A question of courage*, London, Collins

Fiction: good junior readers   Edwardian, WW1

Not strictly about Victorian England but set in the First World War, Emily Palmer is a servant girl who joins the suffragette movement. She also becomes involved in pacifism, because of her brother's determination not to fight. Both young people are descendants of the slave Midnight, and thus mixed race.
KS 2: SU 3a — Victorians/Edwardians

Ride, Sally

Carole Stott, 1988, *Into the Unknown*, 'Women History Makers' Series, London, MacDonald

Juniors, adapt for infants   Late C20th

Sally Ride was the first woman in space.
KS 1: Famous people — pioneers; notable national past events;
KS 2: SU 3b — Britain since 1930

Seacole, Mary

Multicultural Education Service,1986, *Black Heroes and Heroines*, Metropolitan Borough of Wolverhampton

Infants and juniors   Mid-C19th

The story of the Jamaican nurse who financed herself to work in the Crimea, earned recognition at the time, but died in poverty in London.
KS 1: Famous people — pioneers; KS 2: SU 3a — Victorian Britain — public welfare, health, army

Seacole, Mary

Eric Huntley, 1993, *Two Lives: Florence Nightingale and Mary Seacole*, London, Bogle l'Ouverture Press

Juniors   Mid-C19th

Good source bringing these two lives together — lives comparable in some respects, very different in others.
KS 1: Famous people; KS 2: SU 3a — Victorian Britain

Seacole, Mary (1805-1881)

Sylvia Collicott, 1991, *Mary Seacole*, History Stories Set A, London, Ginn

Infants   Mid-C19th

A very simplified version for infants of Seacole's nursing work in the Crimea, and subsequent neglect. See other more substantial versions for supporting material.
KS 1: Famous people — pioneers

Seacole, Mary (1805-1881)

Alex Attewell and Sam Walker, 1992, *Mary Seacole: Teacher's Pack and Learning Resources*, London, Black Cultural Archives with Florence Nightingale Museum

Juniors, teachers' resource, adapt for infants   Mid-C19th

Seacole attended sufferers from cholera in the epidemics in Jamaica in 1850 and the Panama in 1851. She paid for her own journey to Crimea where she worked with the ill and dying British soldiers. Wrote her memoirs in 1857 (see next entry). Despite some official recognition and gratitude from soldiers, she died penniless. This resource pack is full of practical activities and information to support KS 1 and KS 2 history and geography.
KS 1: Famous people — pioneers; KS 2: SU 3a — Victorian Britain

Seacole, Mary (1805-1881)

Mary Seacole, 1988, *Wonderful Adventures of Mrs Seacole in Many Lands*, Oxford, OUP

Resource for teachers   Mid-C19th

The original version written in 1857, when Mary Seacole returned to England from the Crimea.
KS 2: SU 3a — Victorian Britain — public health, medicine, armed forces (original primary source)

Secret Place

Theresa Tomlinson, 1990, *The Secret Place*, London, Walker Books

Fiction: easy read, young juniors   contemporary, 1940s, Tudors

Moves between the present, the Second World War and back into the Tudor period. Two little girls decide to turn the old air-raid shelter in their garden into a den. While cleaning it up, they discover the evidence of children who stayed in the shelter during the war. They think that one of their disabled neighbours is a witch. Through their librarian — who is the disabled woman's sister — they learn in a sympathetic manner about the history of witches in Tudor times, and also the secret of the pictures in the air raid shelter.
KS 2: SU 3b — Britain since 1930 — the war, SU 2 — Tudor times

Sharpe, Sam (?-1831)

Mary Dixon, 1990, *Sam Sharpe and the Christmas Rebellion of 1831*, Birmingham, Handprint, Jamal Foundation

Juniors   Early C19th

The story of ex-slave and Baptist preacher Sam Sharpe, who led the huge Christmas Rebellion in 1831. Though unsuccessful, this uprising contributed significantly to British commitment to emancipation (finally passed in 1838). Sam Sharpe is one of Jamaica's National Heroes.
KS 1: Famous people; notable national past events in other countries; KS 2: SU 3a — Victorian Britain — influence of religion

Shelley, Kate

Margaret Wetterer, 1990, *Kate Shelley and the Midnight Express*,
Minneapolis, Minnesota, Carolrhoda Bks, Inc.

Top infants, juniors   1860s

15 year old Kate Shelley struggled through a storm to warn railway officials of
a broken bridge and saved the lives of the passengers and crew on the
'Midnight Express'. She also helped rescue the passengers of the train which
had gone down with the bridge earlier in the storm.
KS 1: Famous people — courage

Shen Kuo

S.Z. Zhong, 1984, *Ancient China's Scientists*, Hong Kong, The Commerical
Press Ltd.

Juniors, teachers' resource   C11th

Discovered how to make and use magnetic needle for compass; developed
calendar combining solar and lunar calendars.
KS 1: Famous people — inventors and scientists

So Far from Skye

Judith O'Neill, 1992, *So Far from Skye*, London, Hamish Hamilton

Fiction: good junior readers   1840s-50s

Highland Clearances — details about why the families were forced to leave
their crofts and start new lives in Australia in the middle of the nineteenth
century. Excellent material about Scotland in the middle of the nineteenth
century and also the early days of settlement in Australia. Very sympathetic
treatment of aboriginal people's perspective on white settlers.
KS 2: SU 3a — Victorians

Stitch in Time

Penelope Lively, 1986, *A Stitch in Time*, London, Puffin

Fiction: easy read, young juniors   late Victorian

Time travel story about a family who spend a holiday in Dorset and learn
about Harriet, who lived in the house 100 years before.
KS 2: SU 3a — Victorians

'Sun a-shine, Rain a-fall'

London Transport Museum, 1995, *'Sun a-shine, Rain a-fall' London
Transport's West Indian workforce*, London

Primary evidence   1940s-60s

Oral history; reproductions of recruiting and advice literature which was
available in the Caribbean; information about conditions of service and life
experiences in Britain; photographs and teachers' notes.
KS 2: SU 3b — Britain since 1930

Tacky (?-1760)

Mary Dixon, 1990, *Tacky: Freedom Fighter and Folk Hero*, Birmingham, Handprint, Jamal Publications

Juniors, infants   Mid-C18th

The story of Tacky's war in 1760, one of the big slave rebellions which preceded abolition and eventual emancipation.
KS 1: Famous people — pioneers; notable past events in other countries.

Te Whiti (1831-1907)

Hugh Sinclair, 1978, *Te Whiti,* Pack 4 Explore a Story, London, ILEA with Collins, now available from Harcourt, Brace, Jovanovitch

Junior readers   late C19th

Te Whiti was the Maori leader who outwitted armed officers and successfully resisted colonial attempts to take away Maori land. This could be part of the Victorian study of the armed forces.
KS 1: Famous people; KS 2: SU 3a — Victorians

True Confessions of Charlotte Doyle

Avi, 1990, *The true confessions of Charlotte Doyle*, London, Orchard Books

Fiction: good junior readers   Early Victorian

Set in 1832, Charlotte is a twelve year old American girl whose father has come to England on business, bringing the family. He arranges for her to be sent home to America unaccompanied, on a merchant ship from Liverpool. She becomes involved with the mutiny of a rebellious crew against their violent and cruel captain. An exciting story for top juniors, with plenty of authentic detail about life on board a sailing ship.
KS 2: SU 3a —Victorian Britain

Truth, Sojourner (1797/8-1883)

Ray Uter, Virginia McLean, Lesnah Hall and Frank Forde, 1987, *Four Women: Black Makers of History*, ALBSU, London, The Peckham Bookplace

Infants, juniors   C19th

Runaway slave, great orator and campaigner for black and female rights. Famous for her 'and ain't I a woman?' retort to a white male antagonist. Anniversary of death, November 26, 1883.
KS 1: Famous people — pioneers

Truth, Sojourner (1797/8-1883)

Jeri Ferris, 1988, *Walking the Road to Freedom: A story about Sojourner Truth*, Minneapolis, Minnesota, Carolrhoda Books Inc.

Infants, juniors   C19th

With the support of Quakers, former slave Isabelle Hardenbergh became the free Quaker preacher woman, Sojourner Truth. Truth worked as a nurse in the Freedman's Hospital in Washington during the Civil War. She also successfully challenged streetcar segregation — 100 years before Rosa Parkes. In the latter part of her life she spoke out against slavery and campaigned for women's rights.
KS 1: Famous people — pioneers

Tubman, Harriet (1820-1913)

Ferris, Jeri, 1988, *Go Free or Die: a story about Harriet Tubman*, Minneapolis, Carolrhoda Press Inc.

Infants, juniors mid-C19th

Concentrates on Harriet's own flight to freedom but also includes material on her return journeys to bring other slaves out of the South. The Underground Railroad had 'stations' where slaves would be helped on the long and dangerous journey to Canada.

KS1: Famous people — courage, pioneers

Tubman, Harriet (1820/1-1913)

Minority Group Support Service, *Harriet Tubman, Freedom Fighter*, Coventry Education Authority, Minority Group Support Service

Juniors, adapt for infants mid-C19th

One of the best resources on Harriet Tubman; contains details of her life on a plantation as a slave, her own flight to freedom on the Underground Railway, her courage in leading over 500 black people to safety from slavery; her work as a nurse and a spy in the Civil War on the Unionist side.

KS 1: Famous people — pioneers, courage; notable international past events

Tubman, Harriet (1820/21-1913)

Kate McMullan, 1991, *The Story of Harriet Tubman, Conductor of the Underground Railroad*, A Yearling Book, New York, Bantam Doubleday

Juniors, infants (with help) C19th

Biography of Tubman from her early childhood days of slavery through to her death, including her own flight to freedom, her historic journeys back and forth into the Southern States as 'conductor' of slaves to freedom, nursing in the Civil War, and later years, including commendation from Queen Victoria and invitation to royal birthday celebrations.

KS 1: Famous people; notable local and national past events, including in other countries

Tudor Farmhouse

Elizabeth Newbery, 1994, *What happened here? Tudor Farmhouse*, London, A & C Black

Juniors C16th

Based on the reconstructed farmhouses at the Weald and Downland Open Air Museum. Detail about women's lives and ordinary domestic existence based on archaeological evidence and hypothesising from artefactual evidence. Excellent resource for active historical work based on evidence and archaeology.

KS 2: SU 2 — Life in Tudor Times

Under the Hawthorn Tree, Children of the Famine

Marita Conlon-McKenna, 1990, *Under the Hawthorn Tree: Children of the Famine*, London, Viking

Juniors, fiction   mid Victorian

Three young children aged twelve, ten and seven, caught in the Great Hunger of the 1840s in Ireland, when the potato crops fail, struggle to survive. The baby dies, and their mother fails to return. Determined to stay out of the workhouse, they decide to make their way on foot to great-aunts in a far off town. Simple enough for young juniors, a moving story told with compassion, carefully recreating the authentic detail of the period.
KS 2: SU 3a — Victorian Britain

Victorians

Clare Chandler, 1994, *Victorians*, Hove, Wayland

Juniors   C19th

Biographies of various male and female Victorians of note including Elizabeth Fry, Mary Seacole, Julia M Cameron, Charlotte Bronte, Emily Davies and Mary Kingsley. Nicely set out with mixture of drawings and photographs, some primary evidence; includes date charts and suggestions for other people to follow up.
KS 1: Famous people; KS 2: SU 3a — Victorians

Victorians

Jayne Woodhouse and Viv Wilson, 1994, *The Victorians*, London, BBC Fact Finders

Junior resource   C19th

Excellent resource; some primary evidence, photos and drawings on a variety of issues in Victorian period, including women and girls working. Unusally for this kind of textbook, includes material on Trade and Empire — India and Africa — and a few pages on black settlers in Britain.
KS 2: SU 3a — Victorians

Wells, Ida B.

Sue Davidson, 1992, *Getting the Real Story*, 'Women who Dared' Series, Seattle, Washington, The Seal Press

Top juniors, resource for teachers   Late C19th; early C20th

Black woman journalist who worked to expose and counteract racism through investigative reporting on lynching in Southern States; lectured in England.
KS 2: SU 3a — Victorian Britain

What did you do in the War Mum?

Age Exchange, 1993, *What did you do in the War Mum?* London, Age Exchange Theatre Trust

Primary evidence for KS 2   1914-18; 1940

Photographs, adverts and oral accounts of World War 1 as well as World War 2.
KS 2: 3b — Britain since 1930

Wheatley, Phyllis
Merle Richmond, 1988, *Phyllis Wheatley*, 'American Women of Achievement'
Series, New York, Chelsea House Publishers

Resource for teachers, needs adaptation for infants and juniors   Late C18th

Wheatley was captured as a child by slave traders and sold in Boston. Visited
England in 1773 at the height of her fame as a poet. Died penniless aged 31.
KS 1: Famous people — artists and poets

When Hitler Stole Pink Rabbit
Judith Kerr, 1989, *When Hitler Stole Pink Rabbit*, London, Collins

Fiction: junior readers   1930s-40s

A Jewish family's flight from Germany to England: a fictionalised version of a
true story.
KS 2: SU 3b — Britain since 1930

Windows on the World
Tom Larkin and Annette Honan, 1991, *Windows on the World*, Mission
Education Dept, St Columbans, Navan, County Meath, Ireland

Adult and children's resource

Excellent four-part series with ideas for use in classrooms, some biographies
of famous people, work on quilts, stories and the tradition of storytelling etc.
Available from One World Centre, Belfast .
KS 1: Themes, stories, famous people;
KS 2: general work on traditions, heroism etc.

Wollstonecraft, Mary (1759-1797)
Kitty Warnock, 1988, *Mary Wollstonecraft*, 'In Her Own Time' Series, London
Hamish Hamilton

Teachers' resource, adapt for juniors   Late C18th

Wollstonecraft's book *A Vindication of the Rights of Women* (1792) is one of
the earliest feminist tracts and caused an immense stir in its time. She
discusses how girls and boys are and should be brought up. The arguments for
women's education, family rights, employment and suffrage foreshadow those
of the latter part of the century.
KS 2: SU 3a — Victorian Britain — domestic life, work, education

Women and Travel
Dea Birkett, 1991, *Women and Travel*, Hove, Wayland

Juniors, adult resource   C18th and C19th

Unusual range of material, including not just expected information about
notable women explorers and travellers, but also material on nurses sent to
Boer War, emigrants to America and Canada. Uses contemporary lithos and
photos.
KS 2: SU 3a — Victorians

Women in Politics

Ann Kramer, 1988, *Women in Politics*, Hove, Wayland

Good junior readers, adult resource   end of C18th to late C20th

From Mary Wollstonecraft to Joan Ruddock, information on notable women, including several Victorian feminists. Good pictures and quotations. Includes material on education, trade unionism, suffrage, WW1 and 2, Depression and women in the Hunger Marches. Right up to date, with second women's movement, Greenham etc.

KS 1: Famous people; KS 2: SU 3a — Victorians and SU 3b — Britain since 1930

Women leaders in African history

David Sweetman, 1984, *Women leaders in African history*, London, Heinemann

Adult resource   C15th BC — late C19th AD

Short biographies of twelve women leaders from Hatsheput of Egypt (C15th BC) to Nelande of Zimbabwe (1863-98). Original visual sources and maps.

KS 1: Famous people — rulers

Worrell, Sir Frank

Multicultural Education Service, 1986 *Black Heroes and Heroines*, Metropolitan Borough of Wolverhampton

Infants, juniors   Mid C20th

Knighted for services to test cricket

KS 1: Famous people — sports

Chapter 14

Organisations and Bookshops

Bookshops

For a recent list of bookshops all over Britain please consult:

The Radical Bookseller Directory, 1992, *Directory of bookshops, publishers and periodicals in Britain and Ireland*, compiled by Eirdre O'Callaghan (should be available in reference section of local libraries).

Africa Book Centre, Ist floor, 38 King Street, London WC2E 8JS, Tel. 0171 240 6649. Specialises in resources from Africa for adults and children, but some from Caribbean. Superb photographic material and some artefacts.

Black Cultural Archives, 378 Coldharbour Lane, London SW9 8LF, Tel. 0171 738 4591. Small museum, resources on Africa and Caribbean for adults and children; some teaching packs.

Black River Books, 113 Stokes Croft, Bristol BS1 3RW, Tel. 0117 942 3804, Fax 0117 924 4634. Specialises in resources from Africa and Caribbean for children and adults, black studies, some material from Asian sub-continent.

Centerprise, 136 Kingsland High Street, London E8 2NS, Tel. 0171 254 9632, Fax 0171 923 1951. Good collection of material on local history, including from other parts of Britain; books of photos etc; some feminist and black cultural studies.

Eastside Books Ltd, 178 Whitechapel Road, London E1 1BJ, Tel. 0171 247 0216 (formerly THAP). Good collection of material on local history, including from other parts of Britain and on the Asian communities.

Federation of worker writers and community publishers, 23 Victoria Park Road, Turnstall, Stoke on Trent, ST6 6DX. Has lists of community bookshops and groups, and also lists of books which you can order direct (e.g. oral history publications).

Harriet Tubman Bookshop, 27 Grove Lane, Handsworth, Birmingham, Tel. 0121 554 8479.

Letterbox Library, Unit 2D Leroy House, 436 Essex Road, London N1 3QP, Tel. 0171 226 1633, Fax 0171 226 1768; specialises in multicultural and non-sexist fiction for children, especially material published abroad; also keeps a small supply of non-fiction and resources for teachers. (Phone for catalogue which is updated every quarter, or to visit.)

New Beacon Books, 76 Stroud Green Road, London N4 3EN, Tel. 0171 272 4889. Specialises in material from Africa, Caribbean and some from Asian sub-continent. A radical bookshop with material on education, workers' issues and women, poetry and fiction. Some children's books.

One World Centre, 4 Lower Crescent, Belfast BT7 1NR, Tel. 01232 241 879.

Peckham Bookplace, 13 Peckham High Street, London SE15, Tel. 0171 701 1757. Community bookshop with local history, children's books, multicultural and feminist resources.

Peepal Tree Books, 17 King's Avenue, Leeds LS6 1QS, Tel. 01132 451 703, Fax 01132 300 345. Specialises in Caribbean fiction and poetry.

Soma Books, 38 Kennington Lane, London SE11 4LS, Tel. 0171 735 2101. Specialises in material from and on the Asian subcontinent and Asian communities.

Timbuktu, 378, Coldharbour Lane, Brixton, London SW9 8LF, Tel. 0171 737 2770. Specialises in African and African-Caribbean resources.

Organisations, Specialist Libraries

Age Exchange Theatre Trust, 11 Blackheath Village, London S.E3 9LA, Tel. 0181 318 3504. Produces considerable amount of material on oral history, reminiscence history etc. Also has loan boxes of artefacts for hire.

AIMER, Access to Information on Multicultural Education Resources, Reading and Language Information Centre, University of Reading, Tel. 01734 318 820. Database project offering information on multicultural, anti-racist teaching materials.

Anne Frank Educational Trust, P.O. Box 432, Bushey, Herts WD2 1QU, Tel. 0181 950 6476, Fax 0181 420 4520. Promotes democracy and human rights through preserving the legacy of Anne Frank. Touring exhibition for hire, and a variety of children's and adult resources for sale.

Birmingham Development Education Centre, Gillet Centre, 998 Bristol Road, Selly Oak, Birmingham B29 6LE, Tel. 0121 472 3255.

Ethnic Community Oral History Project (ECOHP), Hammersmith and Fulham Urban Studies Centre, The Lilla Huset, 191 Talgarth Road, London W6 8BS, Tel. 0181 741 7138, Fax 0181 741 8435. '... aims to make accessible the voices of people from ethnic community groups in their own words and on their own terms.' Has archives of tape recordings and produces publications — current list includes resources on Irish, Polish, Iranian, African-Caribbean, Greek Cypriot, Chinese and Somali experience in Britain.

The Fawcett Library, London Guildhall University, Old Castle Street, London E1 7NT, Tel. 0171 320 1189. This is the most comprehensive library of historical and contemporary material relating to women in Britain. In addition to copies of virtually everything you need written by and about women, there are archives of posters, original manuscripts, back editions of journals and magazines, and an incredibly helpful staff headed by the legendary David Doughan.

The Feminist Library, 5a Westminster Bridge Road, Southwark, London SE1 7XW, Tel. 0171 928 7789. Lending and reference library of contemporary feminist material, mainly books and journals. Open Tuesdays and Saturdays. Phone to make sure.

Greater London Records Office, 40 Northampton Road, London EC1R OHB, Tel. 0171 606 3820, Fax. 0171 833 9136. Holds archives of old prints, maps, photographs, school, hospital and other official and institutional records. Essential resource for Londoners but you will need to visit. Phone for an appointment.

The Historical Association, 59a Kennington Park Road, London SE11 4JH, Tel. 0171 735 3901. Some useful publications for primary history teachers and historians generally, particularly its journal *Teaching History*. Organises conferences on teaching of history.

Inkworks Community Centre and Jankore Library and Resource Centre, 20-22 Hepburn Road, St Pauls, Bristol BS6, Tel. 0117 942 1870.

International Broadcasting Trust, 2 Ferdinand Place, London NW1 8EE, 0171 482 2847, Fax 0171 284 3374. Videos and published material on a variety of Development Education issues, anti-racist and global education.

Leicester Centre for Multicultural Education, Harrison Road, Leicester LE4 6RB, phone 01533 665451, Fax 01533 680117. Produces own publications.

Manchester Jewish Museum, 190 Cheetham Hill Road, Manchester M8 8LW, Tel. 0161 834 9879. Museum, resource centre and bookshop.

Oxfam, 274 Banbury Road Oxford OX 2 7DZ, Tel. 01865 311 311.

Oxfam Education has an office in Wilton Road, Victoria, London SW1, with an excellent selection of resources and very helpful, knowledgeable staff. Tel. 0171 976 5056, Fax. 0171 828 8955.

Oxfam Education (Brighton) 134a Western Road (Rear Entrance), Brighton BN 1 2LA, Tel. 01273 207 014

The Pankhurst Centre, 60/62 Nelson Street, Chorlton on Medlock, Manchester M13 9WP, Tel. 0161 273 5673. Museum, resource centre and bookshop — a memorial to the historic women's suffrage struggles in the restored houses where the WSPU started.

Ragged School Museum Trust (for Barnados archive material), 46-50 Copperfield Road, Bow, London E3 4RR, Tel. 0181 980 6405.

Save the Children Fund, Mary Datchelor House, 17 Grove Lane, Camberwell, London SE5 8RD, Tel. 0171703 5400.

Tower Hamlets Humanities Education Centre, Professional Development Centre, English Street, London E3 4TA, Tel. 0181 983 1944, Fax 0181 981 9956. Holds the humanities resources which were previously in the ILEA Humanities Centre. Archive collection and material for teachers; some publications, e.g. *Talking Time — a guide to oral history for schools.*

Working Group against Racism in Children's Resources, 460 Wandsworth Road, London SW8 3LX, Tel. 0171 627 4594. Produces articles and lists; will give advice.

Publishers

Magi Publications (Dual language), 112 Whitfield Street, London W1P 5RU, Tel. 0171 388 9832. Children's picture books.

Mantra Publishing, 5A Alexandra Grove, London N12 8NU, Tel. 0181 455 5123. Mainly books for children, including non-fiction.

Minority Group Support Services, Southfields Old School, South Street, Coventry CV1 5EJ, Tel. 01203 226 888, Fax 01203 525 752. Publishes dual language materials and packs with posters, teachers' notes and pupils' booklets: current list includes packs on Harriet Tubman, Martin Luther King, Mary Seacole, Gandhi, Sri Guru Nanak.

Roy Yates Books (Dual language children's books) 40 Woodfield Road, Rugwick, Horsham, West Sussex RH12 3EPW, Tel. 012403 822 299.

Tamarind Publications, PO Box 296, Camberley, Surrey GU 15 1QW, Tel. 01276 683 979. Children's picture books.

Trentham Books, Westview House, 734 London Road, Oakhill, Stoke on Trent ST4 5NP, Tel. 01782 745 567, Fax 01782 745 553. Professional materials for teachers, strongly anti-racist. List on immigration law.

Who's afraid of the big bad wolf?
by Hilary Claire

With acknowledgements to all the other traditional and alternative versions

One spring day I was sunning myself on my favourite rock in my home in the woods. I was keeping a watchful eye on my three little cubs, who were gambolling playfully within sight when I heard the tell-tale rustle of footsteps. Then into the clearing came a little girl, strangely dressed all in red. She wore a big cloak wrapped around her body and her head, as if she didn't want to be recognised. An arm poked out through an opening in the cloak, holding a wicker basket, also completely covered over with a red and white checked tea towel. I was immediately suspicious. Who could this be creeping so quietly through my forest, so strangely disguised? I quickly pushed the cubs into our home behind the rock and went up to the intruder.

'Good morning,' I said politely. 'Fine day isn't it?'

The red-cloaked stranger ignored me and, thinking she hadn't heard or seen me because of the hood wrapped round her head, I stepped right out in front of her, smiling to show I meant friendship.

'Good morning,' I said again. 'Stranger round here are you? Where might you be heading for on this bright spring morning?'

'Scram, wolf!' she cried, to my surprise. 'Scram! get away! I don't speak to strangers.'

What an insult! A stranger in my own home! I was born and brought up in these woods, and so was all my family, going back many generations. It was she who was the stranger here, not I.

I stood my ground and said firmly 'I beg your pardon? I think there must be some mistake. I live here. Please tell me what you are doing and where you are going and then you can pass on your way.'

'Get out of my way *now*,' she cried. 'I'm going to visit my granny with this basket of food, so let me pass.' Then she pushed right past me and ran off down the path, rudely chanting: 'Who's afraid of the big bad wolf, who's afraid of the big bad wolf.'

I was shocked by this behaviour and knew that her granny — who also lived in the forest and was a friend of mine — would be too. I told my cubs to play quietly while I was away and hurried off through the forest to the granny's house, intending to get there before the bad-mannered little girl with the red cloak arrived.

When I arrived, the good old lady agreed that her granddaughter had been very rude and we made a plan to give her a little lesson in manners. She hid under the bed while I put on her mob-cap, glasses and nightie and climbed into the bed, pulling the sheets right up under my chin.

Soon the little girl arrived and sat down on the bed, pushing the hood back off her face. She was all rosy-cheeked and really quite attractive and I felt more kindly towards her until she spoiled it all again.

Peering at me and giggling she said:

'What big eyes you have, granny!'

Now granny's glasses were quite strong and probably did make my eyes look bigger, and actually I couldn't see very well out of them anyway. I said 'All the better to see you with, my dear!' and took them off, offering my cheek for a kiss. Instead, the little girl drew back saying, 'What big ears you have, granny!'

Now I have had to put up with personal insults about my ears before so I just said:

'All the better to hear you with my dear!' and gave a friendly smile.

But now to my surprise, the little girl who'd been so sure of herself before seemed quite alarmed.

'What big teeth you have, granny!' she cried.

Now granny and I had planned to give the little girl a bit of a shock, and then have a talk about good manners, and this seemed like a good moment.

I jumped out of bed, pretending to be fierce and growling

'All the better to eat you with, my dear!'

Of course I had not the slightest intention of eating the little girl. I knew far better than that and there was plenty of food in the forest anyway. However, the silly little thing rushed round the house screaming 'Help! Help!'

I pulled off the nightie and cap and tried to calm her down, just as I would my own cubs, by giving her a small cuff and then holding her firmly. But this just made it worse. She became quite hysterical, beating at me with her fists and kicking at me with her little red shoes.

Granny peeped out from under the bed, winked and started to crawl out so that we could deal with the little girl together. But just at that moment our plan went badly wrong. There was a crash at the door and a huge Forestry Commissioner appeared with an axe in his hand.

'What's going on here!' he cried, striding into the small room. 'Don't worry, little girl, you're safe now. And you madam, he said to me, stepping forward, 'are under arrest.'

I made a very quick decision not to try and explain the true story, and with one leap fled through the open window.

I would like to say that everyone lived happily ever after but it would not be true. I really don't know whether granny tried to tell people what had happened. Perhaps no one believed her. I kept away from humans after that, feeling they could not be trusted. And sadly, I found that they became even more suspicious of me, and ready to hunt me down, believing the stories that I was wicked and cruel and ate little girls.

Appendix 2

Immigration and Emigration Patterns in Britain over the past two millennia

IMMIGRATION

1st — mid C5th AD
Romans, including many legionnaires, traders and craftspeople from other parts of the Roman Empire, including Middle East, Greece and North Africa.

Mid C5th
Angles, Saxons invade and settle in Southern England.

End C8th — end C10th
Viking invasions and settlement in Britain

Mid C11th
Normans invade and establish themselves with William the Conqueror as King.

C12th
Close connections with France through House of Plantagenet. Jews come into Britain from Northern France.

C13th and C14th
Increasing numbers of cloth merchants, leather craftsmen etc from Europe living and working in England (estimated 3,000 aliens out of population of 50,000 in London in 1501).

EMIGRATION

1290
Massacre of Jews in York, rest of Jews driven out of England

IMMIGRATION

From 1532
Dutch and French Huguenots fleeing from persecution take refuge in England.

1680-85
40-50,000 French Huguenots fleeing religious persecution after Revocation of Edict of Nantes find refuge in England.

C18th
Large numbers of black people coming to Britain as result of slavery (estimated 20,000 out of 676,250 in 1764). Many are freed or escape and live as free people. Irish people arriving to find work.

C19th
1840s, large numbers of Irish come to England seeking work, following potato famines.

Mid century on — Asian professionals and merchants.

1870s onwards — Jews seeking refuge from pogroms in Russia, Poland and Eastern Europe, settle mainly in large towns, e.g. London, Birmingham, Leeds, Manchester, Glasgow.

Indian 'ayahs' and 'lascars' left behind or voluntarily settle in Britain.

Numbers of Indian intellectuals and professionals spend time in England — mostly studying or on business.

Some Chinese sailors stay on in Britain, particularly in London and other ports.

EMIGRATION

1610 — onwards
Settlement of American colonies Virginia, Maryland and New England (1620 'Pilgrim Fathers').

1646 onwards
Bahamas, Jamaica, Tobago, Bermudas occupied by British and first plantations set up.

Large numbers of Irish to America.

From early in C19th — Scots to Canada and Australia as result of Highland Clearances.

From 1806, Cape Colony becomes British, and English emigrate to South Africa.
1820 — sponsored British settlers to Cape Colony, South Africa. Establishment of English missions in Southern Africa.

1830s 'Children's Friend Society' sends several thousand destitute children to Canada, Australia, South Africa and Mauritius.

After India brought under direct Imperial Rule (1858), British families sent to manage the 'British Raj'. English missionaries go out to India.

1850 onwards — assisted migration schemes to New Zealand — English, Scots and Irish, including single women.

IMMIGRATION	EMIGRATION
Some Africans, particularly from West Africa, spend time as students in Britain.	1850s — gold rush in Australia — attracts migrants from Britain.
	1860s — New Zealand gold rush 1880s onwards — South African gold rush.
	Settlement schemes to Canada for English and Scots (including single women).
	1880s onwards, British colonisation of parts of West, East and Central Africa, small numbers of British leave to settle (e.g. Kenya, Tanganyika, Northern and Southern Rhodesia.

C20th
1918-

After WW1 Asian, Chinese, African and Caribbean sailors stay on. 1920s — Sikhs from Punjab	1920s assisted migration schemes for Irish, English and Scots to New Zealand and states of Australia.

1930s

Radical and Jewish refugees from Nazi Germany

1940s

Poles in exile in Britain stay on after war and bring families	After war: assisted migration schemes to New Zealand and Australia.
1948 onwards — first sponsored workers from Caribbean islands. Caribbean immigration continues till mid-60s.	Voluntary migration to Canada and South Africa.

1950s-1968 — main immigration of Indian and Pakistani men to find work, including through invitations; later joined by families.

1960 onwards — main immigration of Cypriots, though small numbers already in England from 30s.

1960s — early 70s — East African Asians voluntary and enforced migration from newly independent Kenya, Uganda and Tanzania.

1960s onwards — increasing numbers of Hong Kong Chinese join small communities of Chinese, dating from turn of century.

1970s onwards — refugee groups granted asylum: e.g. Vietnamese, Central Africans, Latin Americans, Somalis, Kurds, Bosnians.

INDEX

Africa 11, 44, 65,131, 134, 203-4, 210, 225, 233

African-Caribbean see Caribbean

African
  contribution to WW2 165
  in C19th England 138-141, 225, 243
  in C20th England 243
  in Tudor England 109, 115, 120, 243
  slaves 111, 116

agriculture
  female work in C19th 148
  in C19th 125
  in Tudor period 107

Aldridge, Ira 224

Alfred the Great 96

Anderson, Elizabeth Garrett 72, 158, 224, 232

archaeology 43, 58, 99-100, 110, 207, 208, 210, 211

Archer, John 224

Armada 105, 106, 114, 115

artefactual evidence
  classroom collection 53
  for Romans 99-100
  for work on Tudors 109
  from Benin Empire 207-8, 217, 220
  using fiction 43-49, 53
  using museums 92, 109
  with infants 23, 34

Asian people
  in London in C19th 140-42, 243, 255
  immigrants in C20th 174, 243, 255,

assessment 91

autobiography 153, 177

Aztecs 206

Baddeley 43

Barnados 34,139, 177,193, 274

Besant, Annie 200, 225

Bettelheim, Bruno 42

bias 64, 87, 96
  using fiction to teach about 50-53

Blackwell, Elizabeth 158, 224

Bodichon, Barbara 136, 156, 157, 160, 225, 236, 270

Boer War (South African War) 157, 232, 233

Boudicaa 98, 100, 101, 247-8

brass casting 212, 218, 220

Brent, Linda (Harriet Jacobs) 136-7, 159, 160

Bruner, Jerome 1,2, 5, 41, 83, 85, 205

Burnett, John 133, 149, 160

Cable Street 200

Caribbean 85, 199
  connections in Tudor period 115-119, 246
  contribution to WW2 165
  immigrants experience 173, 243, 247, 255, 256, 265

Catholics
   in Tudor period 104-6, 144
   in C19th England 132, 144-5, 230
Cato Street uprising 200, 229
Celts 97-8
Chadwick, Edwin 158, 190
Chartism 123, 195, 196, 199, 228
child development 5-6, 9-10, 42, 46, 54
childhood
   history of 22
   historiography 133
   work with KS 1 23-4
Chuma, James 137, 225
Civil War mid-C17th 194
class 9, 10, 15,147
   working class Victorian women
      149-155
   middle class Victorian women 155-8
   and consumerism in C20th 175
   and philanthropy 189
cloth trade
   in Tudor period 107-8
   cotton textiles in C19th 127-8
   Indian cotton 129-30
Coleridge Taylor, Samuel 161, 226, 249
colonialism 84-5
Columbus, Christopher 111
Constantine, Lord Learie 226
controversial issues 205
   sensitivity with young children 16-18,
      56
   introducing through fiction 56-61
cotton 127-9, 234
   cotton mills in C19th 152
Craft, Ellen and William 57, 136, 138,
   223, 226-8, 237
cross-curricular themes 21,22, 26-8, 43,
   71, 73, 204, 209
   for Benin history 209, 216
Cuffay, William 137, 199, 223, 228
Cuguano, Ottobah 228
curriculum planning 88-9
Darling, Grace 71, 74, 254
Davidson, William 137,200, 229
Davies, Emily 157, 230, 236, 268, 270
Depression 175-8, 252, 270

Despard, Charlotte 188, 230
domestic service 148, 153
Douglass, Frederick 57,136, 223, 246,
   250, 251
Drake, Sir Francis 84, 114-119
drama 51
   about anti-slavery campaigns 135
   about Benin 221
   about Boudicaa   100
   about famous people 70, 74,143
   about Jarrow March 176
   about Tudors 118-9
   about women doctors 158
   from autobiography 153
Earhart, Amelia 230, 250
East India Company 84, 120
economic and industrial understanding
   124-5, 143
Eddershaw 43
education
   for working class children in C19th
      149-50, 193, 194
   for middle class children in C19th
      150, 192-3, 229
Edwards, Samuel 231
Egypt 6, 12, 203, 206, 207, 270
elderly people 33, 112-3
   in fiction 44, 47-9
Elizabeth 1 104-6,113-4, 120
emigration 169-173, 183-5, 279-80
English Woman's Journal 156, 225
equality 7-8, 40, 47, 50
   in the KS 2 curriculum 86-7
Equiano, Olaudah 86, 223, 231, 239
Esigie, Oba 213
ethics 16, 33, 208
ethnicity 11
Eurocentrism
   in the curriculum 7, 8, 12
   choices of famous people 64-5
evacuation 167
evidence
   with KS 1 23, 42
   missing 53, 87-8
Ewuare, Oba 213

explorers
  Tudors 108, 117,119-120
  Victorian 65-6, 232-3, 269
family history 56
  confidentiality 24, 28-9
  historiography 133
  in KS 1 curriculum 23-26
  in local study unit 184-5
  starting with fiction 44, 49, 55
fascism 165, 168, 230, 235, 238
fiction
  about anti-slavery campaign 135
  about Highland Clearances 146
  differentiating from fact 40-44
  for famous people 74
  for family history 44, 49, 55
  for Roman period 97, 101
  for Tudor England 109-110
  for working class C19th life 151-2
  in KS 2 89-92
  to develop historical skills 39, 41,
    42-6, 51, 91
Foley, Alice 154-5
Frank, Anne 65, 167, 231-2, 252
Fry, Elizabeth 155, 157, 252
Gandhi, Mahatma 65, 72, 230, 234, 253,
gender 8, 10, 205
  absent evidence 87, 207-8
  and education in C19th 149-50, 158
  and race 14-15
  in 1940s and 1950s 168-9
  in non-Western societies 206
  in Roman British history 100
  in Tudor period 86-7,111-114
  in Victorian period 146-150
  in WW2 168
Gies, Miep 168, 231-2, 239
grandparents
  projects on 25-6
  working from fiction 47-49
Great Exhibition 1851, 124, 138, 227
Hadrian's Wall 98
Harnett, Cynthia 90, 121, 258
Hatcher, Richard 13-14, 19
Hawkins, Sir John 84, 110, 114-119
Hazareesingh, Sandip 37, 93

health see medicine
Henry VIII 107-8, 110
Heyrick, Elizabeth 134
historical concepts 1-2, 24, 207, 209,
  216-7
  with KS 1 5, 22, 23, 26, 35, 39, 41,
    44-5, 46, 50, 70
historiography 7-9, 24, 183
Hobhouse, Emily 157, 232
Holocaust 17, 107, 167, 206, 231-2
  using fiction to introduce 58
immigration 36, 83, 169-173, 279-280
  (see also Caribbeans, Indians, Irish,
  Jews)
Imperialism 8, 66
India 11, 44, 199, 209, 225
  cotton textile industry 128-9
  East India Company founded 84, 120
  First War of Independence, 1857 129
  visited by Ralph Fitch, 1594 120
Indians
  contribution to WW2 165
  immigrants in C20th 174
  in Britain, C19th 139-142, 234, 237
  KS 1 project 25
industrialisation 124, 127,144, 151
International Women's Day 25
interpretation 46, 50, 64, 66, 71, 217
  using fiction 52, 53
Ireland 89, 104, 107
  Home Rule 230, 234
  potato famine 144
  subjugation in Tudor period 104-5
Irish 230
  immigrants in C20th 174
  in England, C19th 132,144-5
Jarrow March 176-7, 200, 238
Jews 17, 24,109, 200
  refugees in 1930s 165-6
  in Europe 17, 58,167, 231-2
Jex-Blake, Sophia 70, 72,157
John, Trevor 90-1
Johnson, Amy 232, 255
Jones, Claudia 72, 173-4, 188, 233, 256

Key Stage 3 history
    connections with Key Stage 2 history
        6, 83-4, 124
King, Martin Luther 65, 72, 257
Kingsley, Mary 65, 137, 157, 160, 209,
    233, 239, 269
Kung, Hans 106
law and order 193-5
Little, Vivienne 90-1
Livingstone, David 66, 137-8, 225
Malcolm X 65, 72, 258
Mandela, Nelson 59-60, 72, 259
Mandela, Winnie 72
Match Girls Strike 200, 225
Mayans 206
Mayhew, Henry 132, 144, 145, 160
medicine
    black doctors 231,233, 235, 238
    in C19th 190
    in Tudor period 112
    women doctors 67, 72, 157, 224
Midgley, Clare 160, 239
mining
    female labour 147
Mitchell, Hannah 153
Moody, Dr. Harold 234, 246
Morant Bay uprising 237
multiculturalism 18-19, 169
    in infant history curriculum 24-27
    in Roman period 99
    in Tudor period 108-110
in Victorian period 131, 136, 138-144
murals 58, 196-7
museums 36, 92-3, 109-10
myths and legends 40-1
Naoroji, Dr. Dadabhai 234, 260
Nightingale, Florence 65, 67, 70, 157,
    225, 260
non-statutory guidance for history 18-19,
    21, 22, 31, 39, 41, 48, 54, 70, 71, 225
ONeill, Judith 91,146, 159, 265

oral history 15, 34, 49, 192
    avoiding exploiting interviewees 33
    for Benin 209, 211, 220
    for Britain since the 30s 164-167, 174,
        243, 246, 249, 252, 256, 265, 268
    from C19th 148, 153
    in KS 2 163-4
    methodology 31-33
    with children 25, 30-31, 163-4
Pankhurst, Christabel and Emily 197,
    230, 234, 262
Pankhurst, Sylvia 150, 197, 234-5, 237,
    239
Parkes, Rosa 71, 262
patchwork quilting 56-57, 75
peace movement 73, 230, 232, 235, 238
perspectives 50, 55
    and egocentricism 46
    and equal opportunities 47
    black perspective in Victorian unit
        135-144
    British rather than English 89
    in oral history 164-5
    on famous people 70
    on Benin history 217
    on law and order 194
    on the Roman invasion 96-99, 101
    on Tudor pirates 117-8
    using fiction with infants to develop
        46, 51-2
Peterloo 197, 229
Philip II King of Spain 114
Piaget, Jean 2, 41, 46
pictorial evidence see visual evidence
pirates 117
Pitt, Baron Pitt of Hampstead 235
polygamy 206
Poor Laws 189-92
Prince, Mary 138, 160, 236, 239
progression
    chronological 88
    in KS 2 curriculum 88
Protestants 105
PSE 28-9, 46, 170
Purkis, Sally 104
Quakers 134

race 11
  and gender 14-15
racism 11, 13, 46, 203, 226
  anti-Irish 144
  exploring through fiction 45, 57, 59
  resistance to 200, 231, 233, 235, 236-7
  whole school policies 13-14
Raleigh, Sir Walter 110, 119
Reformation 105
refugees 18, 27-30, 37, 60-61, 280-1
  Huguenot 105, 108, 280
religion
  conflicts in Tudor period 105-7, 118
  and anti-slavery campaigns 134
Remond, Charles 236
Remond, Sarah Parker 138, 223, 228,
  236-7
sailors 199
in C19th 139-41
Saklatvala, Shapurji 237
Salmon, Phillida 33
San Juan 116
Sancho, Ignatius 237
Scobie, Pamela 91, 152, 159, 200
scolds 113
Scotland 89
  Roman period 98-9
  Tudor period 104-5
  Highland Clearances 146
Seacole, Mary 67, 70, 72, 137, 157, 161,
  238, 263-4
Septimius, Severus 98, 99, 243
Shaftesbury, Lord 147
Sharpe, Sam 134, 264
slavery 11, 13, 87-8, 205, 206, 210
  Saints church in Clapham 197
  and Benin 209-10, 214-5
  and British ports 199
  anti-slavery campaigns 133-6, 228,
    231, 235-6, 247, 250, 259-60, 261,
    264, 266
  black resistance 134
  for cotton production 111, 127-8
  for sugar and tobacco production 111
  in Roman Britain 97-98, 100
  in Tudor period 84, 115-6

in USA 227-8
middle passage 17, 134, 209
teaching through fiction 56-7
Underground Railroad, USA 56-7, 75,
  250, 255, 261, 267
women and anti-slavery 135
Sojourner Truth 72, 74, 266
South Africa 204
  Boer War 157, 232, 233
  using fiction to teach about 59-60
spiral curriculum 83, 85
stereotypes 203, 204, 207, 216
Stevens, Olive 6, 86
Strangers Home, East London, 139-141
subjectivity
  as inevitable in history 82
suffrage
  female 72, 156, 195-6, 197, 199, 224,
    225, 230, 234, 237
  male 196, 197
sugar 111, 214
  boycotts in anti slavery campaign 135
Susi 137, 225
Sutcliff, Rosemary 90, 97, 101
Swanwick, Helena 237-8
sweated labour 148
tea 130
television
  children's knowledge of the news 6,
    54, 86
  for role-play 143, 119, 176-7
Temperance 130, 231
Three Wise Men 6, 21
time-lines
  for Benin 209, 216
  for female labour 147-9
  for immigration/emigration 172, 185
  for Tudor period 118
  for Victorian period 143
personal with KS 1 23, 25, 27
tobacco 110
Tolpuddle Martyrs 196, 200
Tomlinson, Theresa 91, 151, 152,

trade 233
  Benin 209, 211-3, 218
  concepts in KS 1 36
  in Tudor period 84, 107
  in Victorian period 124-6
transport
  black contribution in C20th 36, 173
  cars 125, 175
  cycling 154-5
  in Victorian period 145
  Irish contribution in C19th 144-5
  women in WW2 168
Troyna, Barry 13-14, 19, 107, 121
Tubman, Harriet 57, 65, 74, 75, 267
value judgements 2,23, 52, 118, 205, 206
visual evidence
  black and white photos 46
  for Benin 217, 219, 220
  for C20th 169, 172, 178
  for local history 188, 195,
  for Victorian period 149
  from Tudor period 107, 109
  in oral history 34
  indicating change 187
  using fiction 42-49
  where to find 34-6, 195
  with infants 25, 34-5
Visram, Rozina 86, 141, 159, 160, 243, 255

Wainright, Jacob 137, 225
Wales 89, 98, 104, 176
walls 58
  Berlin Wall 99
  Hadrian's Wall 98
  in Belfast 99
Wells, Ida B 138, 268
Welsh 104
Whig history 7-8, 149
Wilkinson, Ellen 176, 238
witchcraft 112-3, 194
Wollstonecraft, Mary 189, 269
Women's Movement
in C19th 56-8, 193, 230, 236-7
in C20th 8, 14, 169
workhouses 189, 190
working classes
  and Co-op movement 200
  education 36, 149-50, 193
  life in C19th 30
  poverty 189-90
  using oral history 163-4
  women and children 147-9, 153-4
World War Two 58, 61, 165, 168, 178-9, 246, 252, 254, 264, 269
  Commonwealth contributions 165
  Women in WW2 (including black women) 168, 247, 251, 268, 270